ON DEADLINE

MANAGING MEDIA RELATIONS

THIRD EDITION

CAROLE M. HOWARD
WILMA K. MATHEWS

WAVELAND
PRESS, INC.
Prospect Heights, Illinois

For information about this book, contact:
Waveland Press, Inc.
P.O. Box 400
Prospect Heights, Illinois 60070
(847) 634-0081
www.waveland.com

Copyright © 2000, 1994, 1985 by Carole M. Howard and
Wilma K. Mathews

ISBN 1-57766-086-2

Printed in the United States of America

7   6   5   4   3   2

This book is dedicated
to all the bright young students and professionals
who are following in our footsteps and branching out beyond.

CAROLE M. HOWARD, PRSA, ABC, writes, speaks and leads seminars on media relations, global PR, employee communications and marketing. She is the retired vice president of public relations and communications policy for The Reader's Digest Association in New York, where she had worldwide responsibility for PR, was president of the Reader's Digest Foundation, and also served on the corporate Management Committee. A former reporter, she worked for AT&T in Seattle and New York for 18 years in various public relations and marketing positions. She is the author of scores of articles on PR, marketing, advertising and management, and a contributor to six other books. Her speeches have been published in *Vital Speeches* and in three textbooks. She is a contributing editor of *Public Relations Quarterly;* on the advisory boards of *Journal of Employee Communication Management, Ragan Public Relations Journal*, and *Public Relations News*; and a frequent speaker to public relations and business organizations and at universities around the world. An accredited member of the Public Relations Society of America and International Association of Business Communicators, Howard is a past member of Women in Communications, Inc. and National Press Women. She is listed in the *Who's Who of American Women* and the *World's Who's Who of Women.* In 1990 she was named one of the top 40 "Corporate PR Superstars" by *Public Relations Quarterly.* Having been a member of the Board of Directors of a public company as well as for several nonprofit organizations and foundations, she brings an unusually broad perspective to the practice of media relations. She lives in southwest Colorado with her husband Bob and cats Molly and Mac. E-mail: *tailwinds1@aol.com*

WILMA K. MATHEWS, ABC, has 30 years in international and domestic public relations management including media relations, marketing communications, crisis communications and planning. She is director of public relations for Arizona State University, the third largest public university in the United States, and heads her own media training and consulting firm. Mathews worked for AT&T for 15 years in various public relations and media relations positions. She also has directed programs in nonprofit organizations and began her career with magazine and newspaper experience. A Fellow and accredited member of the International Association of Business Communicators, Mathews has received the association's Gold Quill Award of Excellence for Media Relations. She is author of *Effective Media Relations: A Practical Guide for Communicators* and a contributor to the second and third editions of *Inside Organizational Communication* and *The Communicator's Guide to Marketing.* She has spoken before numerous professional, civic and academic audiences around the world, contributes articles to trade and professional journals, and conducts media relations seminars and workshops. Mathews is listed in *Who's Who of American Women* and the *International Who's Who of Professional and Business Women.* She serves on the advisory board of *communication briefings* and the executive board of the IABC, and is a member of the Public Relations Society of America. E-mail: *wkm23@asu.edu*

CONTENTS

Foreword   ix
Preface   xiii
Acknowledgments   xix

1   **Technology and Tabloids** How the New Media   1
      World Is Changing Your Job

2   **Getting Started** Setting Up Your Program   11

3   **News** What It Is and How It Gets to the Public   29

4   **Tools of the Trade** From News Releases   47
      to Background Briefings

5   **Reporters** Helping Them Meet Their Objectives   69

6   **Spokespersons** Training and Briefing Them   105
      for Their Role

7   **Ethics** The Golden Rules of Media Relations   133

8   **Media Events** How to Make Them Work for You   147

9   **Going Global** How to Manage International   187
      Media Relations

10   **Crisis Planning** How to Anticipate and Manage   215
      Emergency Situations

11   **Measurement/Evaluation** How to Know if   271
      Your Program Is Working

12   **The Future** Expanding Your Counselor Role   283

Notes   323
Bibliography   335
Index   337

FOREWORD

After all the research has been done and the organization has set its policies; after the news releases have been written; after management has approved them and the lawyers have cleared them, there remains the "small" task of distributing them to the news media.

If the news release has been soundly conceived and professionally prepared, chances are reasonably good that editors will accept it for publication in one form or another. But alas for all of us in public relations, a large percentage—perhaps even a majority—of media contacts will be handled poorly. Milliseconds after news releases have arrived electronically or on paper, editors will hit the delete key or toss the paper in the "Big Round File." For the most part, the releases will concern events or include information of no interest to the medium receiving them.

No form of media contact—phone call, hand-written note, e-mail, fax or whatever—will provide a return on the investment if it conveys the wrong message, or has been sent to the wrong medium, or to the wrong person at the right medium, or has been sent in the wrong format or at the wrong time. Wasted effort, wasted time, wasted money. It is no wonder, therefore, that editors who screen such material form a low opinion of public relations and its practitioners. News releases may be only the tip of the iceberg of media relations as some believe, but certainly as professionals we deserve to be judged by how well or how poorly we perform this essential function.

All too often one hears that media relations isn't really public relations; it is "merely" publicity. Carole M. Howard and Wilma K. Mathews explain why media relations, properly practiced, must be preceded by policy determination, issue analysis, counseling and the like. They demonstrate convincingly that solid planning skills are necessary to practice successful media relations.

Almost all business today—profit and not-for-profit—is global. The transformation has come subtly but overwhelmingly. Organizations today plan and act globally, not nationally, to survive. Those that understand world cultures and world markets are thriving. That is why international public relations now carries greater responsibilities and shares greater opportunities to serve.

The time is right for another update of *On Deadline: Managing Media Relations*. It is appropriate and wise that Howard and Mathews have greatly expanded their coverage of international public relations and the electronic tools that support it. Few professionals actually have directed and participated in so many precedent-setting and worldwide public relations activities as they.

They also have added new information on how the Internet has affected the practice of media relations. And, because we have moved beyond counting clips, column inches and ad equivalencies, they have upgraded their discussion of measurement to focus on changing opinions and behaviors.

Readers will benefit from their generous sharing of their experiences on behalf of The Reader's Digest Association, AT&T and Arizona State University, as well as the many new case histories from other organizations that are included in this third edition. For their unstinting sharing of this information, the entire public relations profession is in their debt.

By limiting this book to the subject of media relations and enlarging the definition of this function, the authors restore media relations to its proper position. Both Howard and Mathews have worked in media relations for many years; their individual experience equals that of some entire corporate departments. There are few types of difficult situations they haven't already coped with successfully. You can be certain that their recommendations are based on experience in the "real world."

The third edition of *On Deadline: Managing Media Relations* is virtually an encyclopedia of media relations. Without stint or reserve, the authors share herein the breadth and depth of their experience. This book will provide much help to those who must "meet the press" (or interviewers from television, radio, magazines or cyberspace). Whether you are responsible for calling an editor, posting news on your organization's Web site, or managing a full media relations program, you will discover that Howard and Mathews have provided you with sound counsel.

Chester Burger
Life Member
Counselors Academy
Public Relations Society of America
New York, New York
June 1999

PREFACE

We were in the midst of training a new person who had transferred into our media relations group when a colleague mentioned a similar situation at his company. "He's pestering all of us for hints on how to do his job," our friend said. "Why isn't there some book I can give him to read?"

"It sure would have been nice if someone had written it all down for us," we joked. And then, "One of us really ought to write that book." But even two robins do not make a spring. The conversation veered off in another direction, and writing the book became a dormant topic.

Shortly thereafter we responded to a late-night query from the *Wall Street Journal* after the leak of a layoff announcement. We had to coordinate responses to internal and external queries with spokespersons in 20 locations across the country. At one point a public relations manager in a manufacturing plant remarked, "You really ought to write this up—it would make a perfect case history."

Some time later we canceled plans for dinner together, one to write a speech on corporate media relations to a Public Relations Society of America chapter in Louisiana, the other to plan a workshop on media relations at the International Association of Business Communicators annual conference. At each of these functions we heard similar comments from members of the audience: "You have had so many different experiences with the news media you really ought to write a book." Thus, the idea came to life again. The fundamental tools of our trade are words. How flattering—and how humbling—to be told there is a need to sit down at your computer and bang out the story of how you spend your working life.

Successful sales of this book's first edition, initially in the hardcover edition and later in paperback, led to another request—to update the book and include a separate chapter on international media relations because of its growing importance to our profession.

Now, five years later, it is time for a third edition. The Internet has rapidly changed the way we communicate with each other, and e-business is transforming entire industries. Measurement has become more sophisticated than merely counting press clippings or Web site hits; rather it involves tracking changed opinions and modified behaviors. And globalization has become even more important for almost all organizations, large and small, in our worldwide, interdependent economy.

Education and training, even of a very high magnitude, are not enough. You also need experience. As cosmetics tycoon Helena Rubinstein put it, "First you've got to get educated—and then you've got to get smart."

Our approach in this book is to cite anecdotes and case studies from our combined six decades as public relations practitioners in the corporate and nonprofit worlds and from the experiences of others who have graciously shared their stories with us. We hope you will find in them a freshness of vision that will enrich your own insights. Our goal is to provide direction, not directives. We will talk about the media relations job from both a strategic and a tactical point of view. We also will temper our advice with knowledge gained from our days as working reporters.

Start with Planning

The third edition of *On Deadline: Managing Media Relations* first gives an overview of how the new media and the current focus of traditional media are affecting how you communicate your organization's news events. Next, we delve into the critical first step of planning a media relations program. There is nothing so wasteful of our resources or our energies than activity without insight. We also include a detailed description of setting goals and measuring results, for only with such operational systems in place will you be treated as equal members of the business team by others in your organization. We will offer tips on how to get your management's approval *before* you begin and keep them informed of your progress and any changes in external or internal conditions as you proceed, so that your contributions are appreciated by the decision makers of the organization.

Architect Mies van der Rohe once said, "God is in the details"—and this is no less true of our profession than it was of his. With that in mind we offer specific suggestions on how to improve your relationship with reporters—including hints for ensuring that reporters can reach you at night, keeping your news release distribution lists up to date, creating interest in your organization with regular Web site updates and background mailings, deciding whether to announce your news in the morning or the afternoon, modifying your office coverage to match the media's hours, getting the most mileage out of clipping and electronic monitoring services, and deciding when to be responsive and when to say no.

We also provide detailed instructions on how to background both your organization's spokesperson and the reporter before a major interview, because the preparation you put in before they meet often makes the difference between success and failure. We will guide you in becoming a part of the decision-making process within your organization. You can take advantage of the instantaneous public opinion polls you can get from your ongoing contacts with reporters and from the Internet to counsel your organization's officers and board before practices and policies are set.

Aimed at a Broad Audience

We have written the third edition of *On Deadline* for a broad audience. Students of journalism and public relations should find insight into their fields no matter which side of the profession they choose. Chief executive officers and other key spokespersons for organizations may find that parts of the book offer valuable background on how the media operate. The third edition of *On Deadline* may be useful as a handy reference before a reporter comes in for an interview. Perhaps even reporters will find it interesting to glimpse the inner workings of the world of media relations. It may make them understand why we practitioners view ourselves—when we are doing our job well—as performing a valuable service that makes us not barriers to information but rather indispensable translators of the needs of both reporters and our organizations.

Most of all, the third edition of *On Deadline* is written for those people who are, or plan to be, responsible for an organization's or client's day-to-day relations with the news media. Whether you work for a bank wanting to publicize expanded financial services, a utility explaining the complexities and benefits of deregulation, a social service agency desiring to generate attendance at a new job-counseling clinic, a trade association lobbying for legislation or a large corporation marketing a new product, the media's coverage—or lack of coverage—of your news will be an important factor in the results.

Influence Decisions as Well as Report Them

A natural avenue into the world of public and media relations is to join a company or organization after a few years of experience as a reporter. For those of you who fell victim to the siren's song of journalism, the transition should not be difficult. Dealing with the media from this side can be just as stimulating as chasing after a story and a byline. Indeed, we would argue more so, because you now have the opportunity to influence decisions and activities rather than just report them. You will have the same almost instant feedback as the media covers your organization's news on that evening's newscast, in tomorrow morning's newspaper, in the next issue of a magazine, or in an on-line article.

On the other hand, for people who have not spent time as reporters, producers or editors, a move into the media relations position can be an abrupt change, requiring flexibility not only in *your* lifestyle but also in your family's as you strive to adapt to the media's sense of urgency. The workday's planned activities are forsaken when a reporter asks for information on your agency's fundraising expenses and it takes you several hours to gather the facts, arrange an interview and brief a spokesperson. A dinner party is interrupted when you receive word that there has been a chemical spill at the plant and reporters are clamoring for information. A weekend outing is canceled when you must move up your planned news conference by a week because of a leak that has surfaced on the Internet. A night's sleep is lost when the clock is stopped during union bargaining as your organization works to negotiate a contract and avoid a walkout.

If you like order and predictability and prefer to take a great deal of time to enunciate your views orally or in writing, media relations is not the job for you. But if you ar stimulated by being at the center of action, enjoy responding to stimuli from several directions at once, can rapidly formulate thoughts and clearly articulate positions, find it exhilarating to bring definition to ambiguity, then media relations may be the field for you. Your energy and your ability to learn will be tested. The job requires people who can remain calm and focused in a crisis—and above all, keep a sense of humor and perspective. Your reward comes from the people you meet and the events you influence.

We hope the third edition of *On Deadline* will help all present and future media relations practitioners to do a better job of walking the tightrope as you strive to balance a reporter's demand for fast and accurate information with the organization's need to guard competitive secrets and avoid violating the privacy of employees; to become as adept at bringing valuable information into the organization as at getting the news out. For the beginner it will serve as a textbook; for the more experienced person, a reference book. For neither should it be dull. Media relations is an exhilarating field. If our prose reflects the excitement of being part of news events as they unfold—and contributes to more accurate coverage of the activities of corporations and other organizations—then we will have adequately achieved our objectives and served our profession.

ACKNOWLEDGMENTS

Deciding whom to thank when you work with colleagues and journalists who are so willing to share ideas and experiences is a very difficult task. However, there were some who were especially helpful with editorial advice, manuscript reviews and unflagging interest from the time we got the initial idea for the book to the day the first edition of *On Deadline: Managing Media Relations* was published. These include Chester Burger, Bob Burke, Hal Burlingame, Bill Cooper, Bob Ehinger, Roy Foltz, David Manahan, Brian Monahan, Bill Mullane, Elizabeth Park, Jack Sauchelli, Deb Stahl, Mike Tarpey, Al Wann and Candy Young. We also want to pay tribute to Mary Sokol, whose magic fingers keep us on our toes as well as on schedule.

For support and suggestions on the second edition we gratefully acknowledge the contributions of Stephanie Carpentieri, Carol Cincola, Lesta Cordil, Helen Fledderus, David Fluhrer, Chris King, Craig Lowder, Linda Milone, Martha Molnar, Lynn Munroe, Tara Phethean, and Don Ranly. Valuable assistance for the third edition came from Barbara Griswold, Chris King, Lynn Munroe, Debbie Tully and the staff of the Pagosa Springs, Colorado, library. As well, Mac and Molly provided close and much appreciated supervision of the manuscript.

As always, special thanks to Bob Howard, who is our greatest supporter and most constructive critic. We also very much appreciate the ongoing counsel and contributions of the Waveland Press editorial and marketing team—Tom Curtin and Jeni Ogilvie—who have become both publishing partners and good friends.

Chapter 1

TECHNOLOGY AND TABLOIDS
How the New Media World Is Changing Your Job

As the world has become more complex, business and financial journalism has changed. It used to be relegated to the back pages of newspapers or to filling air time on slow news days. Then increased consumer involvement in the stock market, significant advances in research, dramatic corporate mergers and acquisitions, as well as massive organizational restructuring and layoffs put economics, finance, technology and business subjects onto the front pages.

In newsrooms throughout the country additional reporters are being assigned to cover the economy. More pages are included in business sections. More publications are dedicated to the economy. More air time, including entire cable channels' programming, is devoted to financial events. Economic issues have become personal issues—and thus, news.

Those of us who make our living by helping reporters translate such news into terms the general public can understand often feel as if we are living in an enormous clothes dryer—events are tumbling around us and we around them in a frantic, haphazard way. It is, after all, somewhat scary to see the words you spoke yesterday to a reporter on the phone set in type in this morning's *Asian Wall Street Journal* or *The New York Times*.

1

Trend Toward Tabloid Journalism

Unfortunately, business journalism suffers from the same trend toward shallow reporting and soundbite editing that has afflicted the general consumer media. The traditional double-source rule is fast disappearing if not gone, with rumors and gossip too often mascarading as news.

Grant N. Horne, retired vice president-public relations of Pacific Gas and Electric Co., says that "TV/radio news formats and much of the print press increasingly take their reporting cues—especially a harsh, confrontational style—from the psycho-babble of their talk show cousins." As a result, Horne points out, "Increasingly, people recognize that the media business, and especially television, is more about entertainment, provided by entertainers, than it is about fact."[1]

Veteran PR executive and teacher Fraser Seitel reinforced that concern when he said, "Leaks and lies and innuendo no longer become the province only of the tabloids. Journalistic survival, even for mainstream media, means a greater willingness to stretch the truth to become more categorical and controversial."[2]

Even respected journalists are joining in the criticism. Calling her 1999 autobiography the story "of my ride on the decline of network news," CBS correspondent Lesley Stahl spoke harshly of the drop in TV news standards: "There was a new ethic at CBS . . . going for the buck was first, second and third priority," she wrote. She felt that management "was downgrading us to some second-rate tabloid." Stahl added, "The lines between tabloid shows and us were blurring, and it wasn't just how we looked. More and more we were covering their subject, the world of personality. The private lives of famous people were becoming our territory too, as the competition for ratings heated up."[3]

Meanwhile Robert MacNeil, famous for his nearly 40 years in broadcasting, wrote a blistering, behind-the-scenes novel in 1998 about network news today—a world in which crazed competition drives serious journalists into the tabloid feeding frenzies Americans increasingly see on their screens. In a promotional piece Walter Cronkite wrote, "MacNeil calls it a novel but here, in delightfully readable style, may be the best explanation yet of that which ails television news."[4]

As *60 Minutes* creator and executive producer Don Hewitt put it, "I would like to believe that the [networks'] founding fathers, were they still around, would have stood fast on what was, for them, an article of faith: News is news and entertainment is entertainment, and crossing the line between them is often dishonest and always bad broadcasting."[5]

Print media also denounce the trend toward tabloid journalism. *Newsweek* noted that word of the President Bill Clinton-Monica Lewinsky affair broke first on a Web site and then rapidly was picked up by the mainstream media: "This scandal may be remembered as the moment at which the status quo in the news business finally crashed and burned." In what the magazine called "today's anything-goes news culture," *Newsweek* opined, "It's not that news standards have slipped; it's that news standards are now irrelevant to whether a story gets into the media bloodstream."[6]

What appears on the Internet, then, has great impact on what we will see on our TV news that night and read in our newspapers the next morning. As the editor of the *American Journalism Review* put it, "One thing is clear: The phenomenon is not going to go away no matter how much journalism purists and reformers decry it. The day when the elite media could make the call on whether something comes to light is far behind us."[7]

Internet Transforms Our Lives

Cyber-savvy children cruise the Internet and search for information on Web sites from the time their fingers are firm enough to strike the keys of a computer. Even senior executives have become comfortable with the new technology. According to a Yankelovich Partners Inc. study in 1998, 91 percent of executives responding listed Internet information services as a primary news source.[8] And many journalists look first to an organization's Web site before calling in to the media relations contact for information.

As we enter the new millennium, more than 90 million individuals and businesses are connected to the Net. That figure, reached from a virtual motionless start less than five years ago, represents a rate of growth more than five times as fast as the acceptance of television two generations ago. The 1998–99 holiday season saw an explosion of Internet shopping as a record number of on-line shoppers spent $3.5 billion in the fourth quarter of 1998.[9] As a result of the Internet, every organization is now a 24-hour business, with customers—and journalists—expecting constant accessibility and immediate response. John Gilfeather, a managing partner at Yankelovich Partners Inc., put it succinctly: "Electronic communications and your Web site never sleep."[10]

It is true, as Polaroid PR vice president Anne M. McCarthy has observed, that "the Net can be accused of manufacturing, merchandising and marketing more than its fair share of 'vaporware' or hype." Regardless, its phenomenal growth is "redefining the global economy and creating a considerable amount of wealth in its wake."[11]

Consider the following statistics: From *USA Today*—"It took radio 30 years to reach an audience of 50 million and TV took 13 [years]. The Internet took just four years."[12] And it keeps on growing. Conservative forecasts estimate as many as 550 million users will be surfing the Net by the year 2000. That's 10 percent of the world's population.[13]

Direct Channel of Communication

The Internet has the advantage of being a direct channel of communication between an organization and its stakeholders. Stuart Z. Goldstein, managing director at National Securities Clearing Corp. in New York, has noted that companies can now become their own news bureau, writing and distributing print, audio and video stories via the Internet and satellite.[14]

"The problem isn't so much the ability to communicate," says Michael Bloomberg, CEO of Bloomberg L.P. He heads a company with 100,000-plus Bloomberg terminals around the world delivering not only immediate changes in bond and stock prices, their histories and comparisons with one another, but also a full range of business and financial stories reported by Bloomberg journalists. "It's the ability to find the one piece of information you need amid all the clutter. I think that's why a lot of focus in Internet and technology stocks is on [Web] browser companies that help people find their way. I don't think that there's a lack of information out there. Quite the contrary: There's so much information nobody can find anything."[15]

As McCarthy put it, "[It's] unnerving for some and inspiring for others." She went on, "One thing is for sure—the Net is not for the faint-hearted, the impatient or the insecure. . . . Communications professionals have two choices: Observe this phenomenon with millions of browsers sitting on the sidelines or hop on the magic carpet."[16] *PR Week* writer Jonah Bloom believes that "the Internet and PR were made for each other." He says, "They are both about making a connection, about establishing one-on-one relationships."[17]

Print Is Not Dead

Yet publishers of print publications are not about to cede their entire future to cyberspace. *American Journalism Review* editor Rem Rieder reminisces with a chuckle about Ted Turner's prophecy in 1981, shortly after the launch of CNN, that newspapers were dinosaurs and in 10 years or so they would be a fond memory. "Well, newspapers turned out to be a fairly hardy breed of dinosaur," Rieder observed. "Nearly two decades later, they not only are hanging on, they actually seem to be thriving." To continue to be successful, print media should play to their strengths and "do what they do best—covering substantial matters with depth in as compelling a way as possible, providing insight and context harder to come by in other media, digging well beneath the surface to break stories," he says.[18]

Baltimore Sun editor John Carroll reinforces that point: "On your visit to the *Sun*, you might also note an absence of hand-wringing about television and the Internet. Our staff knows that a newspaper can have far more influence in a community than all its electronic competitors combined, and that only a newspaper can seriously aspire to be the conscience, and the goad, of a city or of a state."[19]

After all, even in this Information Age where our communications channels are dominated by e-mail, Web sites, faxes, television and satellite networks, most people still read newspapers. In the late 1990s more than 80 percent of adults still say they've read a daily paper at least once in the past week. And six out of 10 say they read a daily newspaper yesterday. That figure is down from nearly eight out of 10. But Sunday newspaper readership has remained steady at seven out of 10 adults. The concern is that younger readers, those in their 20s and 30s, do not read as often as their elders do. And in most American markets research has shown women are especially hard-pressed to read the daily paper, although they read Sunday papers as much as men do.[20]

Changes in Media Mix

Although newspapers remain an important information source, they have been disappearing at an alarming rate. Major U.S. cities have changed from multi-paper towns to one-paper towns. Other papers like the *Wall Street Journal, USA Today* and *The New York Times* are becoming truly national papers.

This change in the newspaper field is one of many media changes documented by Ronald E. Rhody when he was executive vice president of BankAmerica Corp., in a speech in San Francisco. He also pointed out that:

- Cable TV is blossoming as a major competitor for both print and traditional broadcast media, with network TV losing much of its audience.
- Radio is in a resurgence.
- Special interest magazines are making serious inroads into the circulation of traditional news and general readership magazines.
- Bloomberg's wire service has come out of nowhere to give Dow Jones and Reuters a run for their money.
- Major media organizations have come to find out they are mortal too, as corporate raiders came into their lives.

"Particularly important are the management changes that have been taking place almost everywhere in the media," Rhody said. "Far too little time is given in assessing how those changes impact the conduct of news operations. Regardless of the rhetoric offered about consistency of editorial policy, changes in management of the editorial function of news organizations substantially affect the way the news is gathered and reported. And those changes almost always put heavy pressure on writers and editors to do it differently, or do it better to beat the competition. Because that's the way the score is kept."[21]

As well, as cable companies buy telephone companies and vice versa, and as entertainment companies acquire TV stations, the traditional lines between industries have blurred. Said the *Wall Street Journal*, "As the deals pile up, U.S. regulators and lawmakers keep saying they are concerned that consolidation could bring all telephone, television and Internet services under the control of a few large and powerful companies."[22]

Other Technological Changes

"New technologies are bearing down at high speed on the old engines of information," said *Newsweek* in an analysis of recent changes in the media world.[23] The use of complex information management technologies is now a normal part of growing up. Our children's early exposure to computers as both learning tools and playthings means they are already trained to receive, generate and interact with text and graphics on a TV screen. Increasingly sophisticated communications networks allow the media to speed news via satellite and optic fiber networks around the country, across borders and over oceans.

A live video "feed" from the other side of the world is seen in true-to-life color and real time many thousands of miles away. Cell phones and small video cameras allow citizens to report the news live as they are experiencing it, even in disasters. Thanks to video or radio satellite tours, spokespersons can "travel" to scores of cities in one day to publicize a new book or to drum up support for a political campaign without leaving their hometowns.

Truly, the Information Age is here and the Information Highway is well developed. We are only beginning to realize the opportunities and benefits for the exchange of information and news. In fact, possible applications are limited only by the imagination of the users of these technologies and of those who would serve us with interconnected networks, sophisticated terminals, expanded data bases and software programs.

The public's thirst for information never seems to be quenched. As Dan Rather opined: "In a world where it seems we're inundated with news, I think we're only inundated with . . . well, mutations of the news, imitations of the news, variations on the news. When it comes to real and serious and important reportage we're not glutted. We're starved."[24] And Robert MacNeil wrote in his autobiography; "In most of the stories television cares to cover, there is always 'the right bit,' the most violent, the most bloody, the most pathetic, the most tragic, the most wonderful, the most awful moment. Getting the effective 'bit' is what television news is all about. . . ."[25]

Changes in Media Relations Jobs

Demands on the people responsible for relations with the news media also are increasing. If we have not changed with the requirements of the job, then we have no doubt lost opportunities to serve our organizations, clients and profession. As Will Rogers put it, "Even if you are on the right track you will get run over if you just sit there."[26]

It was not so many years ago that the press job in an organization was a seat-of-the-pants, reactive position. All we had to do was keep up friendships with reporters at local press association functions, keep our sense of humor when they phoned with tough questions, and keep the company's name *out* of the newspapers. Many corporations and organizations believed their decisions and actions were none of the media's—or the public's—business.

Today that has changed. For one thing, the name of our job has changed. It is *media* relations now, reflecting the ever increasing importance of television, radio and the Internet as sources of news. For another thing, today's management expects more of us: Not only must we be able to get the organization out of a mess, we also are expected to *keep it from ever getting into the mess in the first place*. Our work has become accepted as a valued management and strategic function.

Issues Management and Strategic Planning

Media relations people, like all public relations professionals, are moving rapidly into the more complex—and more ambiguous—world of issues and issues management. Not that we have moved out of the fire-fighting, news-releasing, question-answering business. That will be as important a part of what we do tomorrow as it is today. But it will not be the major thing we do, and it cannot be the only thing we let consume our time. It no longer is enough that we be good communicators with a broad knowledge of our organization and its product lines. Now we must be familiar with everything from equal-opportunity laws to environmental-protection legislation, from worker's compensation to antitrust actions, from global issues to regulations governing the buying and selling of stock on Wall Street. In short, our skills and our work are expected to make a positive, measurable contribution to the organization's goals.

Good media relations requires thoughtful plans and targeted strategies. It is much more than churning out news releases on new products. It is searching for other opportunities and news events that can be turned into positive media coverage. It is taking time to develop a rapport with key reporters in order to sell them on the news value of your organization's activities.

Walter K. Lindemann, a senior vice president of Ketchum, the New York-headquartered multinational PR consulting firm, describes the substance of media relations in the past. His words serve as a reminder of another significant change in our function. For years our focus had been "almost exclusively on the communications of key messages to selected target audience groups," he said. "If we could somehow appropriately disseminate the messages and themes that organizations were interested in conveying to others, if we could somehow begin to show that the appropriate audience segments were indeed being exposed to the messages, were receiving them, understanding them, and retaining them, and finally, if we could somehow prove that the messages that were sent had changed public opinion, then most of us felt that we could argue that [media] relations has value." [27]

Changing Behaviors and Building Relationships

Today the criteria are more difficult to achieve. Much of the time our goal is actually to *change behaviors*— or to preserve the behaviors that we want to continue. Kathleen Ladd Ward, former chair of the Public Relations Society of America's research committee, wrote in 1998 that although communications are important, "the ultimate objective is to build and maintain beneficial relationships between organizations and their publics." She defined positive relationships as "those in which both or all parties perceive that they benefit" and says trust is the primary attribute of any good relationship. [28]

Of course, media relations is not a stand-alone function. It is one part of your organization's arsenal to meet customer needs and increase shareholder value. In fact, Eli Lily CEO Randall L. Tobias believes that in today's corporation "most effective functions are becoming increasingly more *virtual* than functional." To be valuable to your CEO, he advises, you need to spend your time focusing on issues—not trying to preserve your traditional function as it was practiced in the past."[29]

Some argue that to serve well we must be retained as outside counsel *of* the organization rather than *in* it. In fact, we must be both. We must be able to explain to a reporter why we may *not* be able to give out certain information, and a few minutes later argue equally convincingly with an organization officer as to why we *should* disclose it. Representing at different times the perspective of the reporter, the public and the organization, we become the official split personality. It is a much more difficult and more interesting role.

Chapter 2

GETTING STARTED
Setting Up Your Program

Getting started in media relations means understanding your role and your objectives and sticking to both. But what is your role? Referee? Propagandizer? Shuffler of news releases? One fact that few executives or organization leaders seem to appreciate is that your role is to make a reporter's job easy, to help that reporter meet his or her objectives and, at the same time, to help your organization meet its objectives.

This tightrope-walking exercise means that when you speak to a reporter you are representing the organization; when you speak to the people in your organization you are representing the reporter. You do not need a split personality to achieve the balance, but you do need a sound understanding of everyone's goals and objectives. The reporter's objective is to get a story to help his or her editors meet a goal of having a newspaper that will sell or a television newscast that will attract viewers. Now, what are your goals and objectives?

What Kind of Program?

There are two possible kinds of media relations programs: passive or reactive, and active. A passive program means that your organization has determined, for whatever reason, not to seek the attention of the public eye. A passive posture may be initially frustrating to reporters. Once the word gets around, however, the organization generally is left alone, except in crises. Any other mention in the media about such a company often is speculation. Privately held companies sometimes engage in this practice and can do so because they are not required by law or regulation to divulge earnings or other financial data.

Even an organization obligated to divulge information to the public can still have a passive program. In this case, nothing beyond what must be reported is given out. This stance does not win friends among the media, but respect from journalists is probably not a goal. There is no need for a media relations person in such an organization because attorneys and accountants can prepare the basic required releases for the public.

If, however, you are with an organization that wishes to have an *active* media relations program, you need to understand what active means. Perhaps, more importantly, you need to know that active does not mean: churning out a release a day; taking reporters to lunch all the time; holding a news conference at the drop of a hat; scheduling all of your subject-matter experts on every radio and television talk show in your area; counting inches of copy or seconds of air time as the sole measurement technique; or creating glitzy video news releases.

Active does mean that you plan, implement and measure a well-conceived media relations program that supports your organization's goals and objectives. The way to do this is to set up your own media relations goals, objectives, strategies and timetables.

Developing a Communications Policy

Media scholar Harold Lasswell has said the communications process must be considered in terms of "who says what to whom, through what channel, with what effect."[1] This applies most significantly in media relations where you need to know—before the telephone rings—who will speak on behalf of your organization and to what purpose.

Beyond designating the official spokespersons, a communications policy can set the tone of all your media activities. The policy needs to be endorsed by, and disseminated from, the leadership of your organization.

Early in his tenure, Theodore Vail, the first president of AT&T, wrote a communications policy that has withstood the test of time:

> The only policy to govern the publicity (of AT&T) is that whatever is said or told should be absolutely correct, and that no material fact, even if unfavorable but bearing on the subject, should be held back. When we see misstatements, make it certain that those making them have the correct facts. This will not only tend to stop the making of them, but will lessen the influence of them by decreasing the number of misinformed, and any excuse for misstatements. Attempted concealment of material fact cannot but be harmful in the end.[2]

You should not be creating your communications policy while the reporter is waiting at the door. If your organization does not have a clear communications policy that covers publicity, it is your responsibility to write that policy.

The basis for your communications policy can be found in the guiding tenets of your organization such as a code of conduct, mission statement, rules of ethical behavior and business principles.

Your policy should address—in clearly understood words (skip the legalese here)—your organization's proactive or reactive stance, guidelines for disclosure (what is proprietary and what is not) and who will be authorized spokespersons for the organization.

The communications policy must be understood, approved and endorsed by the senior management of your organization. More important, the policy must be adhered to at *all* times. The strength of a communications policy will be tested during a crisis or negative coverage.

With a policy in hand and mind, you now can go on to more detailed plans.

Writing It Down

The first step in setting your media relations goals and objectives is to know thoroughly the direction in which your organization is headed. This includes knowing its overall strategy, goals and objectives. You then can create your own program.

First, look at each of the organization's goals carefully. Then, write down all the ways in which you can help your organization meet those goals. For example, if your organization is like most, it will have a goal concerning finances. It may be a declared statement about the amount of return on investment, or it may be a desire not to have to raise members' dues. Your support could include a series of briefings for financial analysts, placement of articles relating to organizational growth in magazines that reach investor audiences or making sure the public knows of the many services your organization provides.

Another organizational goal probably relates to human resources: the intention to maintain a well-trained, well-paid, employee universe with a low percentage of turnover. If you think this is an internal matter only, ask yourself where the employees come from. They come from the public at large. Your role in this area can be to make sure the public is aware of your organization's hospitable environment by issuing announcements of promotions, retirements, long-term service anniversaries, suggestion award winners, employee club activities, plant/office improvements, corporate donations, tuition reimbursement programs, on-site day care centers and travel opportunities.

This exercise of writing down ideas helps you marshal your thoughts, ensures that you truly do understand your organization's key objectives and helps you recognize how you can fit into the overall structure. Put aside your list of ideas; they will be used later.

Next, gather the work plans and goals/strategies from other departments, such as marketing, community relations, product development, labor relations and legal affairs.

Your media relations plan also should support—directly or indirectly—these departments. You may find it helpful to create a separate media plan for each department so that individual departments and you know what is expected and who will do it.

Even if you're not in a position to provide direct support to each department, having their plans helps you anticipate possible issues, schedule media events around key activities or just serve as an advisor to the department. At a minimum, knowing what is in these plans prevents you from unknowingly causing harm or conflict.

The Formal Structure

There are numerous ways to structure your media relations program. Select the way that best suits the day-to-day management techniques, language and operations of your organization. The following example may be of help, as will the case study at the end of this chapter.

Media Relations Program: XYZ COMPANY

GOAL I. To support the company's goal to attain financial stability through increased investments by the public.

First Objective: To provide the financial media with timely, accurate earnings information.

Tactics

1. Establish contact with a key person in the finance department who will provide information to media relations department on prearranged schedule.
2. Create a checklist of financial reporters in general, also business and trade publications that reach targeted audiences.
3. Prepare questions and rehearse answers in advance to inquiries by journalists about the organization's finances.
4. Issue earnings announcement each quarter.
5. Provide detailed briefings for financial reporters at the annual meeting.

Second Objective: To help encourage targeted audiences to invest in the organization by making them aware of the solvency and growth of the company.

Tactics

1. Determine the key investor audiences by working with the investor relations department.
2. Determine which publications or types of publications those audiences are likely to read.
3. Attempt to place six articles, which reflect the growth of the company, in those publications.

Third Objective: To help financial media have a better understanding of the organization's future.

Tactics

1. Select three key financial writers who reach an influential target audience.
2. Arrange for each writer to have an interview with a selected specialist in the Finance Department; each interview should occur at separate times, covering separate stories.
3. Mail updated information kits to all financial journalists on the mailing list.

GOAL II. To support the organization's goal of hiring and maintaining a well-trained employee body with a low percentage of turn-over.

First Objective: To inform the public of the accomplishments of long-term employees.

Tactics

1. Work with personnel; establish a way to be notified of all personnel advancements and retirements.
2. Create a brief form to be filled out by each promoted or retiring employee that will give information to be used in a news release.
3. Upon notification of a promotion, issue a release to selected business and trade media within five days. Issue a release to employee's hometown papers and his/her alumni magazine within two weeks.
4. Upon notification of a retiring employee, issue a release to business and trade press, hometown papers and alumni publications at least two weeks before retirement date.

Second Objective: To show the organization as a good corporate citizen.

Tactics

1. Compile a list of all employees involved in civic and volunteer activities.
2. Select possible feature-story ideas from that list.
3. Interview the employee and his/her supervisor about the activities.
4. Try to place the resulting story in area weekly newspapers or sell the story idea (if visual) to the local television station.

While the XYZ Company example is somewhat simplistic and altruistic, it does show that a media relations program can be planned by writing concise goals, objectives and tactics. Of course, each tactic should have a specific time frame and budget included with it, as well as the name of the person responsible for that tactic.

When the plan is completed, it should be sent to the key executives in your organization for review and comment. This action serves several purposes. First, it shows your top management that you are attuned to the workings of your organization because your departmental activities are geared to support the entire organization and its objectives. Second, it allows each person the opportunity to have some input to the plan. Everyone likes to be asked his or her opinion of something; most people like to respond with a suggested change or two. A word of caution: Do not automatically incorporate all suggestions into your plan. Look at each suggestion and, as objectively as possible, consider both its source and what happens to related activities if it is incorporated.

The reason to take some time with these suggestions is that not everyone sees the world in the same way. The vice president of labor relations will have concerns quite different from those of the vice president of financial relations who, in turn, will focus on different issues than the vice president of marketing, who will see things very differently than the general attorney.

Understanding each person's viewpoint will help you understand the suggestion he or she made. At that point, you can see what the implications might be if you automatically incorporate that person's suggestion about your media program. You may find that all suggestions are actual improvements on your plan; you may find that none of the suggestions will improve the plan but that they reflect territorial concerns rather than overall organization issues.

Of paramount importance is making sure you and your organization's legal counsel have a clear understanding of your individual roles, and a good working relationship. You need cooperation and mutual respect to be effective.

After incorporating any new data, make sure these same people see the final document labeled as your "working document." This is the plan from which you will work day by day. This also is the basis for the measurement of your program and your individual performance. Each person on the media relations staff should have a copy of the final plan as well. It should be referred to often and updated regularly.

If you and your staff think of the media plan as a "List of Things To Do," it will help bring that plan into the day-to-day reality of the job. We all know the satisfaction we get from completing and then crossing through an item on a list; the same holds true with a well-written plan because you can cross off each tactic and, ultimately, each objective on the list.

Getting the Office Prepared

Generally speaking, not enough effort is spent outfitting a media relations office. Much time and frustration could be saved if more preparation were put into the physical items needed in your working area. If you were a dentist, would you open up shop without the proper equipment? And a lawyer would not think of hanging out a shingle without making sure the necessary reference books were nearby.

The physical equipment for media relations may be determined by the way in which your business operates. You may get a simple word processor or a computer complete with Internet capability, database software and graphics support, if that is how your company thinks. You may need plenty of filing space and work space, or you may be able to work from a cubbyhole or from your home office.

The telecommunications system is important. Reporters should never be frustrated in their attempts to reach you because your telephone and/or fax line is busy. You need either more than one line to your office, successive lines that automatically reroute to a secretary's or subordinate's line when your line is busy or a cellular phone. Whatever system you select, remember that the objective is to make sure a reporter can reach you when he or she wants to—not when it is convenient for you.

The use of e-mail as a delivery tool is extremely important as more and more newsrooms accept material electronically. Make sure your e-mail system has a good broadcast capability and a personal address book.

Finally, you'll need a fax machine, preferably one with memory, multiple distribution capability and plain paper feed. Direct line access to public relations news lines or even newsrooms is a high plus.

Your office should be a veritable library of resource information. Among the books, software and other materials that should be readily accessible to you are:

1. An up-to-date dictionary
2. Style manual (your own or one such as the *AP Stylebook*)
3. Thesaurus
4. Your organization's annual reports for the past five years
5. Professional/academic journals/books relating to media relations
6. Company-produced material, such as recruitment brochures, product promotion material, benefits booklets
7. Copies of your organization's internal publications
8. Media directories

9. Organization charts
10. History of the organization (if one doesn't exist, consider writing it)
11. Company data/statistics
12. Calendar of events for the organization (earnings releases, product announcements, speeches to be given by the president, trade shows, annual meeting, seminars, fund drives)
13. Information kits consisting of, for example, the most recent annual report, a fact sheet about the company's products or services, the president's most current or best speech; keep about 25 available at all times
14. Business cards
15. Corporate goals and objectives/media goals and objectives
16. Atlas

All of this material will be used in some way at various times. Reporters can ask obscure questions, and you have to be ready to reply as quickly as possible. In adding to the above, you should subscribe to the publications with which you'll be dealing and set up a monitoring service for broadcast media and a clipping service for print.

Of key importance is the compilation of company/organization statistics. Journalists adore numbers: they are easy to read, easy to compare, work well in headlines and impress readers. Get a head start on potential questions involving numbers by composing such questions yourself. The result should be a file on statistics that can answer questions about:

1. Employee numbers. These could be broken down by management/nonmanagement, union/nonunion, male/female, percentage increases in different universes, location/geography, ethnic growth and distribution over the years, how many retirees, number laid off in the past year and the last five years. Member profiles follow a similar pattern.

2. Facilities. How many factories or office buildings or sales offices or service centers do you have? In what states? Countries? How much square footage? If large, how many total acres? When was each facility built? What are their street addresses? Who decides where to buy/build a facility? How many facilities have you closed? Sold? Are you adding new ones? Where? When?

3. Miscellaneous information. What are the key dates in your organization's history? What are key dates of inventions? What is your best production/service record? What are the odd hobbies among your employees? Who is the founder of your organization?

4. Executive information. What are the biographical data on each of your organization's executives? What is the percentage of male/female, ethnic division, local/national/expatriate? What about your board members? Who are they and where are they from?

5. Financial statistics. Beside the earnings and other information available in an annual report, compile information on how much payroll your organization paid out in the last year. How much in state/local taxes? How much to local/state suppliers? How much to minority suppliers? How much to suppliers outside your country? How much did your organization contribute to community or service programs?

6. Environmental statistics. How much did your organization spend to meet environmental standards? How much did the company recycle in paper/trash/aluminum/plastic? How many employees were involved in some environmental clean-up campaign? How many campaigns did the organization sponsor?

Because you do not know until the phone rings what might be on a reporter's mind, it is best to start gathering material now and to keep adding and updating constantly. Convenient ways to store material are in your computer (with backup) or even in easily accessible, indexed binders to facilitate use when you're not around. Whichever method you select, remember the object is to have material at hand that you can get to quickly and easily when a reporter asks you a question. A reporter will remember you if you are able to respond immediately without having to say, "I'll get back to you on that."

This is also a good time to begin compiling a list of subject-matter experts within your organization. When reporters call for an interview or general information, they do not begin by asking to speak specifically to "Mr. Jones, the manager of personnel statistics." Instead, the reporter is more likely to ask to interview someone who can talk about personnel statistics. The reporter does not know the people in your company—that is your job.

Start a list of subject-matter experts by thinking like a reporter and asking yourself: who is knowledgeable about pricing policies? Labor relations? Purchasing? Individual products?

Transportation services? Food services? Financial statistics? Member services? Global markets? Quality? Environmental affairs? Government affairs? If you list the subjects alphabetically and then beside each entry list the subject-matter expert (with office, home, pager and cell phone numbers and e-mail address), you may find your job much easier the next time a reporter calls.

Introducing Yourself

Now that you have a media relations plan and a well-coordinated office, it is time to start letting the media know who you are. With your media relations plan in mind, you need to select the persons within the media whom you need to meet. Do not assume that you have to know all the editors and program directors at all the newspapers, magazines and television and radio stations in a 500-mile radius or around the world.

You should select only those media, and only those editors, who can help you meet your goals and objectives. Those are the people critical to your efforts. Once you have made that list, do not rush out and attempt to call on all persons at once, nor immediately call and invite each one to lunch. Instead, take the time to think about what you want to do and plan your activities accordingly. If none of the editors know you because you are new to the job and/or new to the area, then your primary reason for contact is just to get to know these people.

Select your list of people and begin calling to set up appointment times when you can drop by and introduce yourself. Make sure you call at the least busy times: after the newspaper has been put to bed, after the television crews have received their assignments and have gone on location, after the radio newscast, after the bureau chief has filed the latest report. In making these appointments, you should ask for just a brief amount of time. Do not try to crowd all your appointments into the same day because you also want to be on time for each appointment.

As you meet each editor, assignment director or program director, present him or her with some basic material about you and your organization: the information kits mentioned earlier, several of your business cards and perhaps even some slides or photographs of your chief executives, your key product(s) and your company logo.

Ten "Be" Attitudes for Successful Media Relations

1. Be cooperative. Recognize that newspeople face constraints and expectations that most of us never dream of, and that if you can say "yes" to a request for information or an interview, you are making their job much less of a hassle.

2. Be accessible. Don't even think about restricting your availability to the media to regular business hours. Give out your home, cellular phone and pager numbers freely, and encourage reporters and editors to use them. If your organization is a 24-hour-a-day operation and someone else can handle routine inquiries after hours, it may be perfectly acceptable as a matter of policy to direct those routine media calls to that person. But if the reporter calls you first, don't ask him or her to jump through hoops by saying, "Why don't you call so-and-so"; give the answer yourself and suggest that the next time the reporter call the person on duty. Let the reporter know that you are always available if a question cannot be answered by someone else satisfactorily. Try to return all phone calls from the media within an hour.

3. Be direct. When you can't help a reporter, say so, and explain why. Don't be defensive, don't sound pained and overburdened and above all, don't display arrogance. You should be genuinely sorry that you can't help a reporter, because it is a missed opportunity for both of you.

4. Be fair. Don't give opportunities for in-demand interviews only to certain media outlets and not to others. If your chief executive officer is suddenly thrust into the spotlight, for example, and agrees to just one block of time for an interview, don't offer that time only to the news organization screaming the loudest.

5. Be a resource. It you can't arrange an interview or answer a question for a reporter, whenever possible suggest someone else who can. It is always better to end a conversation with a reporter by giving him or her another direction to pursue instead of a dead end.

6. Be an authority. Learn all you can about your organization and its industry: history, financial condition, goals, future, mission. And learn everything you can about how newsrooms—both print and broadcast—operate. Your goal should be to inform newspeople of important trends as well as converse knowledgeably with them about their business.

7. Be an educator. You need to educate two very different constituencies—your co-workers and media representatives—about each other. Hold workshops, informal meetings and media training seminars if appropriate, to defuse distrust and misunderstanding.

8. Be an advocate. It's sometimes tricky to walk that tightrope between two sets of clients—those within your organization and those in the media. Although one of your primary responsibilities is to present your organization favorably to the media, it is just as important to reinforce the value of the media to your organization.

9. Be a strategist. This is where "proactive" media relations comes in. Don't make the mistake of thinking that if you're not out there pumping up the organization's agenda every time you have contact with a media person you're not doing your job. Be selective in what you promote about your organization.

10. Be a team player. This rule is really the internal version of Rule Number One. You'll find that becoming a team player is a great way to let your organization know how successfully you are practicing the preceding nine rules. Seek out information from key people throughout your organization so that you can stay informed about critical developments. Keep others in your department who don't work in media relations apprised of your activities. What does all this lead to? Building relationships and credibility—both inside and outside your organization.

Debra Gelbart, Phoenix, AZ

You should not try to sell something on this first trip out. Your objectives at this time are to let the media know you, to recognize you and to know how to reach you. If you come asking for air time or editorial consideration, you could be considered a hard-line salesperson instead of a media relations professional. The personal contact should be maintained throughout the year in various ways. Do not wait until you need the media to be on your side in a tough situation.

If you cannot personally visit each editor, reporter or program director occasionally, at least keep up by telephone, fax, e-mail or by dropping a note to them. One way to do this is to have these people put on the mailing list to receive your employee or member publication. This keeps the company in the editor's mind and also provides an opportunity for that editor to come up with his or her own ideas for stories.

Always take advantage of meeting with and working with the media at your organization's key trade shows and conferences. Often, this will be the only time you will get to see many of these people.

Another way to enjoy contact without compromise is to join, if it is possible, a local press club or some other association frequented by the news media. You may want to attend workshops, seminars or lectures conducted by the news media. This gives you the benefit of learning more about the audience that you serve while, at the same time, letting the media know by your presence that you take your position seriously and professionally.

Don't let globalization lead you to thinking you have to fly across the ocean to meet and work with key editors overseas. Initially, you can work through a local bureau editor and take advantage of visits by editors from other countries to trade shows in your country. Also, plan to work via fax and/or e-mail.

Meanwhile, Back at the Office . . .

If you are out meeting the media, attending lectures, dropping by the press club or attending trade shows, who is minding the store? Office coverage, both when you are there and when you are not, is another element of media relations that is too often overlooked. Such an omission courts disaster. You must, in essence, be prepared to serve the media 24 hours a day, seven days a week. The people who work for you and the executives you support must understand that, and be knowledgeable in how to help you serve the media. Reporters working for the morning newspaper might need you before the late night news. Radio could need you any hour on the hour. If you deal with global media, compound this by numerous time zones. Make sure your home, pager and cell phone numbers are on all your business cards and news releases along with your fax number and e-mail address. If any of those numbers change, that is a good reason to contact all your media to notify them of the change.

Make sure your office staff knows how to handle any media inquiry. They will need to get the name of the reporter (accurately!), the name of the medium he or she represents, the telephone number where the reporter can be reached (check that number twice), the deadline under which the reporter is working, and the nature of the request. In short, you are attempting to get any of the same information that would normally be requested of a caller. With a reporter, however, the timing is often more critical.

When you issue a release, make sure that you (or the person listed on the release as the contact person) are at the office through late afternoon to catch any calls from reporters working the morning papers or from television news directors for the evening news. The effort you just expended on issuing that release is wasted if you leave the office at 4:30 P.M. and the journalists do not come on their beat or shift until later. A cellular phone is useful, particularly if you have a long commute or spend a great deal of time driving to appointments. Journalists may try to reach you in the car or at home. If you have any dead time when you cannot be reached at any of your numbers, an opportunity may be lost. Be prepared for middle-of-the-night calls to accommodate media in other countries and time zones.

Also make sure that during lunch there is always someone to answer the media department's telephones. You know from personal experience the frustration of hearing a telephone ring for some minutes, especially a telephone you know should be answered because it is a business number. You also know that your opinion of the people at the other end of the line decreases in direct proportion to the number of times the telephone rings or the vagueness of the recorded message. You work very hard building credibility with the media; do not let it disappear because everyone went to lunch at the same time. If you do not have voice mail at the office and at home, get them. And check your voice mail constantly to make sure you're not missing a critical call.

There is an adage that says "Failing to plan is planning to fail." This is true of most things, but it especially proves itself with media relations. Whether you are setting up a year's program, a visit with an editor, office coverage or a delivery system of news releases, planning will help you do your job more efficiently, more quickly and with more assurance. With planning you should attain your objectives, one of which is to help the reporter meet his or her objectives.

Case Study: Honeywell Bylined Authors Program

Honeywell's Home and Building Control Division had a daunting challenge in 1998—to change the building media's perception that the company was not a proactive industry leader in technology.

In order to create positive relationships with key building decision makers, Honeywell needed to change its image in the media from passive and reactive to innovative and proactive.

Need/Opportunity

Honeywell, with the help of Tunheim Santrizos Company, conducted a thorough media audit. Both the need and opportunity for the program were determined by the following five findings:

Finding I: While acknowledged as an industry leader, Honeywell is not perceived as interesting or dynamic by the media.

Finding II: Honeywell's key messages, visions and strategies are not reaching the trade media.

Finding III: Honeywell's Building Control key management does not have a solid relationship with the trade media.

Finding IV: Honeywell's Building Control communication efforts are viewed as reactive and passive.

Finding V: While in general most reporters believe Honeywell provides quality, useful media materials, Honeywell's Building Control communicators are not consistently meeting the needs of editors and reporters.

Intended Audience

Honeywell's Home and Building Control Division determined that in order to reach its key audiences, it needed to develop its media communications skills and foster strong relationships with influential trade publications. Honeywell broke down its key audiences into two tiers—influencers and decision makers.

Influencers: Honeywell targeted editors and writers in trade publications willing to create a working relationship with Honeywell experts. These members of the media were a direct link to important decision makers in the building control industry. Without eliminating the existing communications barrier, Honeywell could not reach its other key audience.

Decision Makers: Despite years of developing the industry's finest building control products, additional efforts were needed to reach vital decision makers. Honeywell needed to bridge the communications gap to key customers and potential advocates by reinforcing its position as an industry leader and expert.

Objectives

After completing the research, Honeywell developed the following two objectives:

Objective I: Change the media's perception of Honeywell from reactive and passive to proactive and innovative, by providing editorial and informational services on new technology and industry trends to key editors in the building control industry.

Objective II: Create a successful trade media relations program, to increase coverage in targeted publications.

Program Summary and Solution

Honeywell created a bylined authorship program to act as the backbone of its nationwide trade media relations campaign. Honeywell evaluated its media relations efforts, researched trade media perceptions, connected Honeywell experts with targeted editors and, ultimately, changed the media's image of the company while receiving improved coverage.

Honeywell immediately began developing the Honeywell Bylined Author Program by identifying key trade publications and discovering what editors and reporters wanted and needed to hear. Stories were pitched to editors selected through media research and interest from the publication.

Honeywell communication managers identified internal experts to act as official writers and supervisors of the bylined articles. Capitalizing on Honeywell's Building Control depth of technical expertise would be essential when discussing the importance of the articles with editors.

Honeywell identified pertinent themes and drafted outlines for the technical pieces. "Sourcing Sessions"—informal interviews and conversations between Honeywell experts and communication personnel—helped develop appropriate messages for the features. Stories ranging from "Access Control" to "Building Automation" were written, distributed and approved, and eventually secured in trade publications.

Limitations and Challenges

The challenge before Honeywell's Home and Building Control Division was significant. Three serious limitations accompanied the obvious challenge—reinvent the division's image in the building media. The limitations included:

* Coordinating the busy schedules of Honeywell experts and communication personnel to ensure deadlines were met.
* Convincing editors and reporters that Honeywell's Building Control technical expertise was valuable and relevant to each publication's target audience.
* Producing a successful media relations program throughout 1998 on a modest budget; a budget of $40,000 was proposed.

Evaluating Program Success

Honeywell achieved its objectives as follows:

Objective I: Honeywell developed an expert bylined authorship program that will serve as the cornerstone of its continuing trade media relations campaign. The results were achieved by:

* Obtaining positive responses from influential trade editors and reporters. Media perception of Honeywell has changed dramatically since the program was instituted. Honeywell has documented stronger relationships with the media, as well as continued requests from editors for more bylined articles on new building control technology, trends and services.
* Generating positive feedback from Honeywell experts and "authors" who now feel comfortable working with and speaking to members of the trade press.
* Increasing credibility and visibility for Honeywell's communicators as experts in their field, as evidenced by correspondence from media members and feedback at industry trade shows.

Objective II: As of December 1, 1998, the Honeywell Bylined Author Program has been a success. Honeywell has reached more than one million industry professionals with coverage in 33 targeted trade magazines. Trade placements featuring Honeywell's bylined articles on its superior technology, products and services include coverage in *Computer Life Engineered Systems, Contracting Business* and *Plant Engineering*, among others.

Chapter 3

NEWS
What It Is and
How It Gets to the Public

The Internet and the explosion of cable and satellite TV channels are blurring the boundaries between news and information. This does not mean the end of newspapers or TV news programs. It surely means that they will lose influence and dispense less "traditional" news.[1]

—Robert J. Samuelson
***Washington Post* Writers Group**

The increase in opinion, speculation and argument documented . . . in the American press, especially on television and radio, seems incontrovertible . . . This kind of programming serves more as entertainment than information and is cheap to produce and disseminate in nearly limitless quantity. News, by contrast, is expensive, especially the kind of investigative reporting called for in the Lewinsky scandal, and in scant supply.[2]

—James B. Stewart
Review of *America in the Age of Mixed Media*

Times change. And along with them, definitions change. Trying to pin down what is "news" becomes an endless exercise, with as many definitions as there are public relations practitioners, journalists and academicians. Or even playwrights. George Bernard Shaw opined that the media are "unable, seemingly, to discriminate between a bicycle accident and the collapse of civilization."[3]

Modern-day observers of the media are bemoaning the obsession of networks with "infotainment," a hybrid of news and entertainment, designed to hold viewers longer. Is this the definition of news?

Bill Kovach and Tom Rosenstiel conclude in *America in the Age of Mixed Media* that "a true and reliable account of the day's events has been undermined and displaced by whatever passes for continuous news. Power has shifted from reporters to sources whose agendas are often hidden. Argument and opinion, the more strident the better, have supplanted information. And there is a fixation on the big story that will deliver a large audience and ratings, with O.J. Simpson as the model."[4] Is this the definition of news?

Surveys continue to cite television as the primary source of viewers' news and information yet, according to Ralph Nader, "News programs are now down to 8.2-second sound bites when covering elections, compared with 42 seconds in the 1960s."[5] Is 8.2 seconds the definition of news?

Sometimes, though, the simplest definitions are the best.

A company newspaper once interviewed some construction workers at a site in Texas, asking each the questions: "How much of what you read in newspapers and what you see on television news shows do you believe? Why?" An equipment foreman ended his answer with the statement: "We only get to see and hear what they [the news media] want us to."[6] That answer is, in essence, a definition of news.

If information does not get past the final editor's desk, it does not get printed, it does not get read on radio, described on television or put on-line and, thus, it does not become reported news. Such editorial processing of information is not unique to the news media. All of us make decisions each day—about which pieces of information we will keep to ourselves and which pieces we will share with peers, subordinates, superiors, families and friends. It is a process that appears benign except when in the hands of news media personnel. In that arena, the process seems to be a show of power with a blatant disregard for the "real" truth.

For the media relations professional, the task is not the delivery of news to an editor. A more accurate characterization is the delivery of properly prepared material that might be passed on by an editor to become news. What criteria do editors use in determining whether or not material will become news?

Michigan State University conducted a survey for the American Society of Newspaper Editors and the Newspaper Readership Project to answer that question. The journalists queried defined news as having the following characteristics:

1. **Consequence**. Educates and informs; is important to lifestyle or ability to cope; has a moral or social importance; is "should know" material

2. **Interest**. Is unusual, entertaining, has human interest, arouses emotions or would cause people to talk about it

3. **Timeliness**. Is current; is a new angle on events or a new trend

4. **Proximity**. Pertains to local issues, trends or events

5. **Prominence**. Concerns famous people, famous events; has received other media coverage[7]

Other perspectives emphasize different factors. A public relations textbook asserts that news is "anything timely that is interesting and significant to readers or viewers." A handbook on media relations gives two definitions of news: (a) the first information about any event that interests a large number of people; and (b) not what you want to tell other people but what other people want to know about you.

The *Public Relations Journal* reported a change in the concept of news: "For the TV networks, news encompasses more than just major headlines. It also includes human-interest stories, entertainment, sports, fashion, and even food news. This broad-spectrum approach is found on the evening TV news and in newspapers as well. It is no longer unusual, for example, to see Dan Rather or Tom Brokaw reporting on a human-interest story such as the demise of a small mining town, the latest fashion shows in Paris, or the return to popularity of American softball."[8]

Whichever definition you choose, remember this: news is a perishable commodity. Nothing dies more quickly than yesterday's news.

For the media relations practitioner who has been given the edict to "Get this news out right away," determining if that material has a chance of becoming news is not as intimidating as you think. Your information must be good enough to meet the ultimate definition of news: it's whatever the editor says it is. Basically, there are six questions you can ask yourself about the material. These questions correlate well with what most journalists believe to be news criteria:

1. Is the story local? Does it have a local "hook" to it, something that will interest readers or viewers in this area? For trade or specialty publications, is the material of interest to the targeted readership?

2. Is this information unique or unusual? Is this the first, the latest, the last, the biggest of something?

3. Is the material timely? Is this something happening now or that will happen in the near future? Does the material relate to another item that is currently being discussed publicly?

4. Is it timeless? Is this a topic with a long shelf life, such as AIDS, the environment or ethics?

5. Does this information concern people? Our curiosity about the lives and events of others is evidenced by the strong sales of periodicals devoted just to people and the growing number of "people" shows on television.

6. Does this material create human interest? Pathos? Humor?

If the answer to any of these questions is yes, chances are your material will get an editor's attention and perhaps be placed in the newspaper or on the evening news.

Hard versus Soft News

News generally falls into one of two categories. Hard news most often happens by itself. An explosion or fire is hard news. The results of a board meeting can be hard news. A strike at the factory is hard news. This is news that the public needs to know. Soft news, on the other hand, is news that the public does not need to know. Soft news is a story about a teenager who volunteers to help the elderly. It is the dedication of a war memorial. It is the story of a blind operator at a keyboard. Soft news also is called "evergreen" because it most often has a long shelf life and does not have to be used today. Hard news must be used immediately or it perishes.

Media relations practitioners probably will find, if they examine their placement activities, that they deal most often with soft news. Hard news items that must be planned for and placed each

The James E. Lukaszewski, APR, of the Lukaszewski Group, created a checklist for determining newsworthiness. The list is based on attributes reporters believe that news has:

- *Surprise:* News is about things turning out differently than we had planned. These outcomes aren't always bad, but most of the time they are.

- *Affect:* News has emotional appeal—it affects people—which means that news of machines breaking down is not very newsworthy.

- *Effect:* News is about what the result is—things like death, injury, homelessness, personal harm, etc.

- *Secrecy:* News is about whatever you want to hide. The media wants whatever the world isn't supposed to know.

- *Conflict:* News is usually about conflict arising from one or more of four sources: from *insiders*, like whistle blowers and disgruntled employees; from *outsiders*, like our competitors or competing interests; by *organized opposition*; and/or by *unprepared spokespersons*.

- *Reporter's interest:* News is more worthy if it hits close to home, i.e., the reporter's nephew works in the plant that just burned down.

- *Mistakes:* News is about when business errs, because American business is expected to function perfectly at all times (see "Surprise").

- *Change:* Newsworthy by definition.

- *Editor's perspective:* News is what the editor thinks it is. If the editor thinks you have a problem . . . you do have a problem.

year can be determined easily: annual meeting results, quarterly earnings, election of new officers, opening a new office, launching an on-line business, announcing a new product, global expansion, increase of services. Such items constitute a small percentage of the practitioner's effort. The bulk of work likely deals with soft news placement—trying to interest the media in timeless material that can inform, educate or entertain readers or viewers.

Many practitioners fail to take advantage of soft news placement opportunities because of the preconceived notion that the media would not be interested in the story of a company-sponsored fishing tournament or the planning involved in setting up a major exhibition of agency services. To keep from falling into this trap, remember that what may be "old hat" to you because of familiarity may be considered news by an editor unfamiliar with your organization. If a story idea passes the five-question test outlined previously, it could become news.

Looking for News

Whether you practice media relations full-time, part-time or as a volunteer, the way to find news in your organization is to become a reporter. If you think as a reporter trained to ask questions, you will find that you are constantly coming across story ideas.

Do not just accept the existence of your company's training or engineering departments. Why are they there? What role do they play in the accomplishment of overall organizational goals and objectives? What relevance can they have to today's concerns such as the environment, the Internet, loss of job security, downsizing, literacy, child care/elder care? Why does the organization invest in these departments? If you look closely, you will find a mine of interesting stories.

Do not assume that personnel news would not be used. Promotions are newsworthy not just to the business, financial or trade press, but also to the person's hometown papers, alumni magazines and professional society journals. Notices of service anniversaries, training courses completed, retirements and honors received are welcome at various publications; the trick is to match the medium with the message. Some of these items, depending on visual appeal, could interest television as well. All of these items are good fodder for your organization's intranet as well as its news site.

An excellent source of story material about your organization is the internal newsletter or newspaper. Sending this publication out to editors in your area—either via a printed copy or on-line—often can generate a flow of activity as the media seek to expand a story or to get a different angle on it.

Items covered in an internal publication that could interest journalists include:

1. Suggestion award winners and entrepreneurs. Rewarding an employee for ingenious thinking makes for a good story beyond the company gates, as does a story about an employee who acts as an internal entrepreneur.

2. Company-sponsored blood drives. Finding out who has donated the most blood for the most number of years can help an editor get a story idea. Perhaps there is an employee who has traced his/her donation to see who received it. Perhaps blood collected at your facility was sent to a disaster site.

3. Unusual hobbies. The significant word here is "unusual" because a hobby truly must be that before an editor will consider the idea. However, almost every employee has a hobby and the possibility exists that some are unusual.

4. Unusual jobs. Not all jobs are glamorous, nor are they dull and boring. There are, within most organizations, jobs that do not fit the normal mold. For example, who inspects the cables that haul up the elevators in the World Trade Center?

5. Service projects sponsored by the company or by the employee clubs. Employee clubs often will have a designated person to contact media about these projects but the company media relations person could be nearby as well to serve as a consultant.

6. Introduction of new technologies, equipment or software. The information age brings with it an abundance of items about new, labor-saving, information-sharing, global-connecting devices and software. Depending on the function, there probably is a story. Technology stories work well in the media of developing countries.

7. Seasonal events. Special activities planned for major holidays should be brought to the media's attention as soon as possible. There are more organizations wanting to highlight their activities than there are media slots in which to place them. Look for what makes your activity different or unique. Humanize it.

8. Production records. Turning out the zillionth widget can be an item worth noting if your organization is the first to make a zillion widgets, or if you did so in record time. For the nonprofit area, there can be production records in terms of time, numbers of people served or other units of measurement.

9. Construction news. If your organization is building a new facility or renovating an existing one, information about the progress may be welcomed by the media as a possible visual story or, at the very least, a reminder that a story will be coming when the work is completed.

10. Visiting dignitaries. If a home-office executive is visiting the local plant and can make appearances or be available for interviews, the media would like to know. The same holds true for national or international officers of civic or professional organizations.

11. Organization milestones. There are always anniversaries of one kind or another to commemorate; often, these dates will be relevant to the community or offer an opportunity to reflect on changes brought about by your company or service organization.

12. Organization awards. Vendors, government agencies, service groups and others often present awards to organizations for achievements in such areas as conservation, quality and community support. Both groups benefit from publicity on the award.

This list is far from complete, but it shows the possibilities for news that already exist within your organization.

Coming up with a list of story ideas that can be presented to editors is like preparing a menu: there will always be regular offerings for customers, and there should also be daily specials to entice customers to return. Do not be discouraged, however, if the editor decides he or she does not want anything from your offering today; tomorrow, that same editor may decide your fare is the best in town.

Directing Your Story to the Right Medium

"A newspaper is as much a product as an automobile or a pair of shoes. The selling features of each particular product make the difference between it and its competition."[9] Too many media relations professionals forget that television shows, periodicals and radio newscasts are businesses and not services. As a result of this initial misunderstanding, these professionals often try to market the wrong story to the wrong medium.

One way to help direct your stories to the best possible medium is to break that medium down into its component parts—or products. Understanding the selling features of a medium's product will help you more carefully place your story. Editors will appreciate your understanding of their marketing process and will doubly appreciate that you are not wasting their time. Starting with

From the editors of *communication briefings* come these ideas on ways to generate media interest in your organization:

- Look for logical connections between your business and the goodwill services you may be able to offer your community at little or no additional expense. A manufacturing company with a large grounds-keeping staff launched a neighborhood tree-planting program.

- Consider launching a public information service aimed at educating consumers on issues you and others in your organization are experts on. A hospital uses nurses and doctors to talk about child care. A detergent company uses its technicians to discuss the best ways to care for furniture, clean stains and organize housework.

- Never miss the chance to develop a year-end wrap-up story on your organization's successes during the past 12 months. *Also:* Consider doing a look ahead as each new year approaches.

- Spend some time developing local angles for your organization during national awareness weeks and days

- Always include freelance writers on your news-release distribution list. While this may not result in an immediate story, it will keep you and your organization in front of folks who frequently develop magazine and newspaper feature stories.

- Look for ways to promote a cleaner environment in your city. Donate materials (trash bags, trucks, refreshments and so on) to groups sponsoring litter clean-up programs.

How to Get Results With Publicity
© 1992 by Communication Publications and Resources, Blackwood, NJ.

five main media categories, you can develop your own selection list for the particular media that you wish to attract.

Newspapers

Whether published weekly or daily, newspapers are divided into sections: national/ international news, sports, business, entertainment, home living, technology, real estate and other sections.

Knowing who makes the decisions for each section, what the requirements are for that section and the schedule for the section's production are prerequisites to deciding where you should attempt to place stories. It is possible that one story might have several angles and could be of interest to several section editors. For example, the business editor would want to know the financial impact of your company's new product announcement and how it relates to the local business community. If it is a consumer product, the home or leisure editor would be interested in knowing what the product does for the customer. The lifestyles editor might want to know of your organization's new services. Each editor serves a different constituency and is interested only in what each story means in terms of the interests of that constituency.

Newspapers also have columnists, local and/or syndicated, who specialize in areas that may support the sections or reflect the general editorial stance of the newspaper. Columnists can be strong selling features for newspapers, so getting to know them is important.

A columnist writing on economics is a good target for an in-depth explanation relating to new pricing policies for your industry's products or services. The columnist in the family section who provides household hints wants only "how-to" material and cannot use detailed or lengthy background information. The columnist catering to farmers and gardeners would be interested in your company's new herbicide. A medical columnist might welcome information about your organization's new counseling and referral services. The columnists on the Internet and Web sites need almost-daily grist for their mills.

When marketing a story that has several angles or possibilities, make sure each editor, columnist or writer knows you are talking to the others. You should never assume that internal communications on a newspaper are at peak efficiency. If your story appears twice in the same edition, you have lost your credibility.

Newsletters

Newsletters, whether in print or on the computer screen, are a popular—and still growing—medium in a world crowded with publications. Their rise can be attributed in part to the format of the medium. Newsletters offer bite-sized chunks of information in a small publication, or e-pub, that can be easily stored—or just as easily tossed away or deleted. Because of their brevity, newsletters can concentrate on one specific topic within a broad area of interest or can be devoted to a particular broad issue. For example, you might find a newsletter written for investors in petroleum products only, another designed for all investors, still another for collectors of antique silver and another for human resource professionals.

Newsletter staffs are small and generally appreciate your news releases and story offerings as long as the information is geared to their newsletter's audience. In serving newsletters, you should inquire whether they are interested in photographs or graphics.

Be sure to check publication schedules. A printed newsletter has a set publication date where an electronic one may vary in publication dates and/or updates.

Magazines

The proliferation of specialized print and electronic magazines is making placement in this medium easier in terms of identification but more difficult in terms of quantity. The first step is to identify which magazines reach your particular audiences. You may have to compile several breakout lists if your media operation is extensive. For instance, you may find you need magazines that reach your customers (by level of decision making, by geography, by financial status), your industry (by specific area of technology, services, support) or the public at large (for business, leisure, product or consumer issues).

Like the newspapers, each magazine may then be divided into sections, such as marketing, finance, technology or people. However, because the magazine itself serves a special constituency, there will not be as much subdivision. The same rules of careful analysis apply to magazines with one added feature: magazines are candidates to run photographs and graphics supplied by you. Often, a photograph of a new product or one representing a new service may be run as a stand-alone piece if there is not room for the entire story. Check the magazine's requirements carefully, however, to avoid sending a product photograph to a publication or e-line that never uses them.

Many magazines run special issues or annuals in conjunction with trade shows, fairs or seasonal events (back to school, fashion, city-wide events). You may decide to target these special issues instead of broadsiding the publication throughout the year.

Radio

Radio is perhaps the least complex of the media and, very possibly, is the most overlooked. Radio stations follow the trend of print by specializing and appealing to distinct, segmented audiences. This audio specialization produces a good product for the radio station but can frustrate the media relations professional who does not take the time to thoroughly investigate the medium.

The broadcast range of radio stations is an important factor for you to know. The stations with the widest, most powerful ranges are the ones you need if you have an emergency, such as an urgent call for blood at your hospital or updating the public on a chemical spill that may necessitate evacuation. You need these power stations no matter what kind of music they play! Your personal preference may not lean towards country music, hard rock or classical, but if you need powerful broadcasting strength, go to the source.

You need to determine the product line of each station to help you decide which stations to cater to at which times. There are all-news stations, all-classical stations, all-country stations and all easy-listening stations. The majority of stations are a mix of talk, music, commentary, news, sports, special programming—each station trying to find its niche in a rapidly growing radio audience.

Most radio stations manage with small news operations. They depend primarily on material that comes over the wire services, is delivered to the station or is called in to the news director. Many radio stations, large and small, like to use "actualities" to liven up the newscast. An actuality is a live or taped comment from you or some other organization spokesperson. Being willing and available to provide an actuality will often enhance your position with the radio news director who makes the decision about your story offering.

Stations that offer call-in talk shows may be of interest to you if your organization is involved in a sensitive or volatile issue and you need to set the record straight or to respond to the public's concerns. Specialized radio programs offer opportunities to present in-house experts on a particular subject matter talking about consumer items, technology or farm-related topics.

Talk with radio news directors and program directors to get detailed information on a station's opportunities. Then target your material carefully to a listening audience. For example, early -morning and late-afternoon talk shows can have a large "driving audience" of automobile commuters.

Television

Because television offers both sound and sight, because the industry is fragmenting its audiences through cable television channels and because television channels now double up with their own Web sites, a media relations specialist must approach this medium with a different perspective. Most people believe they get their news from television. However, television news shows account for only a small percentage of the station's offerings. Supporting the newscasts are network shows, locally produced variety/entertainment/talk shows, syndicated specials, documentaries, movies and network-produced, live coverage of events. Even the news show itself is so fragmented that only 8–10 minutes of a 30-minute show can be called "news."

Unless you are in charge of national media for your organization, you should be concerned primarily with locally produced shows for your story and news offerings. The local news shows are the prime targets for your releases. Assignment editors at the television station determine which stories will be covered for the early- and late-evening news. They make the determination based partially on the real news value of the item and partially on its visual qualities. Television is a motion picture medium, which means that your news or story idea should include suggestions about how the story can be shown. A slide of the president of your company may be visual, but it gets dull after just a few seconds because it does not move. If your item is short, then the slide may be all that is needed. Decide carefully if you can support your soft news story visually before offering it to television news.

Local talk shows provide an excellent medium for your subject-matter experts—if they are well trained—to talk about, demonstrate and respond to issues. The show's producer can give you more detailed information about the requirements for the show, time needed for booking guests and capability for live demonstrations.

Cable television provides channels on health, sports, news, music, history, biographies, travel, religion, country music, movies and many other interests. In some markets, there may be foreign-language channels. Working closely with your in-house video production team, you can provide certain cable channels with programs produced by your organization to meet your target audiences.

Analyzing all the factors related to each medium will help determine where to send your message. One story idea may not appeal to all media, whether hard news or soft news. Quarterly sales results, for example, are considered hard news, but figures and percentages should be seen to be best understood. Newspapers and magazines may have the space to run this material, but a television assignment editor probably will decide the information is not worth the effort to create the graphics. Radio editors have no means of conveying visual information and may decide the material would require too much explanation in an already crowded newscast.

Conversely, a story idea about a picnic for disabled children may get excellent response from television because of its visual capabilities, no response from radio because of lack of imagery capabilities and mild response from print media because of the amount of space needed to create empathy with the project through feature writing or still photography. The key, of course, is to carefully determine which medium should be connected with which piece of material.

Directories and Mailing Lists

With the profusion of new media concepts comes the potential difficulty of tracking each medium, editor, writer, schedule and requirement. There are numerous directories available to a media relations practitioner. They cover print and electronic media from international to local levels. Determining which directory best suits your needs may take some time and study but will be well worth the effort.

Before rushing out to purchase an expensive directory or the latest CD-ROM, visit the public library to peruse the directories available there. In looking through the media directories, ask yourself these questions and any others you can think of that suit your specific situation:

1.   How often is the directory/CD-ROM printed? Updated?
2.   What geographic region(s) does it cover?
3.   Does it include trade publications? Specialty magazines?
4.   Does it list radio and television? Cable networks?
5.   Does it give the names of editors? Columnists?
6.   Are there editorial and photo guidelines?
7.   Is the circulation for the publication listed?
8.   Are the viewing audiences for television and the listening audiences for radio listed?
9.   Does the directory list television talk shows?

10. Are scheduled print/air times listed?
11. Does it give names of individual contacts?
12. Are photo, video, audio, graphic criteria listed?

As a check on what you select from the directory, talk with your organization's marketing department. They can tell you which trade publications they think are important. You can then learn the names of editors and write for editorial and photo criteria if they are not listed in the publication. At the same time, you can get the latest editorial calendar.

Talk with your advertising department or agency. Your editorial media strategies should, at a minimum, coordinate with those of the advertising group. Preferably, the strategies should be integrated. Advertising must research publications to discover which ones reach a critical buying audience. From this you can easily learn which magazines target a key audience for your message.

Ultimately, you will want to create your own directory. In doing so, try to create the listing in a way that best reflects your media efforts. For example, if you deal almost exclusively with business news, you probably will not need a listing of sports editors. Your breakouts can be in various categories and even cross-referenced by geography, business publication or broadcast capabilities.

One directory breakout could look like this:

I. Local
    A. Business publications
        1. Magazines (editor, columnists, criteria, phone/fax numbers, e-mail address)
        2. Newspapers (editors, writers, deadlines, reach numbers, e-mail address)
        3. Newsletters (editor, deadlines, criteria, frequency, e-mail address)
    B. TV Business Broadcasts (assignment editor, lead time)
    C. Radio Business Broadcasts (deadlines, criteria)
    D. Wire Services (editors, beats, deadlines)
    E. Syndicated Columnists (topics, schedule)
    F. Web sites (topics, links)

II. National
    A. Business Publications

      1. Magazines
      2. Newspapers
      3. Newsletters
   B. TV Business Broadcasts
   C. Radio Business Broadcasts
   D. Wire Services
   E. Syndicated Columnists
   F. Web sites

  III. Global
   A. Business Publications
      1. Magazines
      2. Newspapers
      3. Newsletters
   B. Wire Services
   C. Embassy press secretaries
   D. Web sites

Under each category should go all the information you can possibly get about each publication or electronic service. Perhaps the most important item is the name of the person with whom you will most often communicate. Remember, **you do not deal with newspapers or television, you deal with people**.

Some of the information you will need is

1. Name of publication/station/show/service/Web site
2. Name of editor/reporter/columnist
3. Street address (for delivering packages)
4. Mailing address (for ordinary correspondence)
5. Telephone number(s)
6. Facsimile number(s)
7. E-mail address
8. Deadline(s)
9. Photography requirements
10. Accepts case studies, by-lined
11. Issues editorial calendar
12. Use of actuality
13. Circulation

14. Broadcast range
15. Times of pertinent broadcasts
16. Special issues
17. Accepts video or audio for Web sites

Directories should be updated constantly. Keeping a directory on a computer is one way to make this chore easier, but there is nothing wrong with writing in the changes and updates by hand as you get them. The important thing is to have available an easy-to-use and fully functional directory.

Clearly, determining what news is and where it should be directed involves more than just writing a release and sending it to every medium in your area. Careful analysis of the information itself and the media to which it should be directed will help you achieve your media goals.

Chapter 4

TOOLS OF THE TRADE
From News Releases to
Background Briefings

The tool kit for the beginning media relations person contains many items; some familiar items used daily and obscure others needed only for the trickiest of chores. And, the tool kit continues to get larger and different, as technology improves old tools and has created new ones.

News Releases

Of the many ways to get into the media, the most commonly known and the most often misused is the news release. The cries of editors seem to be heard only in the wilderness as practitioners repeat mistakes under the guise of, "But, my release is different." If, indeed, that release is different, the information contained in it will appear in the newspaper or magazine, or on radio or television.

Most releases are not different, according to those in the know: the editors. These over-surveyed guardians of the media repeatedly cite horror stories of grammatical and typographical mistakes, cutesy-poo press kits, out-of-date mailing lists, lack of local angle, missing information, an abundance of meaningless management commentary, releases that are out of date or too long and corporate jargon that is indecipherable.

News releases are not designed to take the place of a reporter. Instead, a news release is a for-your-information memorandum to an editor. A release simply acquaints an editor with the basic facts of a potential story, just as a memo would. The editor will then decide if the proposed story warrants attention; if so, a reporter is assigned to gather more information and rewrite the material to fit the format of the print or electronic publication, radio or television.

The idea, simply, is to get editors to read the release—a difficult task when editors are bombarded with faxes, e-mails and pieces of paper only thinly disguised as news. Just as a memorandum should be short and to the point, so too should a news release. There also are basic components to a release:

1. The name of the organization. There is no need to go overboard with multicolored flashing letters and brilliant ink. A simple company or association letterhead will suffice. The name tells the reader the source of the release and gives credibility to the information. For electronic releases, use the organization's letterhead for faxes and the company e-mail address and name as the source of delivery.

2. Contact name and numbers. At the top of the release should be the name of the person to call for more information. All pertinent numbers (office, home, pager, cellular/digital, fax) should be listed (do not forget the area code or an "800" listing) as well as an e-mail address. The rationale for including several lines of contacts is simple: the media do not operate in a uniform nine-to-five day; even if they did, they are not all in the same time zone or the same country. Remember, also, that the pages of a news release sometimes are separated, so it is a good idea to have the contact name and numbers on the last sheet of a faxed or printed release as well.

3. A headline or tag line. This piece of information is not intended as a substitute for the publication's headline writer's efforts, Instead, it gives the reader a capsule phrase summing up the essence of the release. If this were the memorandum, the headline would be the same as the "Re:." Consequently, the headline tells the reader if this is something that needs to be attended to right away or if it can wait. For e-mail releases, you may want a header that pulls strong visual attention. Tina Koenig, writing for The PR Network, suggests following the Yahoo model: "When you have the choice between a ho-hum word and a hoo-haa word, go with the latter."[1]

4. A release time. This information, also at the top of the release, says when the information can be published or broadcast. It can read "Release upon receipt" or "Release immediately" or "Release Friday, December 16, 20__." A word of caution, however. Do not embargo information unless it is required. Editors know that embargoes on stories about a company open house are coy attempts at making the information seem more important than it is. There are times when embargoes must be honored; editors know and respect those times.

5. A date. Put down the date on which you are issuing the release; repeat the date in the release instead of using "today."

6. An ending. Of course a release ends, but editors, copyreaders and reporters are accustomed to looking for a "-30-" or "###" mark to say that the release is ended. Otherwise, a release that comes close to the bottom of a page could be misconstrued as only part of a longer story.

Those are the components of a release—the building blocks, as it were. Of equal importance is what the release says and how it says it.

Other suggestions for news releases are:

1. Follow an accepted journalistic style of writing. Get a copy of *The Associated Press Stylebook and Libel Manual* and use it!

2. Go easy on the length. There are no hard and fast rules about the length of a release; however, two typewritten pages, double-spaced, is considered the approved length. If your release is several pages long, you may wish to consider either breaking it up into several releases, each dealing with a specific topic, or issuing a short release with a longer fact sheet accompanying it.

3. Avoid breaks. It makes for easier reading and more accurate typesetting if you do not split words at the end of a line or split a sentence at the bottom of a page. Write "more" at the bottom of page 1 of the release to indicate there is a second page. If you are printing on both sides of the paper, write "over" at the bottom. If you are sending releases electronically, make sure recipients can tell when the copy stops.

4. Clear writing. Writing a release in corporate jargon, legalese or some other alien language makes as much sense as preparing a release in French and sending it to people who speak only English. Why? As an AT&T executive once cautioned writers: "I have used lawyer-talk out of what seemed to me to be necessary care for accuracy and safety. And it comes out the other end as a credibility gap."

5. Remember the pyramid. The inverted pyramid style of writing is not used just for news releases. The same style applies in writing personal letters, memos, briefs, white papers and other material. *The important information or the conclusion is given first*, with less important information following and, finally, the least important information at the end. Using the pyramid calls for a bit of taste, however. Although the lead paragraph of a release carries the most important information, it is not necessary to cram the answers to "Who? What? Where? Why? When? How?" into that first sentence or paragraph.

6. Adjectives are dangerous. Avoid the temptation to use superlatives in describing your organization's latest product, service or new executive. For one thing, such superlative claims may not be legally defensible; for another, use of adjectival claims hints that the writer had nothing of substance to say about the subject and threw in the adjectives for lack of anything else. An adjective can be used in a direct quote, however.

7. Make it local. One of the key criteria listed for what sells a release to an editor is the local angle or "hook" it has. For example, a national release announcing a new product can be localized by telling when the product will be available in your area, through what outlet and at what suggested retail price. Or, you may want to issue a release saying when a new medical treatment will be available at your hospital.

8. Attribute the news to a person, not a company or organization. Information is more credible if "John Doe, product manager of XYZ Co., today demonstrated the company's newest product" than if "XYZ Co. today announced it has a new widget."

9. Indent the paragraphs. This will make it easier for the editor to read your material.

10. Select a good typeface. This is true for hard copy and electronic versions of a release. You want the recipient to be able to read your material easily.

News Releases for Electronic Media

Isn't a release always a release? No. Not when one is for print and another is for electronic media. Both television and radio have special characteristics that require you to handle your release differently than if the release is going to print media. Primarily, the difference is that radio news is written for the ear; television news is written for the eye and the ear; whereas print and Internet news are written for the eye only.

The best test for electronic news writing is to prepare the release as though it were going to be read directly from your computer screen. Then, read the release aloud to someone and ask him or her to retell the message. You may find a disparity between what you said and what was heard.

Radio and TV broadcast style is not difficult, however. A few easy-to-remember rules will help you through:

1. Along with the release time, put down a "read time" such as ":15" for 15 seconds or ":30" for 30 seconds.

2. Because the material is written to time and not space, everything must be spelled out. There can be no abbreviations, no numerals and all names or unusual words should be spelled phonetically.

3. Sentences are short, with descriptive words before rather than after nouns. For example, "the thirty-nine-year-old vice president" instead of "the vice president, 39."

4. The inverted pyramid rule is not used in broadcast journalism. In print and on the computer screen, a reader can go back and reread a paragraph or a sentence; a radio listener cannot go back. Radio and television journalism is linear. In broadcast style, the release tells what the news is, then tells it again, and then tells it again. Here is an example:

   > The Smith and Jones Company will build a new manufacturing plant here in Anytown. The new facility will employ two thousand people to make the latest in electronic devices. Smith and Jones' newest operation will be ready in two years, cost five million dollars, and add several thousand dollars a year to the local tax base.

The fact that there will be a new plant was repeated three times to the listener.

5. For television, remember that the paramount consideration is visual interest. Your story about new ways to invest money for greater return sounds great and reads better but looks terrible with its charts, graphs and "talking head" expert. In contrast, a story about a white-water rafting trip for children who have never been out of a city reads like many other stories, sounds like a bunch of squealing children against a backdrop of rushing water but looks exciting, enticing and dangerous.

6. More and more, organizations are turning to video news releases (VNR) and audio news releases (ANR) or "electronic news releases" to reach television and radio stations. These are pre-packaged stories—news or feature—distributed either by satellite or on tape. There are pros and cons about VNRs and ANRs you should consider before adding them to your program.

On the plus side, both VNRs and ANRs can be beneficial to smaller TV and radio stations that do not have the capability to send camera crews or reporters to faraway locations to cover a story. Also, including the results of an annual report with either type of release can help boost coverage of an otherwise routine story.

Of growing importance is the value of VNRs to global operations. If having a multination, live tele-press conference is not an option, then issuing VNRs via satellite to support your conference might be a good alternative. Add to this the benefit of being able to add voice-overs in different local languages, and you can begin to see the strength of VNRs.

Perhaps the biggest plus is that you control the message and the footage. This control doesn't give you *carte blanche* to offer an advertisement in the form of an ANR or VNR, but it does help assure your message will not be lost.

On the negative side are a number of concerns as expressed by TV and radio news directors and assignment editors. The stations will not use a nonprofessional tape. This means you need expert help in shooting, editing, scripting and taping releases; such help can be expensive.

TV stations also can't edit or rework a VNR as easily as they can video they've shot on their own. Because many VNRs exceed a recommended length, they seldom will be used "as is." Different technical standards can make it difficult to edit a U.S. tape in other countries, and the quality suffers as a result—assuming a TV or radio station will go to the trouble of editing a tape prepared elsewhere. Further, some stations feel that using a canned release diminishes their credibility.

Measurement also is a key concern. While there have been many advances in measuring usage electronically, there remains the difficulty of learning the context of the usage. It's the equivalent of counting print column inches without knowing if the article is positive, neutral or negative.

Before you decide to add VNRs and ANRs to your tool kit, you need to spend time understanding the time and expense involved as well as the payback. You also need to determine whether a VNR is more appropriate or if "B-roll" footage would serve the same or a better purpose for television, and if call-in actualities might work better than an ANR.

If you decide to issue VNRs and ANRs, make sure they are prepared professionally, are sent to the right person at the right station for the right reason at the right time and in the right format.

Public Service Announcements

If you work for a nonprofit organization, you might be able to take advantage of free radio and television air time for public service announcements (PSA).

It is impossible for stations to use all the PSAs that come their way. To increase your chances of getting your PSA aired, follow some of these tips:

1. Quality over quantity. Because your PSA is competing with professional advertisements, you need to make sure your PSA matches that quality. It is better to have one well-done PSA that gets air time than 10 PSAs that don't. This means having the PSA created professionally, which requires a budget.

2. Focus, focus, focus. Instead of assuming that you need to contact all radio and TV stations in your area, investigate to see which ones reach your intended audience.

3. Stop, look and listen. Spend time with the public affairs or community affairs directors at your stations. Let them tell you if public service time is available and in what format(s) they want your material.

4. Don't get greedy. All nonprofit organizations want to have 60-second PSAs aired; why not offer 15-, 30-, 45- and 60-second versions of your PSA and be grateful for what you get?

5. One at a time. Your PSA should have only one message such as "Give blood," "Immunize your child" or "Get an eye checkup."

6. Redundancy. When you send in an audio or videotape PSA, always include a script—just in case.

7. Be nice. Always thank the station for airing your PSA even if it was at 3:00 A.M. If you're courteous and provide quality PSAs, you might get your PSA moved to prime time.

How to Write for the Ear

Write short sentences. Simple declarative sentences work best. Sentences cluttered with unneeded adjectives and adverbs may not be clear. Make them memorable: "You need room to negotiate." "Brand names will lose their appeal."

Use short words. Think about why people remember proverbs such as "A bird in the hand is worth two in the bush" and "A stitch in time saves nine."

Avoid rows of sibilant sounds such as "Some supervisors seem stifled." They're hard to say.

Try to end sentences with a one-syllable word. It's like having punctuation written in. Listeners can't see periods.

Avoid words listeners might not understand. Use "although," not "albeit"; "polite," not "affable"; "secret," not "arcane."

Frank Seltzer, Dallas, TX, quoted in *communication briefings*,
Blackwood, NJ, November 1993.

Interview

The interview, whether individual or at a press conference, is a highly successful tool. However, its sophistication calls for serious study and preparation. Chapter 6, "Spokespersons: Training and Briefing Them for Their Role," provides the material you need to conduct a successful interview.

Op-Ed Pieces

Another tool for the media relations kit is the op-ed piece. Named for its position in a newspaper—opposite the editorial page—the op-ed piece provides a place where your organization can offer an opinion on a subject or perhaps take a stand on a current issue.

Criteria for op-ed pieces will vary widely. There are some general criteria for op-ed pieces. On the average, op-ed pieces are run every day, from one article to two or three. The length appears most often to be about 750 words. Specifics may vary, but almost all op-ed editors agree wholeheartedly that the pieces must have two things: timeliness and creativity. The best advice is to read your local newspapers to determine their formats. After that, call to ask for specific rules. Some editors prefer to discuss the idea for an op-ed piece ahead of time, others prefer to receive the completed article with just a cover letter. There also may be constraints concerning copyright or usage.

Topics for op-ed pieces are multitudinous, ranging from opinions and analyses of public affairs, politics, education and law, to journalism, health care, religion and lifestyles. Topics can be of a local, national or international nature. They must, however, be timely and related to something that is happening now or is about to happen. No editor likes to receive a piece that already has been run in some other publication, nor does that editor care to receive an article on an issue that has been dead for months. Some editors prefer to avoid extremely controversial issues, feeling that adversary journalism can resemble a ping-pong game. Others encourage publication of diverse opinions on sensitive subjects.

Used judiciously, op-ed pieces can be the answer to many an executive's prayer. How often have you heard a member of management bemoan the fact that "The people just don't understand this issue!"? The op-ed piece may help explain that issue to them.

Op-ed pieces are not to be used as a vendetta medium against some alleged injustice to your organization, nor are they the forum for challenging a reporter's techniques. The key word in considering op-ed pieces is *judicious*. Just define the issue you wish to discuss or state the problem as you see it, provide whatever background or history is needed and then suggest ways the situation can be changed or improved.

PR Week lists eight ground rules for effective op-ed pieces:

1. Pinpoint your market
2. Don't bother to query
3. Write well
4. Act fast
5. Look for multiple opportunities
6. Work to build relationships
7. Make yourself a resource
8. Ask for pay[2] (with tactful negotiation)

Talk Shows

Whether on radio or television, talk shows present excellent opportunities for your media relations efforts. The programmers for these shows have to fill that time slot every day or every week; they are looking for ideas, for guests, for the unusual. You have an abundance of ideas and people available to provide to the programmer. The topics for talk shows are practically limitless and include such standards as education, health care, consumer affairs, technology, law, religion, business, minority affairs, energy conservation, sports, personal finance, globalization, the environment and trends.

Radio talk shows give you and your organization the opportunity to present a new program or a twist to an old program. One media relations staff in Chicago helped a suburban radio station with three half-hour interviews with the company's business managers. The first segment discussed the company's community/education relations efforts as well as minority purchasing and affirmative action commitments. The second and third segments discussed jobs that will have a future in industry—what technical skills and educational backgrounds that industry will be looking for in future employees. The messages were many, perhaps far too many for the print media, and there was not any real news value to the topics. There was, however, some interest, especially to the people who had never heard of the program and might be interested in employment in that company or industry.

Radio call-in talk shows can be a good forum to present your views on a ticklish issue. The possible thorn is that this variety of talk show attracts more listeners but also presents some dangers. Even the best-trained spokesperson in your organization is likely to become agitated over questions from callers, such as, "Did you use drugs when you were a teenager?" Before agreeing to participate in a call-in talk program, listen to several of the shows and determine if there is an abundance of "crank" callers, sensationalist programming or some other deterrent to your organization being there. Good call-in shows, those that are well managed, do provide a forum for your organization that you seldom get elsewhere. They also give you the opportunity to find out what is on the public's mind or to discover that the public did not understand the issue you so carefully put before them.

Television talk shows cover both hard news and feature topics. Of special interest to television talk shows are subjects with visual support. Nothing is duller than 30 minutes of a "talking head." Make the subject and the person interesting. Television is also offering call-in shows on local, national and international levels. Again, it takes a well-trained spokesperson who is willing to place himself or herself on the firing line for any potentially antagonistic caller.

Chat Rooms—A New Place to Talk

As the Internet becomes more ubiquitous, chat rooms are offering an alternative to television or radio talk shows or even in-person briefing sessions.

It's easy to set up a chat room connected with an announcement or in response to a crisis or an allegation—it's similar to setting up an on-line press conference. It's also more user-friendly to spokespersons who have become gun-shy about being verbally assaulted by reporters, radio listeners and call-in television viewers.

Prepare for these on-line sessions as thoroughly as you would for any other media encounter. Anticipate questions, prepare answers, stick to your message.

Also prepare for a longer time in the chat room, as visitors will clock in from around the country and around the world at their convenience, not yours.

A great benefit of this type of exchange is that it is immediate, global and provides hard data on who logs into the chat room as well as "transcripts" of questions and replies.[3]

Letters to the Editor

A letter to the editor intended for publication should not be written every time a minor error, misquote or suspected bias appears in the paper. Remember, a letter to the editor to clarify a serious inaccuracy is welcome, for journalists are as concerned with accuracy and professionalism as you are. On the other hand, a letter written in spite or over a minor error appears juvenile and is treated with the same accord. As with op-ed pieces, letters to the editor should be used judiciously.

Letters to the editor generally are in response to specific articles in the paper and can be used to clarify a point, rebut a charge or simply react to a situation. Letters can also be used, however, to try to create interest in a subject that has not been covered by the media. As with op-ed pieces, your letter to the editor should state the situation, give the background and offer a solution to the problem or a change.

If you decide you need to use a letter to the editor, it should adhere to certain guidelines. The letter should be short, directing its message to only one issue. It should never attack a reporter, and it must be factual.

If letters to the editor are not signed, they will not be considered for publication. To make sure the editor and the reading audience understand the issue is of serious concern to your organization, have the letter signed by the chief executive officer, if possible. This is a stamp of credibility an editor would find difficult to ignore. It is also wise to check with the publication to see if there are additional criteria you must meet.

There is no guarantee your letter will be used, nor is there a guarantee that the letter, if used, will appear in a timely manner. Finally, there is no conclusive way to provide—to yourself or to your organization—evidence that the letter did any good.

News Conference

Just as a release has news as its adjective, so should a conference. After all, why should you call a conference if not to impart news to the media? Unfortunately, the news conference has been badly mauled by publicity-seeking people or groups who offer little more than an orchestrated attempt to gain attention. The news conference should offer both news and a forum for the exchange of information.

First, make sure your proposed announcement is worthy of the time and effort needed to produce a news conference. It will help if you ask yourself some questions:

1. Is this announcement something that will have significant impact on the reading/viewing audience? You will need to hold news conferences during a crisis or high-impact event.

2. Is this a major product announcement? Remember: you can **announce** a product only once; after that, you **publicize** it.

3. Is this a complex issue that cannot be explained with a release? Does the issue demand a forum so that reporters can ask questions?

4. Does the occasion involve a new chief executive officer, a celebrity or major politician from whom the media would want quotes?

In short, always consider whether you can adequately give the information to the media via some other mechanism, be it news release, telephone conversation, e-mail, briefing or op-ed piece, before holding a news conference.

If you decide to conduct a news conference, you need to bargain for all the time and assistance you can get. A major product announcement should come only when all parties are ready to deal with the questions and demands that will result from the announcement, such as product orders, requests for information and product demonstration.

The logistics of hosting a live, in-person news conference are numerous. Questions must be answered concerning the location, the timing, who speaks when, who should be invited, should there be refreshments and what material should be available.

Location. A news conference does not have to be held in the grand ballroom of the best hotel in town. Journalists will go to where the conference is if the event is worthy of the effort. A product announcement could be held in one of several places: manufacturing location, laboratory, hotel, warehouse, trade conference site. Do not be tied down by the traditional; remember, journalists have to travel

to where ribbon-cutting ceremonies and ground-breaking ceremonies are, so they will travel to your event if the event/news is worth it.

Wherever you hold the conference, make sure it meets the
needs of the journalists. There should be room for cameras and
there should be arrangements made for tables and chairs for all
reporters. Make sure any power needs are met as well as any special lighting needs. Check the acoustics so that, if you have to, you
can assist in setting up microphones for better coverage.

On-line conference.   Still in its infancy but rapidly growing
is the e-conference—a press conference on the Web.

There are similarities between in-person conferences and e-
conferences, such as preparation (takes about the same effort and
time) but, there are convenient differences. Instead of renting a
room, having refreshments, renting lights and equipment, you create a Web site; instead of giving directions to get to the land site, you
designate a URL; instead of copying B-roll onto video tape, you run
it as a video component of the press conference; instead of copying
reams of releases, bios, fact sheets and other collateral material,
you load it onto the e-conference site.

Unless you're an expert in this field, you should hire a reputable firm to establish your e-conference. They can determine
quickly, based on your needs, what type(s) of technology—modem
speed, sound cards, video down-link—your reporters will need in
order to access and use the conference.

Costs depend on whether your e-conference is audio-only or
includes video and graphics, so be prepared for fees ranging from
a few thousand dollars to six figures.

An on-line conference can be archived easily and allow the
host organization to determine who logged on to the conference.[4]

Time.   Knowing your local media well means you will have no
trouble determining when to hold a news conference. You should
attempt to have the event at the best "down" time for all the media.
More than likely, this will be during the late morning, after the television crews have been given assignments (one of which you hope
is to cover your conference) and when there still is time for late-
breaking news to go into the final afternoon edition of the newspaper. Reporters for the morning paper will be on duty, and radio
reporters will not have yet completed the "heavy" newscasts for
noon and late afternoon.

Check your community calendar to make sure you are not conflicting with other major events, such as open houses, fairs and demonstrations.

For an on-line conference or global live video conference, select a time best suited for the primary media market you're targeting.

Notification. Alert the media a few days in advance, if at all possible. If you alert the media much before that, you take the chance of a leak. If you wait later than that, you may be too late in that reporters and camera crews will already have their assignments. You may contact the media to remind them of the conference but, if your first notification showed the importance of the conference, a reminder contact can be misinterpreted as pushy.

Protocol. Each member of the media should be greeted when he or she arrives at the conference, even an on-line conference. They should be shown the layout of the conference site, including where the camera crews should go, where print reporters can sit, and the protocol of the on-line, live-feed or in-person questioning.

Start the press conference on time. Just as your speakers have other engagements, so do the media have other events to cover. Stay within the specified time for the announcement itself and try to not let the question-and-answer period linger beyond the point where questions become sparse.

Finally, thank the media for attending the conference. Do not assume they know you are grateful for their appearance.

Available material. The press material you give to the media at the end of the news conference is critically important. The bulk of your preparations probably will center on these items; certainly, the bulk of your time will go into creating and assembling this material into a press kit. In addition to the primary release reiterating what your spokesperson announced, the press kit should have other aids to help the media. If the announcement is a large, complex one, the kit may have several releases with each issue broken down into its component parts. Or it may have just the one release with a fact sheet to back it up. Depending on the situation, you may include photographs of your speakers, products, plants or services in the kit as well as 35mm color slides for television or photos that can be downloaded from the Web site and scanned. You could have prepared actualities for the radio or B-roll footage for the television stations available on site and from the Web site.

Maybe you will need biographies of the speakers and/or copies of the speeches they give. Each kit should be prepared to fit the specific event. Do not force the event to fit the kit.

Prior to the news conference, you should anticipate any possible questions that might be asked both at the conference and later after reporters have digested your material and prepare answers to them.

Emergency Conferences.   Clearly, you need to hold a conference if there is a crisis that demands it, such as an industrial accident or natural disaster. Equally clear is that you will not have the time to locate just the right place and prepare all the right materials and observe the minute details of decorum. In these cases, you operate under the rules of crisis management—you have a plan to cover any eventuality that may occur. Your decisions will already have been made about details such as site, spokespersons and protocol. (See chapter 10.)

The Internet has become a critical factor in the way organizations provide information and respond to the media during a crisis.

Satellite Media Tours

SMTs have been around since the '80s but have changed from their original stiff, talking-head format to upbeat, intricate and highly successful interactive events.

A SMT is a live, "rolling" interview with pre-set interview times, in which one spokesperson can accommodate 10–20 individual interviews with reporters anywhere in the world in just 1–2 hours, from either a studio or on location.

The interviews no longer have to be in a studio, as technology makes remote sites more accessible. This allows you to be creative with the set and spokesperson or celebrity, by having the individual engaged in some activity, conducting a brief tour or demonstrating a product.

SMTs have a great advantage over video news releases (VNRs). In a SMT, reporters get to ask questions and be active participants. A VNR is a controlled tape with no opportunity for exchange of information.[5]

At first glance, SMTs seem expensive but, compared with the cost and time of sending a spokesperson to 20 cities in 20 days for 20 interviews . . . it's a bargain!

Backgrounders, Briefings and Seminars

Not all the tools for getting into the media involve instant returns. Therefore, as part of your ongoing relationships with editors and writers, you should consider having backgrounders, briefings or seminars.

A backgrounder is a written piece that can be given to a writer or editor explaining the history of an issue, including how it came to be an issue in the first place. Often, background material is stated to be "off the record," a misnomer for something vital to the issue that should be on the record. The backgrounder could be a compilation of news stories already written about the issue, technical papers or even internal nonproprietary reports that can be made available to the public.

A briefing, on the other hand, is generally a face-to-face presentation. Journalists are gathered to hear a speaker or speakers talk about an issue instead of trying to rely totally on written material in a backgrounder. A backgrounder package can stand on its own; a briefing requires preparation that might well include a backgrounder package.

Sometimes, a topic will be so complex that it requires a seminar to explain it. These are usually held for specialty writers. The issue, trend, service, technology or theory is explained and examined in depth. Seminars should be conducted by the very best subject-matter experts you have. Seminars are excellent for building long-term relationships with writers and are much appreciated by writers who cover science, technology, medicine/ health care, international finance and other rapidly changing and complex topics.

News Features

An often overlooked tool is the news feature, a hybrid piece that combines the essence of news (after all, it is news if it meets the current criteria) and the style of feature writing. News features are short articles written about aspects of your business or service operation, which are interesting and informative but not necessarily "must have" news.

These features can describe unusual jobs or behind-the-scenes "how-to" operations or focus on one employee or volunteer.

Smaller newspapers and magazines often are interested in these because they seldom have adequate staff to research and write their own features. Always confirm with publications that they want such features. For television, you need to research the story and provide them with the visual appeal of the feature.

Stand-Alone Photographs

A photograph with a cutline that succinctly describes the action in the picture can sometimes be more effective than a full press kit. Unusual photographs that still relay a message can meet both your objective and that of the photography editor to whom you send the item.

It should go without saying that only the finest photography should be considered for this avenue to the media. Whether it is a lucky on-location shot or a carefully planned studio photograph, the final product should be able to stand by itself with just a short message in the cutline. Photos depicting technology, product usage and milestones are a few of the types to be considered. Photographs can be transmitted through media distribution services and sent electronically from your computer as easily as a release, making photographs a valuable, inexpensive way to reach a large audience.

Standby Statements/Qs and As

If you know of an event that could break into the news and cause a reporter to call, there are two pieces of written information you might want to prepare as quickly as possible. The first is a standby statement. This gives the basic facts of the situation and your organization's position. It is not a news release. Rather, it is a piece the spokesperson (the media relations person or whoever else is speaking publicly on this issue for your organization) will use to answer reporters' questions.

The second piece, Qs and As, is expected questions a reporter would ask you and the answers you will give if he or she does. Again, this is not material to be handed out to reporters or to be published in general employee information media. It is for use only to help you reply to questions from the reporters.

To be valuable tools, the standby statement and Qs and As should meet three basic criteria:

1. They should answer the five Ws that every reporter asks: who, what, where, when and why.

2. They should—as much as possible—be cleared in advance so that you are ready to move quickly to answer a reporter's questions. The media's business is news, and a reporter's time frame is usually today. To get your organization's position in a story, you must meet the reporter's deadline. And you are almost always better off when your organization's view is included. In the absence of information, people "fill in"—often with the worst possible scenarios.

3. They should not be words that are cast in concrete. The spokesperson should talk from the material—not read it like a script.

Using the Media Relations Tool Kit

The media relations tool kit is filled with items you can use every day and others that are needed just now and then. The trick is to know how to use each tool wisely and well. Test your use of the tool kit with these situations. For examples of how others have handled similar situations, see chapters 8 and 10.

- Your company introduces a new product that will not be available in your region for at least six months. How do you handle the public announcement? How can you position the company as a forward-thinking organization without raising expectations? Without overhanging the market?

- A reporter calls and wants confirmation of financial data on your company. It is obvious the reporter has figures from a recently held upper-management meeting but has interpreted some of them incorrectly. What do you do?

- The *San Francisco Examiner* is on deadline and needs a statement on the status of a new service offering from your organization. It is 5:00 P.M. in California and 8:00 P.M. in New York. None of the eastern headquarters executives are at home. What do you do?

- There is a wildcat strike at a plant near Washington, D.C. The electronic media show up in force. How do you handle the situation?

- A reporter calls you to do an interview with someone in your area on the deteriorating quality of service in your hospital. From your initial conversation with the reporter, you are sure that the story basically has been composed with preconceived, unfavorable opinions about the hospital pulled off the Internet. What do you do?

- The *Financial Times* of London calls to confirm rumors that your company is attempting to buy out a major European manufacturing concern. It is 11:00 A.M. in New York and 5:00 P.M. in London. Your executives are in meetings. What do you do?

- A reporter says a person who has been laid off by your company just e-mailed him. The reporter says the employee worked in a city that you know has identified a surplus situation. What do you do?

- You have a product announcement, with a major press conference, scheduled for Wednesday. On Monday afternoon the business editor of a leading daily calls you with details about your product, including its name. The story will run in Tuesday's edition, and the editor wants confirmation about the material. What do you do?

- There is a major national trade show in your area. How do you work with the exhibits, product promotion and marketing people to make this a media relations opportunity as well as a sales tool?

Media Terms

To help you familiarize yourself with the language of broadcast and print media, here are some terms familiar in either print, radio or television newsrooms:

Actuality—the recorded words of someone who is part of a radio news story.

Anchor interview—an interview conducted live by a television news anchor with a newsmaker out of the studio.

Art—photograph(s) accompanying a newspaper story.

"B" roll/cover—video accompanying a television news story.

Breaking news—news that's happening right now.

Cop shop—police headquarters.

Live shot—an on-scene television news story reported either as it's happening or shortly afterward.

Nat sound—any audio that's part of a television news story but is not the sound of someone speaking directly into a microphone or to the camera; background sound.

Newser/presser—a press conference.

Package—a prerecorded television news story voiced by a reporter.

Pagination—computerized newspaper page design.

Phoner—an interview conducted by telephone.

Reader—a television news story with no accompanying video.

Sony sandwich—a reporter's on-location live introduction and close for a pre-recorded television news story.

Soundbite/SOT—the recorded words of someone who is part of a television news story.

Talking head—close-up video of a newsmaker or newsperson speaking.

Voice over soundbite or VO/SOT—a television news story with accompanying video read by the anchor that leads into the recorded words of a newsmaker.

Voicer—a prerecorded radio news story voiced by a reporter.

Wrap—a radio or TV news report voiced by a reporter and containing the voice of a newsmaker.

Courtesy of Kathy Kerchner, InterSpeak, Scottsdale, AZ, and Debra Gelbart, Mercy Healthcare Arizona, Phoenix, AZ.

Chapter 5

REPORTERS
Helping Them Meet
Their Objectives

The PR field is in the midst of an evolution where we are moving away "from a time when communication was static and indirect, when we relied on word processors and the telephone," according to Larry Weber, chairman and CEO of the Cambridge, Massachusetts-based Weber Public Relations Worldwide. "Gone are the days of 'spray and pray' press release distribution and press junkets. No longer can you mail an inch-thick press kit to a reporter, expect him or her to sift through the fact sheets and backgrounders, and produce a story on your company or product. In order to get your message out in today's cluttered and complicated world, the approach must be demonstrative, intuitive, experiential, and technology-based."[1]

The emphasis in a media relations program should be on the *relations* aspect—working to build long-term relationships with the people who cover your organization. Good media contacts proliferate once they are established. As is true with many good relationships, they are built only gradually, based on a variety of contacts over time, and strengthened by experiences that foster growing knowledge and respect. They require you to have a thorough understanding of how newspapers, magazines, TV and radio stations, as well as the Internet operate on a day-to-day basis.

In the end, though, this is a people-to-people business. A media relations person deals with writers, editors, producers, and photographers—not with newspapers, television stations, radio microphones, and Web sites. Knowing how to assist a reporter and his or her supporting cast will make the difference in long-term relationships with the media—the only kind to have.

Deadlines Are Critical

The first thing to appreciate is that a reporter's life is controlled by very short deadlines. As former *Time* publisher John A. Meyers put it: "Journalists are fond of the saying that they write the first draft of history."[2] CBS network's Lesley Stahl called it too often being a quick-sketch artist rather than a painter.[3]

In every publication there is a "news hole" that must be filled by a predetermined time when the printing presses start running. At a daily newspaper that process occurs every 24 hours—or more frequently when several editions are published each day. Today's news must appear in today's paper—and tonight's news in tomorrow morning's editions. The reporter's success will be determined by how often his or her stories appear in the paper, rather than being "killed" (newspaper jargon is "spiked") by the editor. And if the reporter writes a particularly interesting or difficult story, he or she will be rewarded with a byline—the reporter's name appears over the story as the writer.

There are equivalent (and usually, more stringent) deadlines for electronic journalism. With the public demand increasing for frequent up-to-the-minute reports, radio stations' past practice of carrying news only on the half-hour or hour and TV stations' traditional two newscasts an evening are obsolete. Numerous spot reports, lengthier regular newscasts, all-news programming on radio and increasing numbers of 24-hour news formats on television (a true legacy of Ted Turner's Cable News Network) have replaced them. Because of the transitory nature of the airwaves, radio stations in particular usually repeat news reports several times. The broadcast journalist thus must meet more numerous and tighter deadlines than his or her print colleagues. Similar to publication bylines, the television journalist's reward for an unusually fine reporting job will be an appearance on camera to report the story in person; for a radio reporter it will be an "actuality" where the interview is carried on the air, rather than having the anchorperson or announcer simply read the story.

Internet Demands Even Shorter Deadlines

The Internet provides stiff competition for the traditional media because of its ability to transmit news virtually instantaneously. The media day has turned into the media hour and now into the media minute or even second. Internet magazines and business/newswire sites such as CBS Marketwatch cover the news, as do publications like the *Wall Street Journal*'s *Smart Money*, which exists in print and also appears on-line with its own news team and unique content. The fifth annual Media in Cyberspace study showed that 1998 was a turning point for the Web, when news organizations began to use the Internet as more than just another means of distributing print version content. In fact, almost 40 percent of magazine respondents with Web sites said at least half the content on their Web sites is original—and that figure is increasing almost daily.[4]

Internet technology has created access to and demand for immediate information and frequent updates. Decisions relating to the media now must be made in an accelerated time frame with little lag time between actions and reporting. Posting your news promptly on your organization's Web site is a must so that a communications channel you control is accurately reflecting your positions at all times.

Two fundamental desires are motivating the reporter: (*a*) to report the story well, that is, accurately and in an attention-getting way and (*b*) to write it quickly. To have the story used, the reporter must meet both requirements; to meet those demands *you* must meet the *same* criteria. A cogent statement or key fact is useless to the reporter today if it was needed as an integral part of yesterday's news story.

The first rule of good media relations, then, is to meet the reporter's deadline. This will usually demand that you respond the same day—frequently, within hours. That is easy to accept in theory. In practice, it often demands the time and authority to stop other work to devote your full attention to the reporter's needs until they are met. If clearances are necessary before you can release certain information, you also will need the influence to ask others to break into their routine to support you.

Learn the Media's Deadlines

You should know the regular and late-breaking news deadlines of all the media that normally carry stories on your organization. Afternoon dailies, for example, usually "close" their inside pages about 9:30 in the morning and their front news pages about noon. Morning papers want all but major news material in by 2:00 or 3:00 P.M. the afternoon before.

Some papers have editions going to different areas; if you are interested in a rural or suburban location, that edition may close a couple of hours earlier than the final or city edition. These deadline times will differ depending on the distance between the paper's publishing plant and its circulation boundaries and the time required to transport copies to the most distant subscriber or newsstand. As well, technology has helped shorten deadlines, as publications now travel via satellite rather than truck. Feature and Sunday sections close several hours, or even days, earlier. Weekly newspapers, which normally publish on Wednesdays or Thursdays, frequently have deadlines a few days before press day, except for major news stories.

The news desk of any publication or station will be happy to tell you its deadlines. You might want to phone those with whom you deal regularly and then make a list of the deadlines that you can keep handy when you are working with reporters.

In any case, it is a good habit to ask a reporter what his or her deadline is each time you get a request for information. This will ensure there are no misunderstandings between you and let the reporter know you appreciate the importance of media deadlines. Over time you will come to a position of mutual understanding regarding deadlines: the reporter will learn he or she can trust you to do everything possible to meet deadlines, even the extremely short-fuse ones. In return, you will expect him or her not to "cry wolf" by creating artificial deadlines—and to give you additional time when the story is of a softer nature not demanding "today" treatment or when the request is for a large amount of information not readily available. If you cannot get all the information promptly, it often is wise to call the reporter to give an update on progress in case the story is being held for your input.

You also will want to avoid phoning a reporter around deadline time with anything but critical information related to that day's news. He or she will be busy writing, talking with the editor, checking last-minute facts or working with the art department on the cutline for a photograph that will accompany the story—in short, getting the news out. There will be no time for chatting about a possible future feature story.

Attention to deadlines also is critical when you are issuing a news release or planning a news conference, because the hour you set as a release time almost inevitably favors some media over others. If you issue your news in the early morning, for example, the afternoon paper and evening TV newscasts will be the first to carry the news. If you schedule the release in the late afternoon you are giving the opportunity for first coverage to the morning paper and making it difficult for the evening TV news to carry anything but a brief mention unless your news is worthy of live on-air coverage. As one TV reporter rebuked a reluctant spokesperson who asked if an on-camera interview could be delayed: "It's the 6 o'clock news, sir—not the six-forty. They'll be on the air with or without us."

If you are releasing copy for a public service announcement, you will want to pay even more attention to a station's or paper's deadlines, because you will not have the status of "real news" behind your request. Here again it would probably be worth your while to phone each outlet and make a list of the public service spot deadlines, because four-week lead times are not uncommon.

Announcement Timing Is Important

The media in your particular area—and your analysis of the importance of each publication or station to your organization—will determine the time you schedule news releases and news conferences. A good general rule of thumb is to alternate between mornings and afternoons if you have both A.M. and P.M. papers in your area—or always to set news events and schedule release times to meet your weekly's deadline if it is the leading newspaper in your community or the key trade publication in your industry. The Internet, radio stations, and all-news broadcasts report just about instantaneously, or at the minimum every 60 minutes, and repeat the news frequently. So the time you choose is not that critical to them.

To meet regulatory requirements relative to release of material information if your organization is a publicly held company, always issue your news releases via AP, the PR Newswire and the DJ Newswire. Also, make sure they are posted on your company's Web site immediately. In addition, if you work for a public company, you will want to coordinate timing closely with your colleagues in investor relations to be sure financial analysts covering your industry get prompt and personal distribution of your news, since reporters almost always contact them for comments on a major announcement. You can issue the same news release to the financial community, but change the contact information from the media relations professional to the person responsible for investor relations. If you are hosting a news conference, plan a separate but identical briefing for analysts immediately before or right after the news conference.

Another good rule of thumb in the United States is never to issue news releases or hold news conferences on Fridays unless you have no alternative. At best you could lose an opportunity to get your good news out to the widest possible audience, because North Americans traditionally listen to fewer newscasts and read fewer newspapers on Saturdays than any other day of the week. At worst you could offend the press and make them think you are hiding something if you are announcing bad news, because it will be more difficult for them to contact you after normal office hours. "You make a big announcement Friday afternoon and then go away for the weekend so I can't ask any questions," a reporter once said accusingly after a utility in Seattle had announced a major rate increase. "It makes me think there's more to this than meets the eye."

The same prohibition applies to late afternoon announcements. Remember that good relations with the media often begin—not end—with a news release. You must allow reporters enough time to contact others about your story, ask questions of you and them, gather visuals to illustrate it, and generally adapt or rewrite your release to meet the interests of their particular audience.

Saturday, on the other hand, can be a good day for nonprofit organizations to issue news releases or to hold news events. They will be covered on that evening's television news and in the next day's papers. Reading the bulging Sunday paper has become a day-long activity in many American cities. Also, you are less likely to have to compete for space with news of business, the stock market, the economy, the government and other organizations that operate on Monday-to-Friday schedules.

Take Advantage of Technology

Unless it is a timeless feature story, you should fax or electronically transmit your news release. This will avoid the problem of your news arriving so late that it has lost its news value. It also will ensure that you get your news to all the media at about the same time, so you do not inadvertently help one reporter "scoop" another.

Address your release to a particular reporter or editor by name so it quickly gets to the right person—and perhaps also phone or e-mail those who cover your beat regularly to tell them a release is on the way if the news is major. Also, if you are sending more than one copy to the same news outlet—for example, one to the assignment editor and one to the reporter who recently wrote a story about your organization—it is a courtesy to add a brief note that says so. Be aware of any distribution idiosyncrasies at the publication or station. To cite an extreme example, if you fail to write "Personal and Confidential" above the addressee's name at the *Wall Street Journal*, the news release likely will be whisked away to the parent Dow Jones News Service for distribution over its wire service. Thus your reporter may not get the news at all, much less by deadline time.

Most reporters check the Web while writing their stories, especially broadbased pieces. Make sure your organization's Web site is updated regularly and easily accessed so that reporters who regularly cover your organization and industry come to consider it a current, useful and trusted source. You will know you have a useful site based on return visits, length of stay and degree of interactivity.

Work with the information technology specialists in your firm to be sure your Web site is registered on various key Web search engines. Reporters will not visit your site if they cannot get in and get out easily, especially when they are on deadline. Your technical people can also help you put your news conferences and special media events on your Web site for reporters who cannot attend in person.

In fact, consultant and author Shel Holtz advises PR people to "make friends with IT [Information Technology]. Go to the technical staff for help, get them to solve problems, take them to lunch," he advises. "You should have a relationship with IT that's no different from your relationship with your printer, video producer or graphic designer."[5]

Your IT people can help ensure that your organization's Web site takes advantage of the technology. You need a design format and visual logic to help people move about the site quickly and easily. Too many Internet offerings mimic static print without reconstructing it to make it appropriate for the medium. Similarly, you will need to learn how to write for the Web. The opening chapter of *Wired* magazine's hardcover book, *Wired Style: Principles of English Usage in the Digital Era*, offers excellent advice. And Shel Holtz' manual, *Writing for the Wired World*, published by the International Association of Business Communicators, is another outstanding source.

Be willing to invest time experimenting and innovating on the Internet. Establish home pages. Post your organization's messages on bulletin boards. Host on-line forums. Promote your products to on-line reviewers. Stage on-line contests. As Shel Holtz said, "The more you use it, the more you'll come to understand its capabilities and how to apply relevant capabilities to your organization's efforts."[6]

Plan Ahead for PSAs

There also are many times when the confusion of last-minute deadlines can be avoided altogether. If your organization has an annual fund-raising event or is planning a major celebration like a fiftieth anniversary, you should write a letter several months in advance to the public service people if you will be requesting help with public service announcements, and a week or two in advance to the news editor if you think there are opportunities for straight news coverage.

Even if you want to keep the nature of the news a secret until the event, a phone call or e-mail advising a reporter who you think might want advance notice to keep the calendar clear on a certain day is the kind of thoughtfulness that helps build long-term personal relationships. A follow-up e-mail the day before the news event is also a fine idea. Busy journalists are reminded of your event, and you can inquire if each journalist will be attending so you get an idea of how many people will be present. But do not overdo it by pestering them for a definite RSVP. Even if an editor has assigned a news team to your event, late-breaking news could result in a last-minute change in the team's assignment.

Accessibility Is Paramount

On a pleasant fall day, the media relations staff at AT&T's New York City headquarters had a luncheon honoring one of their members who was celebrating his fifteenth service anniversary. As was their normal practice, one staff member stayed behind to cover the office over the lunch period in case a reporter called with a request for information that could not wait. Also as a matter of routine, they left the name and phone number of the restaurant. In the middle of the luncheon the person covering the office answered a call from a reporter in Chicago who was phoning to find out why the New York Stock Exchange had suspended trading in AT&T stock. One call to the restaurant and everyone returned to the office to learn that the Department of Justice was about to file a major antitrust suit against the company. Within two hours AT&T was hosting a news conference to respond to the charges and answer questions on what became one of the biggest and most publicized cases in antitrust history—resulting in the breakup of the Bell System.

Holly Golightly opined in *Breakfast at Tiffany's*, "There are certain shades of limelight that ruin a girl's complexion." AT&T would not have wished for such a vivid example to demonstrate the value of its media relations administrative systems. But the fact remains that when an emergency hits and you are making instant history, there is no substitute for routine procedures already in place to ensure the accessibility of key spokespersons. They are crucial whether you work for a large, multinational corporation or staff a two-person office for a trade association.

As much as is practical you should match your office hours to the hours of the key media that cover your organization. Certainly you need a responsible person available throughout the luncheon period. If you have more than one person on your media relations staff, you should consider staggered hours to broaden your office coverage. If you work alone, voice mail and a fax machine are necessities.

In any case, you need to set up a message system that helps you quickly get word of reporters' phone calls so that you can promptly return them. (We know of more than one case where people have waited several days to return a reporter's call—a discourtesy they probably would not inflict on their business associates, and one that forces the media to seek other sources within the organization.) Reporters checking late-breaking news or calling from different time zones should always be able to reach you.

Here's another tip that will demonstrate you truly are accessible: answer your own phone.

Update Your Home Files and Emergency Contact Lists

It also is extremely helpful to keep an up-to-date file of information about your company at your home. Your annual report, most recent financial results, latest organization chart, product catalogues and price lists—such information readily available at home will save you the embarrassment of appearing ignorant of basic facts about your organization. Make a regular practice of taking home every release you issue that day—plus backup information—in case someone calls you there after normal working hours.

Sometimes the topics will be too complex for you to feel comfortable handling without counsel from the person responsible for a specific area. Or sometimes a reporter will want to attribute the response to a high-level executive in your organization. Just as you want reporters to know how to get in touch with you after normal office hours, so you will want the residence, car, cell, and vacation phone numbers of key executives or experts in your organization.

You also will want those executives to be able to call you day or night if an emergency arises that might result in media attention (for example, an injury to a worker in one of your facilities, a plane crash involving your employees, the death of a top executive, or a bomb scare). If your organization does not have such an emergency contact list, you may want to take the initiative to create one, distributing copies to all employees involved and keeping it up to date. Be sure your main office switchboard operator has the list—and be certain all news media calls are referred to you or your staff first, day or night.

We frequently have been grateful that reporters have our home numbers—and we in turn have the numbers of other key company people around the country. A significant case-in-point occurred during a period when the recessionary economy was having a big impact on AT&T's equipment sales. The phone rang at home at 9:40 P.M. It was a reporter from the *Wall Street Journal*. He also was at home, and he was very apologetic. "I'm sorry to call so late," he said, "but some 'looney tune' just called the news desk in New York with a silly rumor that you are laying off 10,000 people and pulling out of the telephone manufacturing business. I know that's crazy, but they wanted me to check it out with you to see if there is any truth to it." As is the case with most crazy rumors, there was a grain of truth behind it. But this reporter knew our business well, so he immediately recognized that, at a minimum, the alleged news tip was highly exaggerated. Like the good reporter he is, he called to check.

We told him that indeed there was going to be a large layoff—1,200 people, not 10,000—that the news would be told to employees beginning with the night shift in about an hour, and that the company would make a public announcement the next morning. We pointed out that the anonymous caller's statement that AT&T was pulling out of the telephone manufacturing business was not true, but unfortunately the declining demand for new home phones as a result of the current economic slowdown was causing layoffs. We gave him some more details and then asked the key question: Did he plan to write a story? He replied that he thought he would.

If you read the *Wall Street Journal* the next morning you might have seen a relatively small five- or six-inch story on the layoff. But what you did not know about was the flurry of behind-the-scenes activity—both late that night and early the next morning—that the story caused. First and most important were the calls that night to our local public relations manager. We had to alert him to the leak, to the fact that there would be a story in the next day's *Wall Street Journal*, and we had to coordinate answers to some more of the reporter's questions. Also we wanted to let the PR manager and his staff know they had to move up their planned announcement to their local media. So they came in early and got their news release out at 7:00 the next morning. After all, it would not do much for their media relations if the local reporters read about a local layoff in the national *Wall Street Journal* before they heard it from our media relations people there.

Also very important were our other major offices and plants around the country. We got a quick alert out to them very early the next morning, so they would be prepared to respond promptly and professionally to the inevitable calls they would get from reporters wanting to know the local situation. And we in New York got ready to handle the queries from other national publications, the wire services and the trade press that we knew the *Journal* story would (and did) cause. It was a busy time. But there was never any confusion or concern about what to do or how to contact the right people even in the middle of the night. The advance planning for the layoff announcement was also vital to the calm manner with which we were able to react to the leak. (Planning layoff announcements will be discussed further in chapter 10.)

Know the News People and Their Media

Another important element in your relationship with the reporters who cover your organization should be your knowledge of their special interests—either because the publication or station has assigned them to the area or because they have a personal interest in the topic. Many times reading the bylined articles or columns of a print reporter, listening to or viewing the programs of a radio or TV commentator, and visiting the Web sites of journalists will give you insight into subject on which they seem to enjoy working.

If you think you have an idea for a feature, try to interest a reporter or an editor in doing it, rather than writing it yourself. Similarly, if you have a good photo opportunity, call the local paper or TV station assignment editor in the hope you can get a photographer or camera crew to come out. As former *Time* publisher John Meyers put it, "Scratch a photojournalist and you will find a reporter who wields a camera instead of a typewriter."[7] Publications and stations are much more likely to use material they have spent their people's time developing. But never talk to two journalists on the same publication, station, or on-line magazine about the same story idea or event—for example, to both the education and business reporters about a high school job fair—without telling each that you have done so.

The Internet is teaming with sites set up by individual entrepreneurs and by major media giants catering to every niche interest imaginable. With so many new and changing sites, it can be difficult to know how and who to contact to place your news.

Gerri Kelly, a senior media relations supervisor at Edelman Public Relations Worldwide's Chicago office, believes that "PR pros must study print magazines to identify who on-line is attracting the buzz. It's all about getting information on a case-by-case basis, and it is different for all our clients. You just have to build on-line contacts and get to know the tech and Internet reporters." She admits, though, that e-mail to the letters page of some of the Internet-only titles is sometimes the only way to get a response. "It's tough to get contact names. You need to read all the trade magazines that review Web sites and look for new opportunities." In addition to Yahoo!, Kelly recommends the *American Journalism Review*'s site (*www.AJR.org*) as a place to seek specific sites of interest.[8]

Drew Kerr, founder of Four Corners Communications in New York City, says it can be "difficult to pitch story ideas to opinion-focused titles, full of individual commentary." But he says there are numerous sites with dedicated on-line staff who are interested in pitches, such as CNet's *News.com*, Wired and *SmartMoney.com*, all of which are technology- and business-oriented sites with significant editorial backup.[9]

Don't Let Failure Get You Down

Don't be oversensitive to failure when you contact a reporter with a news or feature idea. We unsuccessfully tried to interest the Associated Press national photo editor in two pictures before scoring with a unique shot of AT&T's "computer on a chip" paired with a South American fire ant. That placement resulted in the company's high-technology message appearing in more than two hundred publications, including *Newsweek*, the *Minneapolis Tribune*, *Nashville Tennessean*, *Baltimore Sun*, *Dallas Time-Herald* and *London Times*, with a circulation of more than 20 million in the United States and overseas. Twice in recent years at The Reader's Digest Association our news releases were picked up in Ann Landers' column, which is syndicated to 1,200 newspapers in the United States and Canada. One offered free reprints of a *Reader's Digest* article about a home eye test, resulting in 35,000 reprint requests within six weeks. The other offered consumers hints on how to detect sweepstakes fraud.

So keep trying and you'll find ways to succeed. A few strike-outs are worth it if you hit home-runs like that every so often. Conversely, you will want to do at least a little research before you suggest story or photo ideas. It would be very embarrassing to recommend a program on controlling health care costs to a talk show host, only to be told they covered that topic last month.

As valuable as knowing the reporter's interests is understanding the role the publication, station, or on-line magazine has set for itself. The *Los Angeles Times*, for example, defines itself as a national newspaper. In fact, when airline deregulation resulted in fewer transcontinental flights leaving Los Angeles, the *Times* moved deadlines for one edition up 30 minutes so the paper could make the plane to Washington. "We want our paper on the desks of the President and Congress before they get to work in the morning," managing editor George Cotliar explained. "We want to have the same opportunity to influence discussion that *The New York Times* and *The Washington Post* have.[10] Knowing that strategy, you would probably decide to try to interest a *Los Angeles Times* editor in a subject related to a national issue like energy and take an idea geared to a smaller community audience to a suburban paper instead.

If a newspaper is part of a chain like Gannett or Copley, which has a news syndicate, or heads its own news service like the *Chicago Tribune* or *The New York Times*, this association will also have some effect on an editor. He or she is likely to be more interested stories affecting people or communities beyond the paper's own circulation boundaries. (Incidentally, reporters frequently are not told if their stories are picked up by the member papers when they have gone out over the news service or syndicate. You often can build some personal rapport with a reporter by forwarding copies of his or her stories that your clipping service picks up—especially if they are from out of state or out of the country.)

No matter how friendly and frequent your contacts with particular reporters, always remember that they have a job to do and their number one priority is getting the story. As former White House spokesman Marlin Fitzwater put it, "Treat them like professionals and they will be your friends. But treat them like friends and they will betray you every time."[11]

Use Internal Media as Tools

If they carry news of more than employees' bowling scores and the company picnic, internal publications can be effective, inexpensive tools to keep reporters informed about your organization and stimulate interest in feature stories, particularly in smaller communities.

Some organizations include local media people on their mailing list for each issue of the company's employee newspaper or magazine. Others prefer to send only selected issues, with a business card or a note drawing the reporter's attention to a particular feature you think would be of interest. In any case, it is useful to remember that what we take for granted because we deal with it every day can be perceived as news by the local media—particularly if there is a local or human interest angle. Employees participating in Red Cross blood drives and the American Cancer Society "smokeout" days, features on carpools and other employee energy conservation ideas, suggestion program winners, tutoring activities with disadvantaged children, family nights at the plant, safety and handicraft fairs—all these are feature ideas we have placed with local media.

Also, it is important for your management to recognize that once an issue is covered in your organization's employee media it can very easily get out beyond the boundaries of your company. If a story appears internally, you should consider it externally released as well.

You also will want to have handy a standard package of materials about your organization to use as a backgrounder for reporters doing stories on your company for the first time. The annual report and a fact sheet with a list of your key products and services as well as vital statistics, such as number of employees, location and unique features of your office(s), are some of the basics. You can then add other information, depending on the thrust of the reporter's story.

Fact sheets need not be fancy—a plain typewritten sheet is perfectly satisfactory. The important thing is that it be brief (preferably no more than a page), current and carry the date on which it was prepared.

Of course the latest background pieces and fact sheet information also should be posted on your organization's Web site—and updated regularly. Be aware, though, that once on the Internet the information can be accessed by others than journalists so don't, for example, provide your home number on the Web site unless you are willing to receive a multitude of calls from various stakeholders.

Handling Requests for Information

If you have an active media relations program, you are likely to get calls from reporters almost every day. They may want more information on a news release you issued. They could be working on a feature story. Or they might want your organization's view on a major news event of the day. There are, of course, myriad ways in which you can respond to these queries. But one overall rule applies: If you or your organization initiated interest in the topic, you cannot duck or evade reporters' follow-up calls; if a reporter originated the contact, your response will be dictated by your company's objectives, policy and style.

As you are working with people in your organization to write and clear a news release, you will want to remind them that most publications, stations, and on-line magazines will have their reporters call with additional questions rather than use the release as is. That is why you should include anticipated media questions and agreed-upon answers as a routine step in your advance planning and production of any news release (see chapter 4). You will want to ensure your internal contacts are available on the day you issue the release—and stay in your office yourself that day and probably also the following one. You should also brief whoever answers your phone on the importance of the release and the proper and rapid way to handle the calls it generates. Reporters' normal sense of urgency quickly turns to panic as their deadline approaches. Believe it or not, public relations people actually have issued news releases and then gone into all-day meetings, leaving their secretaries alone to fend off frustrated reporters seeking additional information.

On occasion you also may be called by reporters seeking to get your organization's reaction to significant external news events, such as the announcement of a proposed change in international trade or federal tax policy or a local rezoning application for a new industrial park. Whether you are requested to comment on such general public issues will probably depend on the prominence of your organization within your community. Whether you choose to respond will often depend to a great extent on the personal style and civic involvement of your organization's top leaders. You should know or help establish your organization's general policy for handling such broad requests so that you can promptly deal with this type of media request. Follow your local media's coverage of such key issues so you can anticipate and plan responses for the types of calls you may get.

When a reporter asks for information, do not hesitate to ask enough questions yourself so you have a full understanding of the story on which the reporter is working. If you take a single, isolated question, you may not be able to give your expert enough to go on to offer a competent answer. Or the answer to the question, when relayed to the reporter, may lead to another question and you will have to go through the process all over again. Get a good grasp of what the reporter wants. Try to visualize the whole while you are talking about the parts. Anticipate follow-up questions. Be a reporter's reporter.

What you want to avoid is being perceived as a person intent on withholding information or, just as bad, a person who does not have access to information. There still remains a certain skepticism—and sometimes definite hostility—from journalists toward media relations people. The only way to overcome this is to prove yourself every time you work with the media. If reporters continually call other sources within your organization, it is because either they do not know you or you are not meeting their information needs.

Never give away an "exclusive." If a newspaper, radio or TV station, or an on-line magazine develops a feature article on its own and comes to you for information, or is approaching a news story from a unique angle, its rights to exclusive use of that story must be respected. If two reporters seek the same information, however, tell each person that the other is working on the story. It will avoid subsequent conflict and help keep you from being caught in the middle.

Test Your Knowledge, Involvement

There is no sin in admitting you do not know an answer; simply say you will check it out and get back to the reporter. But if that happens very often, you should ask yourself some soul-searching questions:

1. Am I doing everything I can to keep current on company activities and industry trends? Should I expand my regular reading or use of the Internet? Make a point of keeping in touch with people in other departments? Be more active in trade associations or professional societies?

2. Am I anticipating news and activities in this organization that would cause media interest and preparing to handle news queries in advance?

3. Am I—or is my boss—included in planning meetings and in the decision-making process? Do I have the confidence of top management so that I am among the first to know what is happening within the organization? (If not, you cannot be considered a spokesperson; at best you may be a well-qualified reference point.)

Recently, a fellow media relations practitioner complained vociferously that he was left out of the planning and media announcement activities when his company was awarded a major government contract in a bid against the Japanese. But even superficial questioning made it clear he had not kept up with the current highly sensitive government negotiations on lowering foreign import barriers. Nor was he aware of the various Congressional committees conducting hearings on international trade at the time. And he was not a regular reader of the trade press or visitor to Web sites covering his industry. So he was never up to date on what his company's competitors were doing or how the industry viewed his company. Little wonder his boss—and perhaps his CEO—felt that he was not qualified to be the company's spokesperson on this critical subject.

George V. Grune, retired chairman and CEO of The Reader's Digest Association, told the public relations directors of its worldwide operations that one of management's key expectations of them was that they have a thorough knowledge of the business. "That means you need to understand our corporate strategy, our marketing plans, our products, our competition, our internal challenges and our future opportunities. Go out of your way to build working relationships with your operations colleagues," he advised. "They are your clients and excellent sources of information. Attend marketing meetings and ask the product mangers to brief you on their plans. Participate in brainstorming sessions, join task forces and become more proactive in the way you act on key business issues."[12]

Master the Fundamentals

Equally important is that you master the basics of your craft. That means you need to be an outstanding writer and editor in all media—especially news releases and other media relations materials such as photographs and videos.

Watch to see what happens to your news releases. You will soon come to accept the fact that reporters will rewrite your carefully crafted sentences. If they do it too often, however, you might ask yourself why. Are you following the accepted rules of press style? (*The New York Times*, Associated Press, United Press International, Ayer or another widely accepted stylebook is a must to be kept handy as a constant reference source.) Or maybe the reporter's sentences are shorter and easier to understand than yours.

Another excellent feedback vehicle is a media audit—hiring an outside research firm to ask reporters covering your organization (and those who do not whom you would like to attract) how you are meeting their needs. If your question list is short and to the point, most journalists are willing to answer because upgrading your skills and services helps them as well as you. This also is a good opportunity to get their views on the usefulness of your Web site.

A reporter is a lot more likely to get your position right—or indeed, use your statement at all—if it is a "quotable quote." Similarly, the public is a lot more likely to agree with you if you speak in terms they can understand. It is critical that news releases and statements be written in plain English—not in "legalese," and not in corporate gobbledygook. You may feel this point is so basic as to be unnecessary. Unfortunately, our experience has not shown that to be the case. But if it is true, as an AT&T advertising campaign once told us, that to communicate is the beginning of understanding, surely it must also be true that we must all comprehend the terminology. Multisyllable words and diplomatic nuances prompted language expert William Safire to coin the term "Haigspeak" and to quote comedian Mark Russell: "Who would have thought, between Secretaries of State Henry Kissinger and Alexander Haig, the one with the accent would be the one we can understand?"[13]

Organizations bring much of the public's misunderstanding and mistrust upon themselves when they issue news releases and statements full of highly technical jargon and industry lingo. You can get so lost as you read or listen to so-called information sources that you don't know if you have been eating magic mushrooms or wandering around Alice's Wonderland. "You're not more informed," says Tom Rosenstiel, a former *Los Angeles Times* media critic, "you're just numbed."[14]

Mark Twain said that writers should strike out every third word on principle: "You have no idea what vigor it adds to your style."[15] United Press International sent out what it termed a "war on verbiage" message to all of its news bureaus: "Fight the battle sentence by sentence, paragraph by paragraph," the advisory said. "The result will be a sharply angled, concise news story that will deserve every inch of newspaper space it gets. The most effective weapon in the battle to achieve tighter writing is good reporting. Inevitably, the less we know the more we write.[16] All media relations people would do well not only to help reporters follow these guidelines but also to adopt them for their own.

Handling Requests for Interviews

Many times reporters will call an organization asking to interview someone about a particular topic. The natural reaction is to try to find an appropriate person for the reporter to talk to—sometimes a time-consuming and unnecessary effort. Often, a better response is for the media relations spokesperson to be the primary source of information for the majority of requests, reserving the interview for occasions when another person is needed for his or her particular expertise or when the medium warrants an executive-level spokesperson. Having the media relations person be the primary spokesperson will probably mean your organization responds more promptly and more efficiently to reporter inquiries.

When you determine that an interview with someone else in your organization is the best approach, however, there are a number of steps to follow. This section will deal with your support of the reporter in an interview situation. Chapter 6 will cover your work with your organization spokesperson.

The first decision is whether the interview will take place on the phone, via the Internet or video teleconference, or in person. It is a good idea to ask the preference of the reporter. Radio or international reporters normally want a telephone, Internet, or video teleconference interview because it is so much faster. Print or TV reporters' choices are usually determined by their deadlines and distance from your interviewee.

Equally important is your input into the decision, which should be based on your knowledge of the spokesperson's desires and abilities in different situations and your evaluation of the significance of this particular medium and story. If your spokesperson is just one of many sources to be interviewed for a broad survey article in a newspaper or magazine, for example, a phone conversation is probably most appropriate. Telephone interviews are usually shorter because there is less tendency to chitchat. If your organization is to be featured more prominently in the piece— be it in print or on TV—a face-to-face interview is probably best. Your spokesperson is more likely to come across as a personable human being rather than a faceless bureaucrat. But you will want to exert some control over the length of the interview to prevent it from dragging on unnecessarily.

Brief the Reporter Ahead

Regardless of which medium is chosen, you should provide the reporter with a biography immediately—and a photograph, if one is readily available—of your spokesperson. This also is the time to point out how the spokesperson prefers to be addressed, in person and in print; the correct spelling and pronunciation of the name; and the person's particular field of expertise vis-à-vis the story the reporter is writing. Provide this information, along with other appropriate background on your organization and the subject of the proposed story, in advance of the interview—even if this requires having the material delivered by hand. The more you communicate with and provide background to reporters before the interview, the more they are likely to get the facts straight and not waste their and your spokesperson's time with basic "How does it work?" or "What does your company do?" questions.

Tips for Phone Interview

If you have agreed on a phone interview, let the reporter know you will initiate the call at the agreed-upon time. Elementary as this may sound, double-check the time if different time zones are involved—especially with an international reporter. Because many people object to speaker phones, feeling their words are being broadcast all over, it sometimes is best to set up a three-way conference call. After introducing the reporter to the spokesperson, let the reporter take control of the conversation.

You, meanwhile, should take extensive notes of the conversation—verbatim if you can write quickly enough. Neatness definitely does not count when it comes to these notes. The only person who needs to be able to read them is you, so that you can check a quote for the reporter if you are requested to do so or check the finished article for accuracy. If you are dealing with a particularly sensitive subject, however, you may want to write up your notes, including key questions and answers, for your files in case there are questions later about what was said or done. As you monitor the conversation, make notations to yourself if you feel points need clarifying or further data need to be gathered. Resist the urge to intrude on the conversation unless your spokesperson is stumbling and clearly needs you to help with an explanation, or is in danger of giving out proprietary or other sensitive information in response to the reporter's questioning or prodding.

Tips for Internet or Video Conference

If the interview is via the Internet or video conference, you need to decide whether you should be on camera with the spokesperson (probably not, after the initial introductions) or sitting to the side, out of camera range. Also, it is a simple matter to videotape a video conference, so you may want to do that for the record.

Tips for the In-Person Interview

If the interview is in person, arrange to meet with the reporter a few minutes in advance. Then you can get acquainted briefly if you do not already know the reporter and review plans before you go to your spokesperson's office. After making introductions you should again avoid getting involved very deeply in the conversation. Take notes and offer counsel and follow-up where necessary. You should also politely end the interview if the reporter's questions become repetitious or if the time has extended much longer than originally scheduled to a point you feel to be inappropriate. It is rare for an interview to be profitable to both parties if it lasts much longer than an hour.

If a still photographer is accompanying the reporter for shots of the interview, there should not be much extra coordination required on your part beyond alerting your spokesperson. But if you know the photographer wants to tour your operation to take additional photographs, and you have the staff available, you should stay with the reporter and get someone else to work with the photographer and handle critical details like photo permissions, safety and security concerns.

If a TV station wants to send in a camera crew, you should make sure the room where the interview will take place does not have too many windows or a busy or strongly patterned background. Check the crew's space, lighting and electricity requirements in advance. Portable battery belts and hand-held minicams have made horror stories of popping circuit breakers in the executive suite a thing of the past. But the addition of a crew—a cameraperson, probably a sound engineer and perhaps a lighting expert—means added distraction and tension for your spokesperson and requires special attention on your part (see chapter 6). Nonetheless, most TV people consider the video far more important than what is heard, so it is worth your while to think through ways to meet the crew's needs while also getting your key messages across in picture form whenever possible.

After the Interview

After the interview, get the reporter's deadline for any additional data you agreed to provide and ask for a general idea when the story is expected to run. (No reporter can promise a publication or air date. That prerogative is reserved for editors and producers.) Offer to check quotes or verify any additional information needed as the article is being written—a polite way of letting the reporter know you care about accuracy but understand you cannot see the copy in advance.

Once the story appears, if you feel it was a difficult subject handled well or written in a particularly interesting way, you should not hesitate to tell the reporter either in a phone call, note, or e-mail, or the next time you meet in person. Like all of us, reporters are interested in honest feedback and flattered by positive reactions.

If the story does not appear within the expected time frame, it is acceptable to phone the reporter to check the status—as long as you make clear your understanding that editors make these decisions, not reporters. If the story is "spiked"—a term newspaper reporters use when a story is written but never printed—you must not protest too strongly. It is fine to inquire as to the reason, because you may learn from it and thus improve your media relations in the future. Most stories do not appear for the simple reason that news is plentiful, space is limited and editors must make judgments on the value of each story.

How to Handle Errors

The news media have neither the space nor the time to tell the "whole truth." Rather, they carry the part their reporters and editors think important. Under pressures of time and without detailed knowledge of your business, it is inevitable that errors will occasionally appear in news coverage of your organization. Your behavior in this situation will have a major effect on your long-term relationship with the reporter and the publication or station. A natural first reaction is to demand a correction or write a letter to the editor. More appropriately, that should be a last resort. The publication of a retraction, like a double-edged sword, cuts both ways. Errors read only once may be quickly forgotten; read twice, they may stick despite the attempt at correction.

Whether you are approaching the print or electronic media about an error, you will be dealing with a person who naturally can be expected to be defensive if he or she wrote or photographed the offending piece, or protective if he or she is the editor of the person under attack.

Here, in order of consideration and seriousness, is what you should do if there is an error in print coverage of your organization:

1. Acknowledge the difference between what is incorrect and what you don't *like* about a story. List the factual errors; chances are they will be few in number and not all that major. Next, list what you didn't like about the story: the headline; placement of the article in the publication; the three-second sound bite; position of your quotes; quotes from your competitors. Make sure you're considering asking for a correction of important factual errors.

2. In most cases, be charitable and do nothing. Most errors are insignificant in the context of the overall story. They probably will not be noticed by any but the most knowledgeable in the audience who would recognize that there was a mistake. Sometimes it is the headline that offends. Remember that it is written not by the reporter but by a copy editor under incredible space constraints to summarize the essence of the story in a few words. With such brevity can come obscurity or misplaced emphasis. You should not blame the reporter, who probably did not see the headline before the piece was published or aired.

3. In some cases, contact the reporter to request the item be corrected for the record. It often is a good idea to get the accurate information into the electronic files or "morgue" (newspaper jargon for the file room or library where old issues are clipped and catalogued for future reporters' background use). Your purpose here is to politely alert the reporter to the error and ensure it is not repeated in future coverage of your organization. An example of a mistake warranting a correction in the file copy might be a misstatement about your product line, the size of your facility, a name misspelling or an incorrect title of one of your executives. A particularly clever complaint letter was sent by AT&T media relations spokesperson Wink Swain to a reporter who got her companies mixed up: "Oops! As much as I enjoyed [name of reporter's] article on Westinghouse Broadcasting, I'm afraid there was a slight error in corporate genealogy. Western Electric is not the parent company of Group W, though the article was so well done that I almost wish we were," the letter said. "Western Electric is a wholly owned subsidiary of AT&T. The enclosed booklet will tell you all about us. We're certain that the error was innocent, and we don't want to make a big fuss over it. I hope that you and [name of reporter] will accept the friendly reminders that I've enclosed and use them to serve the people of [the town]." Along with a booklet describing the company, Swain sent two pens carrying the corporate logo. The record was corrected and a mistake was turned into a friendly media contact.

4. In a few cases you will want to write a letter to the editor. This can be done when you feel your position was not adequately stated—as compared to being incorrectly stated—and you want to use the forum of the Letters to the Editor column to expand exposure of your views. It might also be appropriate when you want to publicly and formally correct the record, as when your organization is involved in a legal or regulatory action.

5. In rare cases you will be justified in asking the publication to print a correction. This would occur, for example, if your earnings or other pertinent financial information affecting the price of your stock were misquoted. Sometimes a correction can be masked by the addition of updated information; for example, including the time and place of the funeral in a second article when the person's name was misspelled in the initial obituary.

6. In no case should you contact the competing paper to tell them of the incident and to ask them to set the record straight. Ethical journalists will not participate in vendettas against their colleagues. That applies to radio and TV as well. Do not call competing stations and ask them to carry the "true story."

7. If the error is critical, post the correction on your organization's Web site. Remember that two-edged sword, though; many people now will see something they may never have noticed before, so be sure it is worth it.

There are differences, however, when you are dealing with the broadcast media instead of print. If you call up a radio station to complain of an error in coverage, the station often will ask your permission to tape you over the phone then and there, giving your side of the story. They may use your comments live if the program is a talk show with a call-in format. Or they may save the tape for a later broadcast. Before you call you will want to be prepared with two or three key points written down to help you state your position coherently. A TV station could also ask you to appear on a guest editorial giving your position if the issue is controversial or of long-term significance to your community.

You, of course, must be even more swift in correcting any errors that go out in your materials to the print or broadcast media. No matter how careful you are, one day an error is going to slip through your checking and proofreading system. If it is clearly only a typographical error, there is no need to issue a correction and a second release—although you will want to redouble your proofing efforts because even small errors reflect on your professionalism and desire for accuracy. If it is a significant mistake—a name misspelled or a factual error—you must *immediately* get on the phone, send a fax, or issue an e-mail alert to everyone you sent the release to, offer a quick apology and give the correct information. Then you should also send out a revised news release to everyone on the original distribution list, with the words "corrected version" prominently written on the top of the first page.

When to Say No

In spite of the fact that your major role for reporters is to facilitate access to data and people in your organization, there are legitimate reasons for you to refuse to divulge information. There is, however, no occasion we have ever run across when it is appropriate for you or any spokesperson for your organization to reply to a media query with a terse "No comment." That is a desperate response, almost guaranteed to make the reporter search for other sources for the facts.

Tell the reporter *why* you can't discuss an issue in much detail—because it involves proprietary information that will divulge too much to your competitors, because as a matter of policy the company does not discuss rumors in the marketplace that might have an effect on the price of your stock, because you are in the midst of sensitive labor negotiations and want to keep discussion going around the bargaining table rather than on the pages of the daily newspaper, because it is too soon after the accident to know what actually happened, because your lawyers have not yet received the court papers, or whatever is appropriate (see chapter 7). The reporter then has a legitimate quote from you, and yet you have released no inappropriate information to the public. Both the media's and your organization's objectives have been met.

In an interview with *Fortune* magazine, Barnes & Noble CEO Leonard Riggio gave us a perfect example of how to say "no comment" without saying it—and to get a positive point across at the same time—when he refused to divulge his comeback strategy in his company's struggle with Amazon.com: "I have so much I'd like to say that I can't say. It's a very competitive marketplace. What I can tell you is that we have the resources to do many, many entrepreneurial things."[17]

When you are citing proprietary information as the reason for refusing to disclose information, you want to be sure it really is proprietary. One spokesperson refused to acknowledge the existence of a new manufacturing process, only to have the reporter pull out a company brochure with a photo of the alleged secret equipment. On another occasion a media relations person refused to divulge the salary of the CEO and president until caustically reminded by a reporter that the figures were carried in the company's legally required public filings with the Securities and Exchange Commission as well as the annual meeting mailing to shareowners.

On some occasions **you may decide to say no to a reporter's request because of the time it would take to gather the information** or because the information is not available in the form the reporter wishes. These types of requests often come from editors or reporters seeking to localize news of a regional or national company by breaking down sales or financial information at the local manufacturing or sales office level. In these cases, a simple statement that it would be too costly for your organization to keep statistics in every conceivable format, combined with an offer of the information in a somewhat different arrangement, is usually sufficient. Also, many companies do not release sales and profit information for local business units, subsidiaries or product lines for competitive reasons. Reporters will understand if you cite that rationale.

There also are situations **when reporters do not seem to know what they want.** When we come upon a writer whose questions and requests for information indicate a time-consuming fishing expedition rather than a story, we sometimes politely but firmly ask him or her to determine the focus of the piece, at which time we will be pleased to help.

In extreme cases you might want to decline a guest appearance on a TV interview or radio talk show. For example, **if the host has a record of asking loaded questions** or espousing positions contrary to your organization, industry or issue, your appearance may provide only a target for complaints rather than a forum for discussion. If a fellow guest is a bitter ex-employee or vocal union leader complaining of working conditions, your appearance could tend to legitimize the complaint and hurt relationships with your current employees. If the theme of the coverage is not supportive of your objectives—the favorite recipes of a woman candidate for senator, for example—a polite no may also be the best response. Sometimes no publicity is better than frivolous publicity.

Another case where saying "no" is totally appropriate would be **requests to appear on scandal-driven programs** with hosts who care more for ratings than facts. In these situations both the format and the mood of the program are so unprofessional that your appearing would demean both your organization and yourself. Unfortunately, these types of programs are proliferating. As James Fallows wrote in a scathing and powerful piece in *Atlantic Monthly*, too often these days journalists ask questions "with a discourtesy and rancor that represent the public's views much less than they reflect the modern journalist's belief that being independent boils down to acting hostile."[18]

American Journalism Review editor Rem Rieder points out that "in a media landscape with so many voices, it is often hard to be heard. So the temptation to report with 'attitude' and 'edge' to generate 'buzz' is huge."[19]

Even *60 Minutes*, always known for its hard-hitting style, has crossed the line into combative journalism, as it too has fallen victim to the blurring of hard news and tabloid journalism. In her autobiography *Reporting Live*, Lesley Stahl described how the change occurred: "With the falloff in audience, we also began to introduce more conflict into our reports. Actually, the drift toward hostility journalism developed out of the best of intentions. When we realized that the new technology allowed us to squeeze three or four sound bites into one piece, we began to search for 'opposing views' to flesh out our reports. We thought of it as good journalism, but it had the unintended effect of exacerbating a public discourse of disputatiousness. Our bosses began asking for extreme views—a 'stable of arguers'—in the hope that the audience would like the dueling. Soon we were searching for the most polarized views so we could get a real battle going."[20]

In the end, your research into the program, host and other guests—combined with your gut instinct—will no doubt tell you whether to say yes or no.

Other legitimate times to say no may be those rare occasions **when you cannot confirm that a free-lance writer or photographer is actually on assignment** for a publication or station. If you are not familiar with a person who says he or she works for the media, it is a good practice to call the news desk or assignment editor of the appropriate medium to verify the assignment. The editor in charge will be happy to take your call; no publication or station wants unaffiliated people posing as their staff reporters or stringers (writers in smaller markets who occasionally are assigned news stories and features for a large publication).

There may be rare situations when you or your organization have dealt with a particular reporter on several occasions and believe **he or she has such a bias or is so careless** that almost all the resultant stories have been negative or inaccurate. A business-like but candid discussion with the reporter's editor—in person rather than on the phone—will usually result in the assignment of

Does It Pass the Coors Tests?

Anita Russell, director of corporate communications for the Coors Brewing Company in Golden, Colorado, has established criteria to help her staff evaluate requests from reporters:

> Before deciding how to respond, they determine what story they think the reporter wants to tell (knowing he or she might have a preconceived position on the issue), what its importance is to the company, whether Coors has a desire or perceived need to tell its story, what the company's position is on that issue, what the staff's ability is to get their message across, whether they have an appropriate and willing spokesperson, and whether the media outlet is important to the company.

As part of their decision making, they also consider the reporter who is writing the story, researching his or her background including education, past positions, beats, special interests and awards, in order to measure the reporter's credentials and motives. As well, they obtain copies of stories previously written to look for any political bent or special interest slant, and to examine the style of reporting and writing. Depending on the situation, they might also interview the reporter's former editors and track down people previously interviewed by the reporter for their opinions on whether they were treated fairly and quoted accurately.

In the end, Anita says there are four key questions that must be answered in the affirmative for Coors to go forward with a story:

1. Will it help us sell more beer?
2. Will it improve shareholder value?
3. Will it demonstrate that we are customer focused?
4. Is this something to which our company should devote our limited resources?

Anita Russell, "Alternative Media Strategies"
remarks to the Arthur W. Page Society 9/22/97

another person to cover your company if your complaint is deemed valid by the editor. This is a last-resort action that should be taken only in exceptional cases when your allegations are well documented. Editors tend to be defensive of their reporters and profession, especially when criticized by the subject of an article.

Other Helpful Hints

Here are some miscellaneous hints to help you anticipate (and thus be prepared to respond promptly to) reporters' requests:

1. Be wary of sending out news releases with embargo dates. They can be counterproductive to your organization's relations with the news media and to your objective of getting wide coverage of your news if one medium breaks the release date and scoops the others. As *PR News* pointed out in a discussion of the practice, "Traditionally embargoes have been used to give reporters time to digest complex issues or lengthy tomes well in advance of the release date. They've also been used to provide fair access. But that was before the 'press' became the 'media,' with the advent of broadcasting."[21] Unless you have a very special circumstance, it is safer to plan a release time that is good for you and the most important media covering your organization and then release the news with no embargo.

2. When you are issuing a news release on an executive speech, make copies of the full text to have handy in case a reporter asks for it. The request may be caused by the reporter's desire to rewrite or to expand on your news release. Or, the reporter may want to file the talk for use as background or source material in future stories. In any case, your anticipating such requests will enable you to get the speaker's agreement in advance to release the full speech—which can be annotated, if necessary, with the phrase "as prepared" or "as delivered" if there are or could be changes to the typed text. It also is a good idea to have copies of the speaker's biography and photo available to send out to those publications that regularly use photos.

3. Documents filed with a government regulatory agency such as the Securities and Exchange Commission or at a courthouse as part of a trial automatically become part of the public record. You can save the reporter some trouble, buy your organization goodwill and help assure that your position is accurately carried in the story by copying an extra set of such filings if a reporter requests it.

4. Set up a file of biographies and photographs of your organization's key officers, managers and board members. Create a standard form to be filled out, or write up a one-page narrative including such information. Ask for each person's community newspapers if you live in a large metropolitan area; sometimes news of your managers appearing in their local paper or alumni magazine means more to the family than coverage in a big city newspaper. Update the biographical data whenever there is a job change or every two years. Photos should be 5" x 7" or 8" x 10" black-and-white formal studio shots, with identification on the back and new ones taken every five years at a minimum. You may also want to include some candid photos of your top executives—and some color slides if you expect TV coverage. Remember that all television graphics must be 1¼ times wider than they are high to properly fill the screen.

Remember Your Organization's Employees

Your desire to be responsive to reporters' information requests cannot supersede your responsibility to the employees of your organization. They are your best ambassadors or loudest critics, depending on how fast they get relevant information and the context in which it is received. With global wire services, CNN and BBC World News, there is no such thing as "local" news. A layoff in Milan can make news in Madrid; an environmental problem in London can be on drive-time radio in the United States. And negative quotes from uninformed or angry employees can quickly undo an otherwise positive news media effort.

When you are making an announcement to the external media, you will want to coordinate the release time with the person responsible for internal communications so your employees do not read news of your organization in the local paper or on the Internet or hear it on a newscast before they learn of it from management. When there is an external leak ahead of the planned announcement time, you should immediately alert the employee communications person so a decision to advance the internal release can be considered. (Your colleagues should be equally considerate of you and provide advance copies of all employee communications materials so you are aware of what is covered in case they get into reporters' hands.)

Similarly, set up a close relationship with your customer service people. Be sure they have copies of your news releases, standby statements, and questions and answers, so they are giving out the same information to your customers that you are to the news media. When you know media coverage affecting your organization is going to appear, you should also alert your internal communications person. If a positive piece is expected—for example, a feature on one of your workers or an interview with your CEO—your employees will appreciate knowing in advance, especially if it is on radio or television, so they do not miss it. If a negative piece is upcoming, you will want to ensure that employees have your organization's position on the topic in case they get questions from their family, friends, and customers.

Set up a high-traffic area like the cafeteria to demonstrate your publicity efforts in cyberspace and on TV. If the media coverage is significant enough, you should also consider an advance alert via phone, broadcast fax, e-mail, Internet, or letter to your organization's board of directors or trustees, key customers or contributors and perhaps also send them a clipping, transcript, audio- or videotape after the event.

Helpful Hints from Journalists

Here is some advice from journalists on how media relations people can do a better job of meeting the media's needs:

> If you become acquainted with representatives of the media and stay in touch, it will reap rewards for your organization. Pick up the phone and say, "I'm so and so. I work for this organization. I wanted you to know who I was, so if you have questions about what we do out here, you'll know who to call." Follow that up with a letter or e-mail saying, "I talked to you on the phone. Here's what you need to know in the way of phone numbers day and night." Include a suggestion for a story. Say, for example, "You may be interested to know that we just started making widgets along with fidgets, and it might make a story for you." Look around for an interesting employee who would make a good feature article or profile—a fellow who in his off hours collects antique telephones, for example. Then stay in touch with the

media. Make sure they know you're on the scene and ready to help if they have an inquiry.

—Dave Beeder, Business Editor
Omaha World-Herald

The best type of PR person is the one who is receptive when we call—who is willing to tell the company side of the story in bad situations and good. If the company comes forward with whatever they can say about what's happening, then the news media will report that. We are looking for information. We want to know your side of any story. I think the fairest reporting will come when a PR person is helpful and informative when the news is bad as well as good.

—Jim Scott, Assignment Editor
WISH-TV, Indianapolis

We like the hard news, of course—a change in employment or a new product announcement, for example. But we also like little features—a photo of an employee blood drive or a story on a shop crew building a special tricycle for a handicapped girl. Every one that is brought to us will not make the paper, but we like to take a look at them and see.

—Carey Cameron, Business Reporter
Gwinnett (Georgia) *Daily News*

Never lie. If you don't want to answer the question, just say so. If you say, "I can't give you that information right now," I can accept that. I might not be happy as a reporter or an editor, but it won't make me lose my trust. People appreciate realness. If you are accessible . . . if you are open and honest . . . if you say, "Here's what I think and here's why," people will respect you and your organization whether or not they agree with your position.

—Dan Warner, Editor
Eagle Tribune, **North Andover, Mass.**

Return phone calls from reporters immediately. It will make them love you. Do this even if you have nothing to report. If you were waiting for an executive or source to return your call, tell this to your reporter contact, who will understand and value the feedback on the status of the inquiry.

—Tim Padmore, Business Editor
The Sun, **Vancouver, Canada**

Establish a relationship with one reporter at each station or publication. Over time, if you always are honest and straight, rapport will become trust. Then, when a mistake is made, it should be admitted. It hurts an organization more to hem and haw than to come right out and say "We made a mistake." The media will be understanding if you are honest. We only attack when you won't admit you made a mistake.

**—Bobby Batiste, Anchor
CNN Headline News**

What journalists are always after is news. What you want us to cover is propaganda. A good public relations person finds the middle road and meets the journalist halfway. Remember also that reporters are always under time pressure. We need to know what's happening today and what will happen tomorrow—and we usually need to know it now. Your value depends on meeting our deadline.

**—Frederick Ungeheuer, Financial Correspondent
*Time***

If you want to be taken seriously, don't peddle trash and don't waste the reporter's time. Do not try to spin a thinly veiled advertisement into a story; if it does get into print, the reporter will look like a fool and resent you. Don't call the reporter to see if your fax was received (it was, there is just no reason to respond at this point). Realize that their lunch hours, happy hours and weekends may be reserved to run errands, date, attend their children's school functions or see friends—so don't try to schedule business outside of the formal work day. And when you're trying to slip something in under the radar—by scheduling an important press conference at 5 P.M. to screw up print deadlines—understand that we know exactly what you're doing, and we don't appreciate it.

**—Kerri S. Smith
*Denver Post***

Chapter 6

SPOKESPERSONS
Training and Briefing
Them for Their Role

In Joseph Heller's book *Good as Gold*, the hero is invited to go to Washington and be a "reliable source." If he is good at it, he is told, he will be promoted to being a spokesman.[1] It is true that performing effectively as a public spokesperson often brings accolades from within and outside the organization. But, as with all high-risk, high-reward situations, there can be pitfalls.

When you are dealing with the media, any mistake is liable to be a very public one. Visions of a terrible *faux pas* splashed across the pages of the local newspaper or appearing on television screens in countless living rooms throughout the community tend to make our stomachs churn. Indeed, *The Book of Lists* ranks fear of public speaking ahead of death, flying and loneliness[2]—and talking with a reporter for attribution has to be the most public of public-speaking opportunities. No wonder people in our organizations react with something approaching terror at the thought of a media interview, especially on a sensitive subject.

An anecdote cited in journalism circles tells of a city editor who called a reporter to the city desk to point out a mistake in a story. "Well," he said, "you already have made two-hundred-eighty thousand mistakes today and it is only noon." That "two-hundred-eighty thousand" was the paper's circulation figure. The comment impressed the reporter, and it should impress a spokesperson.

Like so many other talents, the skills required to be an effective spokesperson can be practiced and perfected. That associate whom you admire for the apparently natural ability to speak with clarity and confidence undoubtedly is as nervous as you are. But training and experience have helped him or her to master fear—or at least mask it. John O'Toole, retired chairman of the board of the Foote, Cone & Belding advertising agency, pointed out in his book, *The Trouble with Advertising . . .:* "No matter what you do in life, your success at it relies heavily on your ability to communicate and explain your point of view to others in a way that will convince them to share it, or at least consider sharing it. This is called persuasion, and every human being is engaged in it constantly."[3]

A vital part of your job in media relations is your ability to be proficient enough in interview techniques and knowledgeable enough of the organization's policies and products that you can help your spokespersons prepare for news media contacts. At best this interview techniques training should be part of an ongoing program. At a minimum it should be included as part of the routine briefing session you have with your spokesperson before any media interview.

Choosing a Spokesperson

Before discussing the support of spokespersons, it is well to step back and talk about selecting the right one. The choice is not as obvious nor as easy as many people think. Indeed, it is one of the critical elements that will determine the success of your media coverage.

First of all, the obvious and frequent choice—the chief executive officer of your company or organization—is not always the best one. CEOs deal with broad, general, policy matters. Rarely are they involved in the nitty-gritty of the organization enough to know the details of a specific project or issue. Unless your CEO has a personal desire to be the primary spokesperson, you are better off reserving access to him or her for reporters whose article requires comments on overall policy or strategic direction.

Nor is the head of the department involved in the topic always the right person. Promotions in organizations normally are based on outstanding technical or professional knowledge and performance. Department heads may have the ability to make a presentation at an internal meeting or to the board of directors, but this is not quite the same as being able to meet with reporters. When and if the spokesperson is chosen from a middle or lower echelon, be mindful of the sensitivities of that person's superiors in the organization. The top manager usually is known as such in the community. Do not make it look as if someone has usurped the leadership.

While there are varied opinions regarding the effect a person's sex and age have on the impression he or she makes, those attributes should not be relevant to the decision. For example, on one hand, a Boston University study showed that women are more trusted than men, and thus make better public spokespersons, particularly in government, where there was a dramatic difference in trust of male and female spokespersons in similar positions.[4] On the other hand, many people think a middle-aged man projects authority. Our advice is simply to pick the person who can do the best job. As the media relations person, you should become familiar with the abilities of others in your organization so you can choose the best spokesperson for each media opportunity.

Here are the characteristics you are looking for:

1. Above all, **knowledge of the topic** to be discussed with the reporter. Only with a firm grounding in the facts can anyone speak confidently and positively.

2. An understanding of the organization's overall objectives and strategies. There is no way every one of the reporter's questions can be anticipated. You want someone who can think quickly and walk gracefully the fine line between being responsive to the reporter's needs and "giving away the store."

3. An ability to tell and sell what he or she knows—in everyday language and from the point of view of the reporter and the ultimate *audience*.

4. The confidence of top management. This person will be representing your organization to the general public. You do not want to choose someone who is not well respected by those within.

5. A desire to do the interview. If your proposed spokesperson demurs beyond what normal modesty and apprehension would explain, you probably should drop your request. People tend to be honest with themselves; you should take heed when people believe they are poor choices for the assignment. There is a world of difference between being named a spokesperson and serving as one.

6. Overall presentation style. It is important to select someone with presence and personality. Also, your spokesperson should reflect the personality of the organization. A person wearing a three-piece suit is out of place representing a progressive, young computer software company. Similarly, a woman who wears a bejeweled, short-skirted costume does not match the persona of a Wall Street financial institution.

Preparing Your Spokesperson

Once you have determined who will be your organization spokesperson for a particular interview, there is a great deal the media relations person can do to support the one who has accepted this sensitive and important assignment. The fact that many of the steps with your spokesperson parallel those you are taking with the reporter is no coincidence. Indeed, your role as the bridge between the media and your organization is amply tested in an interview situation. Whether you perform a valuable service to both parties or are perceived to be an unnecessary third person by either depends on your professionalism. The quality of your work will be reflected both in the resultant media coverage and in the spokesperson's response to your future requests to talk with reporters.

Immediately after you have set the appointment and determined whether the interview will be on the phone, via video conference or the Internet, or in person, you should communicate with your spokesperson. Whether you do so in person, by phone, by e-mail or by writing a memorandum does not matter. What is important is that your message to the spokesperson contains the following information:

1. **Date, time, place and expected length of interview**. If this is a new experience for this person, state that you will attend to take notes and get any follow-up information needed by the reporter.

2. **Type of story the reporter is working on**—in-depth feature on your organization or survey piece on your industry, for example. Has the reporter's conversation already indicated a clear point of view for the story? Or is he or she doing an overview piece and searching for a local angle?

3. **What the reporter told you he or she wants from the interview**—quotes on your corporate objectives, general sales

plans for a new product line, your organization's opinion of a new community development plan or whatever.

4. What you have provided the reporter. Describe briefly what information you already have given the reporter. List the materials you sent the reporter as part of the background package (see chapter 5) and include them as attachments to the e-mail or memo or go over them in person if you think the spokesperson might not be familiar with them. Your objective here is to let the spokesperson know what already has been said to the reporter so the spokesperson can expand on it rather than merely repeat it.

5. Background on the reporter—if this is the first time the spokesperson has dealt with this particular journalist. Does the reporter regularly write stories on your organization, or is this a first? Does he or she understand your business, or will the spokesperson have to be especially careful to explain the terminology? What has been your experience with the reporter in earlier contacts? Does he or she take notes or use a tape recorder? (You should welcome the use of a tape recorder, since it ensures accurate quotes.) It is a good idea to include samples of the reporter's recent stories—or suggest that the spokesperson tune in to the appropriate program if it is a TV or radio interview and you have enough advance notice. This is particularly important for talk shows like ABC's *Good Morning America,* NBC's *Today,* PBS's *The NewsHour with Jim Lehrer* or their local equivalents, because journalists' interviewing styles vary widely. In some cases, squabbling has replaced dialogue in the pressure to keep things lively.

6. If photography is involved, any special arrangements you are making for the photographer or television crew. Explain the set-up time required for TV production equipment, especially if the interview is taking place in the spokesperson's office. Or arrange to move the interview to another office or location.

7. Suggestions on the main messages and one or two key points you think the spokesperson should stress in the interview. Here is where you make your greatest contribution, not only as a media relations professional but also as a counselor to your organization.

8. Advice on key interview techniques. See the following section, "Hints on Interview Techniques" for a full review of such advice. It is presented as a unit so that you easily can use all or part of the section when working with your spokesperson.

9. Insist on the need to get together to review anticipated questions and possible answers before the actual interview. This initial backgrounding is important. If the interview is two or three days hence, this preparation helps the spokesperson focus thoughts and prepare responses. If the interview is later that same day or early the next (as so frequently is the case) it provides a framework in which to operate. Your briefing session just before the interview is likely to be more concerned with content than logistics.

Prior to the Interview

Media relations people should make it a routine practice to get together with the spokesperson for a briefing before the interview. Executives' calendars are crowded—but a half-hour meeting together before the reporter arrives is time well spent. It gives you both an opportunity to talk about your main messages, review expected questions, constructively critique proposed answers, look at alternative ways to highlight key points and discuss the thrust of this particular journalist and article.

It is a good idea to prepare for the worst-case scenario. Talk about the questions you most hope the reporter will *not* ask, and agree on your answers. Write them down and sharpen them until you are comfortable the spokesperson is presenting your organization's case in the best possible way without being defensive. Get others' input, including legal counsel, if the issues are sensitive.

You also can work out a plan to end the interview if the reporter appears to be getting long-winded or repetitive. You should remind the spokesperson to tell the reporter that follow-up information will be channeled through you. For a phone interview you can alert the spokesperson not to be unnerved by a request to tape the conversation or by the keyboard sounds of a PC, laptop or notebook. Indeed, it is positive feedback that the reporter's questions are being well answered, since many journalists do not take notes until they hear a newsworthy comment.

If there will be photographs, it also can be helpful to remind your spokesperson to be tolerant of what may appear to be strange requests to move objects or rearrange poses. The photographer likely is looking for ways to get an interesting picture out of what is essentially a routine setting. As *Fortune* magazine picture editor Alice George put it: "It takes a special talent to take an eye-opening picture of an assembly line or a boardroom. The only way I know how to deal with the problem is by hiring photographers who have a new way of seeing."[5]

During the Interview

As was covered in chapter 5, your role as media relations person during the interview is to make introductions and then let the reporter take over while you take notes, interjecting only if a statement needs clarifying, a number requires verifying or a promise of follow-up information should be made. If you are physically near the spokesperson during a phone interview, you might want to pass a note if you believe the person has missed an opportunity to make a key point or has made a statement that needs further explanation.

A decision to tape the interview—whether or not the reporter is doing so—should be made with care. Some reporters who consider it normal for a media relations person to take notes are offended if you ask to tape the session. On the other hand, if you are reluctant to honor a reporter's request not to tape because a reporter or program has a reputation for distortion, you may want to insist on taping as a condition for your spokesperson to be interviewed.

Follow-up after the Interview

For the media relations person the job is not over after the interview. At the same time you are following up on your obligations to the reporter, you should devote similar attention to the interviewee.

Right after the interview you should call your spokesperson with feedback—giving both your impressions (helpful for the next time) and the reporter's (whose reaction right after the interview is a good indication of the probable tone of the story and thus should be shared with the spokesperson). If the reporter was critical, you will want to think carefully about how much detail you pass along—and how you communicate it. If the spokesperson is normally proficient but in this case was not, it may just have been a bad day and no value will come from rehashing errors.

If you foresee a potential problem in the resultant coverage that you cannot resolve with the reporter, go ahead and mention it. Your spokesperson would rather be alerted in advance than blind-sided when the story appears. If the spokesperson did a particularly bad job, either confusing the reporter with poorly stated points or blithely releasing proprietary information, you will probably need to find a different spokesperson in the future for that area of your operation.

As soon as the story appears, check the quotations and facts for accuracy. If it is print coverage, always try to get a copy of the article to the interviewee in advance of wider circulation within your organization. Offer your reaction—and get the spokesperson's.

If it is radio or TV coverage, you can purchase a copy of the tape from the station as a courtesy for the interviewee or for your files. If you live in a large metropolitan area such as San Francisco, Los Angeles, Chicago or New York, you can purchase a transcript or a tape from companies that sell such services. Burrelle's also provides electronic monitoring on the Internet.

If it is an Internet piece and you have video equipment available, it can be useful to tape the session.

If it is a print piece, buy copies of the newspaper or magazine yourself. Although you may not intend it, a request to the reporter for a copy of the article when it is printed implies that you do not think enough of the publication to purchase it. Some reporters on hard-to-get association or international publications, however, make it a practice to provide copies to a spokesperson featured in a major article.

Hints on Interview Techniques

Most reporters are far too sophisticated to be impressed by style over substance. Conversely, a fine position can be misunderstood if it is not presented with clarity and confidence. Interviews are not conversations—they are highly structured situations.

Some of television's top news people support your becoming more skilled in interview techniques. "It makes perfect sense to me because people should have every opportunity to make the best case they can for themselves," Mike Wallace told the *Washington Journalism Review*.[6] And John Chancellor added, "It's okay to bone-up for an interview as long as it teaches one not to hide the facts."[7] David Brinkley, questioned by the same publication on his views of spokespersons rehearsing for media interviews, replied: "It's about time they did. . . . They are dealing with the American people through us. . . . They give short, clear answers because they're more effective when they are delivered by us to the American people. I think that is a positive development and I would say it took them long enough to learn."[8]

Similar thoughts were voiced by Irving Shapiro, retired chairman of duPont and also a chief spokesperson for corporate America when he headed Business Roundtable, the organization of CEOs of major industrial companies: "You wouldn't drive a car without practicing, and when you go into the world of professional TV you ought to know what the experience is like. If you don't know that, you're at a huge disadvantage."[9]

Formal media interview techniques training—especially with an outside expert—is well worth the investment, for you and for others who will be spokespersons for your organization. Many former TV people now conduct media training sessions to help executives answer the kind of hardball questions they used to ask. Even if your spokespersons have a great deal of experience, they can make mistakes if they get overconfident or complacent.

Here are some interview techniques that should help you do a better job when you are interviewed by a reporter.

- **Remember your objective**. Is your purpose in doing the interview merely to *inform* the reporter's audience of some event or action? Or are you attempting to *persuade* people to adopt your point of view? *Inspire* them to change their behavior? *Motivate* them to take some particular action? Your ultimate objective will have a great impact on what you say and how you say it.

- **Prepare and practice**. Mark Twain once said it takes three weeks to prepare a good ad-lib speech. Have in mind one or two key points that you want to get across in the finished story. Ask yourself, "If I could edit the article that will come out of this interview, what one or two sentences would I like to see?" Or, "If I could write the headline, what would it say?" Well in advance of the interview, write them out. Try to simplify and shorten them. Some people think if it is complicated it is clever. But Winston Churchill advised, "Short words are best and the old words when short are best of all."[10] Practice saying them out loud so they sound natural to the ear. Perfectly proper sentences in a written text are often too formal and cumbersome when spoken aloud. If it is a phone interview, keep your key points in front of you. Then at the earliest opportunity, try to capsulize your main points in answer to an interview question.

- **Simplify, simplify, simplify.** Communications consultant Ann Wylie says that "what we used to call information overload has gone way beyond that. Now we suffer from 'fact fog' and 'data smog'; we're drowning in an information deluge." She advises spokespersons to rethink the way they deliver information and "simplify, simplify, simplify."[11] That is your best chance to have your message break through the clutter of competing messages and options for your target audience's time and attention. Consider the medieval knights who charged each other on great horses. The problem was that if they fell off, their armor weighed too much to allow them to get back on the horse again. It is impossible to tell everyone everything about your organization. So do not waste effort on unnecessary baggage or battles. Simplify the message and send it with consistency and clarity. Remember the wisdom of Miss Piggy: "Never eat more than you can lift."

- **Place your most important points at the beginning of each response where they will be clear and isolated.** In 15 words or less, what is the essence of your message? In TV or radio interviews, this is especially important because broadcast journalists are looking for a very short "sound bite." Responses like "There are three reasons for that" invite poor editing. Rather say, "Price, performance and reliability are the key factors in our decision." Try to get your main message down to nine or 10 seconds—what CBS's Lesley Stahl call "staccato message bursts on the air,"[12] which, sadly, are too often all a spokesperson gets when the TV editing is complete.

- **Refer to the interviewer by name, early and often.** In print this is a simple common courtesy. In TV it may help get that sentence past the editing process and onto the screen, since stations often like to show that their reporters are well known by celebrity interviewees or in the community. It also gives you some time to think before answering.

- *It is not only what you say but also how you say it that communicates.* The effective speaker is not necessarily polished and perfect. He or she is energetic, enthusiastic and direct. Opera diva Beverly Sills, known as much for her candor as her charm, told *Time* magazine, "There is a growing strength in women, but it's in the forehead, not the forearm."[13] *New York Times* music critic Donal Henahan said admiringly of Sills: "She never has any problem about what she means. She never fumbles for explanations."[14] A forthright, enthusiastic response to a question portrays candor and confidence—in your organization, in your position, in the reporter, in yourself. Long pauses before you answer or a stiff, flat monotone indicate either a lack of conviction or a lack of interest. If the interview is being televised, this appearance of indecision and insincerity will be magnified.

- *You should not feel pressured to respond instantly to a difficult question on a complex subject.* Although we have just mentioned the possible negative effect of a pause before answering, it sometimes is appropriate to take a moment to organize your thoughts. When you are making instant history— or instant policy—you have the right to be comfortable with the way you articulate your organization's role. In a print interview you can verbalize the pause by saying something like, "I hadn't thought of it from that viewpoint before. . . ."

- *Think fast but talk slowly.* If the reporter is taking notes, it will help the accuracy. If you are being taped for broadcast— audio or video—it will help your audience's comprehension. For broadcast, however, you will want to speak a little bit faster because sound bites are getting shorter and shorter.

- *Never forget your ultimate audience.* You are talking to a reporter, but you are speaking to the people who read the publication or watch the program—your past, present and potential customers, employees, shareowners and suppliers. (If none of these audience segments is being reached by the reporter's medium, you can legitimately ask your media relations person and yourself why you are doing the interview.) Frame your answers from their point of view, not your organization's. For example, say "Our customers now have three new colors to choose from," rather than "We have expanded our color selection." Or, "If this bill becomes law there will be significantly fewer parks where you can take your family," rather than "Our industry is opposing this legislation because. . . ."

- *Always include the "me factor."* The Zen masters have a good approach: "Tell me what window you are looking through and I will tell you what you see." It is crucial to appreciate your audience's viewpoint in order to understand how they will react to your message. The key word is *benefit*. If you can enunciate the benefit to each individual's life or family or career or wallet, you will turn a nod of agreement into a spark of interest—and, ultimately, action. People listen and respond in terms of their own lives. What are you telling them that will make their lives easier, more fun, richer or more rewarding?

- *Choose your pronouns carefully*. Don't call the company "it"; you, your staff and your spokesperson should think of your organization as "we" and "us," and your audience as "you." These pronouns convey a personal, interactive image of your organization. "We" demonstrates your synonymy with your organization and eliminates the egotistical ring of "I." Remember also that in advertising copy the two most successful words are "you" and "free." It may not be possible to use "free" in your statements, but "you" should be a regular word in your interview.

- *Humanize your responses by giving a little bit of your own personality as well as the organization position.* Too often when we start to communicate a business message we freeze and start sounding more like a machine than a person. Your field is interesting to you. Make it equally interesting to the reporter. In addition to providing the reporter with a "quotable quote," you may help destroy the myth that all business people are stodgy and boring, particularly if you work for a large corporation. Retired Chrysler Corporation Chairman Lee A. Iacocca gave a similar notable and quotable response to NBC's Garrick Utley who asked, "What about mergers—any marriages yet?" "No," replied Iacocca, "but I think I've been kissed."[15]

- *Be sure your messages reinforce your organization's overall branding.* Each product or service has its own unique character and strengths that you need to articulate and build on to position it clearly with your target publics. Stay focused and pay attention to consistency. As the former president of the University of Notre Dame challenged his students, "We must sound no uncertain trumpets." Whether communicating with reporters or financial analysts, employees or consumers, on the Internet or in traditional media, be sure your messages and key points always support the personality and performance of your brand. Learn from advertising, where repetition is a sacred tool. Repeat anything often enough—and simply enough—and it will be *remembered*. Base it on facts and back it up with performance and it will be *believed*.

- *Do not be embarrassed if a number or detail is not at hand, and do not guess.* Simply tell the reporter that your media relations person will get it. Also, don't feel obliged to accept a figure or fact the reporter cites. Say you are not familiar with it and offer to have it checked. Never—repeat, *never*—have other staff people in the room with you. Surrounded by too many advisers, you may appear to be an obedient Gulliver surrounded by Lilliputians. The reporter wants your views and comments, not facts and figures, from the interview. Your delegating such follow-up detail means your train of thought will not be interrupted and you will be perceived as an expert not concerned with minutia. As well, it explicitly reminds the reporter that the media relations person is and should continue to be the one entrance point to the organization.

- *Do not let a reporter put words in your mouth.* Whenever you hear the phrases, "Are you saying that . . .?" or "Do you mean . . .?" or "Isn't it really . . .?" alarm bells should ring in your head. Mishandling this type of question can result in your feeling your words were reflected back by a fun-house mirror when the final story appears. If you do not like the way a question is stated, do not repeat it in your response—even to deny it. The reporter's question will not appear in print. Your answer will. It is better to respond in a positive way, using your own words, not the reporter's. For example, if a reporter asks if one of your products is overpriced compared to the competition, don't say "I wouldn't want to use the term 'overpriced.'" You just did! Instead, say what you would want to say: "We believe our products provide high value for the price. For example . . ." and go on to list the features. This is particularly important in a television interview, when time constraints will force severe editing. You want to be sure your main point is right up front in every answer, in case you are on the air with only one sentence. Look back at this example to see what a one-sentence edit would do to you.

- **Look for the hidden agenda in questions.** If a reporter is probing your recent hiring of salespeople proficient in certain skills, the resultant article may say that your company is in the midst of a marketing build-up to launch a new product line.

- **Never say you do not know an answer when in fact you do.** A good reporter will know—or find out—that you should have known the information and may be antagonized by your claiming ignorance. If you get a question that is not in the best interests of your organization to answer, explain why. And, as discussed previously, avoid "No comment."

- **Keep your cool.** More and more these days, interviewers deliberately frame their questions in emotional or accusatory tones, going for "attitude" or "edge" in their story. It is just a technique to get you to say something controversial. Do not let it work. It is okay to be angry; it is not okay to lose your cool.

- **Understand that the reporter may be starting out with negative opinions about you or your organization**. These opinions may stem from ongoing publicity about inflated executive salaries, or by the fact that few journalists have training or experience in business. Another gap: Minneapolis-based Pinnacle Worldwide Inc. in 1999 polled 117 executives and 93 journalists asking, "How would you rate business executives' ethical behavior on a one to a hundred scale?" The executives gave themselves an 80 while the news media gave them 30.[16]

- **Avoid tongue-twisters.** We all have heard someone stumble on words like "specificity." Choose words with a minimum of "S"s so you do not sound like a hissing snake—an especially important hint for radio.

- **Avoid using jargon.** When a reporter interrupts with what seem to be basic clarifying questions—or, in the case of an interview with a foreign reporter, if the interpreter pauses and looks puzzled—it may be that you have unconsciously dropped into obscure professional or industry jargon. To the neophyte, reading a wine list can be like interpreting a spy's code book—you know there are delicious secrets buried inside but you cannot get at them. Look for ways to explain your point with simple illustrations or analogies out of everyday life. As the late *Time* financial correspondent Frederick Ungeheuer put it: "Journalists are great simplifiers. We must take complicated technologies and explain them in a brief paragraph." In AT&T's highly technical business we have had success with comparisons such as, "The first transistors looked like little top hats on stilts." Felix G. Rohatyn, the articulate investment banker from Lazard Freres & Company who helped lead New York City's perilous move from the edge of bankruptcy in the mid-1970s, even figured out how to describe that financial concept: "Bankruptcy is like someone stepping into a tepid bath and slashing his wrists—you might not feel yourself dying, but that's what would happen."[17]

- *Avoid "frankly," "to tell you the truth" and "to be honest."* These expressions serve no useful purpose. In fact, they may backfire on you by raising the question of how frank or truthful or honest you have been in all the rest of your interview if you suddenly say that you are going to be "frank" or "truthful" or "honest" with the reporter now.

- *Avoid negatives.* "No, we are not discriminating against women" is not as convincing as "We have a broad program to actively recruit more women managers." President Richard Nixon gave us an infamous example of what *not* to do when he said, "I am *not* a crook." Most people listen selectively and visualize while they listen. So more people pictured and remembered the word "crook" than caught the "not" in front of it.

- *Consider what your words will mean to others.* You don't want to be as parochial as Humpty Dumpty, who told Alice, "When I use a word it means just what I choose it to mean—neither more nor less." Frequently the same word can have different meanings to different audiences. A terminal in the computer business is a piece of equipment—but to many people it is a place where you catch a bus. William Safire offered another example: "To many a depression is what you take to a psychiatrist, not an economist."[18] And in the international arena there are classic stories of misunderstandings caused by a poor choice of words. If your organization actively sells its products or services globally, make sure your spokespersons and translators are very familiar with the language, including local idioms, of each country where you do business. (See chapter 9 for more information on operating in international markets.)

- *Look at each question from the public's point of view*. For example, if a reporter says "You don't have many African-American supervisors, do you?" don't counter with "Our record is terrific. We're doing much better than most companies." That sounds defensive. Instead, be positive in your answers. You might say "We still don't have enough African-American supervisors, although we are making progress. [Such and such] percent of our supervisors are African-American and we have these specific programs . . ."

- *Be realistic in your answers.* Veteran PR counselor Chester Burger reminds us that the best media relations campaign in the world "can't build trust while reality is destroying it."[19] And Arthur Page, an AT&T vice president who in essence founded the field of corporate PR as a strategic management function, taught that while well-thought-out communications programs are vital to an organization's success, they must be based on the reality of its performance and not on Madison Avenue slogans. Page summed up his philosophy in a single sentence: "Public relations is 90 percent doing and 10 percent talking about it."[20]

- *Respond to a simple question with a simple answer.* Short, simple answers are better than long, complicated ones. A few sentences using everyday language give the interviewer less opportunity to misunderstand you. And on TV, where time is measured in dollars, this is especially important. In fact, in a TV interview you should be sure to make your key points in less than a minute—preferably, in 10 or 20 seconds.

- *Never underestimate the intelligence of your audience—and never overestimate their knowledge.* We are not suggesting you adjust your prose to the words used by high-school sophomores, but you must explain your terms, especially when you are covering a difficult subject. Two hours after a recent interview, a reporter phoned the media relations person to plead for a translation: "That interview reminded me of my college physics classes," she said. "I understood it while the professor was talking but when I got back to my room, I couldn't explain it."

- **Speak in the active voice.** Avoid the passive, which places the doer of the action at the end of the sentence or sometimes eliminates responsibility altogether. Say, "We will be moving our offices," not "Our offices will be moved." You want to portray your organization as a group of interesting, concerned people who decide and do things, rather than a faceless, inanimate group. Similarly, don't duck responsibility for difficult actions. Say, "We reluctantly have decided that a layoff of some of our employees is required," not "The economy has forced a layoff." Companies don't make decisions or establish policies—people do.

- **Do not waste your brief time with a reporter by arguing against the other side.** You may want to refute their point of view but inadvertently end up giving valuable media exposure to their position. Instead, stay on *your* message. State your case positively, without mentioning your opponents by name. If you are forced to refer to your adversaries, avoid emotional labels such as "chauvinist" or "radical." Use "less experienced observers" or "the other side" instead.

- **Do not be offended by a reporter's questions about what you consider private or proprietary areas.** As Robert Mac-Neil, founder of PBS's *MacNeil/Lehrer Report* explained in his autobiography, being a journalist is "a lifelong license to follow that most basic human trait, curiosity. . . . It is permission to probe and delve into whatever interests you as thoroughly or as superficially as you like. . . ."[21] True—but as a spokesperson it is your prerogative and responsibility to decide how much you want to say in your answer. If the questioning moves into proprietary or confidential areas, simply explain that providing such information would be too helpful to your competitors. When the questioning gets too personal, wit can be a good defense. Former President Ronald Reagan practiced this technique with the best of them: "Our family didn't exactly come from the wrong side of the tracks," he said of his beginnings, "but we were certainly always within the sound of the train whistles."[22] Broadening your response to divert attention from the narrow, personal nature of the question is a good tactic—

particularly during a television interview. A female politician asked how she balances her duties to her husband, children and the public might reply: "That question clearly illustrates the problems faced by so many American women who are working mothers. . . ."

- *Do not respond to a narrow question with an equally narrow answer.* Rather, take the opportunity to reiterate one of your key points. For example, if you are being interviewed on a plant closing and are asked how many people will be out of work, do not just say "about seven hundred." Instead, reply directly to the question and then immediately expand on it: "About seven hundred, and we are doing everything we can to help soften the blow. We will phase down operations gradually over the next six months. We have generous severance payments. And we are setting up an outplacement center to help our people look for other jobs."

- *Do not answer hypothetical questions.* Instead, particularize them with: "That's a hypothetical question so it is impossible to know what might happen. But let me tell you exactly what did happen in a similar case. . . ."

- *Never, absolutely never, lie to a reporter.* You may get away with it once or twice, but ultimately you will be found out. Then not only you but also your organization will have lost a priceless asset: credibility. As Winston Churchill put it: "To build may have to be the slow and laboring task of years. To destroy can be the thoughtless act of a single day."

- *Be yourself.* If you like to sit around a conference table when you are meeting with your staff, that is likely a fine place for the interview; you will feel comfortable and the reporter will have a surface on which to write and/or place a tape recorder. If you prefer to emphasize your points by drawing diagrams on an easel, do it. If you love sports, it is perfectly appropriate to use an analogy from the football field to illustrate your point. If your taste leans more to music, feel free to make a comparison using an orchestra as a metaphor. The reporter wants your perspective—not that of a well-trained but impersonal robot who gives the impression of speaking fluently but formally in a foreign language.

Hints for Television Appearances

When you stare into the eye of a television camera and see that little red light go on, you are bluntly reminded that there is a huge audience out there who will see and hear whatever you say. Stage fright caused by the camera's relentless gaze and TV's wide exposure is natural, no matter how frequently you are videotaped, whether you are in the comfortable surroundings of your own office or the impersonal setting of a TV studio. There are many things you can do in advance to prepare for the particular demands of television.

Appearances definitely *do* count on television. Its power in politics first became clear in the initial Kennedy-Nixon debate in the U.S. presidential race of 1960. Polls showed that those who heard the debate on radio thought Nixon had won, whereas those who watched the event on TV named Kennedy the winner. These days, executives appearing on C-SPAN while they are being grilled in Congress can appear evasive or "guilty as charged" if they forget the power of the TV camera.

First of all is the choice of what to wear. Gone are the days when a man had to wear a light blue shirt. That requirement was caused by the fact that a bright white shirt would "burn in" a black and white camera—that is, keep it from getting a clear image because of a too-high contrast ratio. A blue shirt became *de rigueur* because in those days that was the only other color shirt most male executives had. Now virtually all television programs are shot in color. Blue is still a fine choice for both men and women. But most other colors are equally good. What you want to avoid are extremes—either small busy patterns or large, bold stripes on your tie, shirt, blouse or dress. Solid colors are best, but you should leave pure white or solid black home in the closet.

Do not wear a large amount of jewelry, especially if it is bright, because it will cause the cameras to "flare," distracting viewers with a starburst of light. Men should wear calf-length socks in case you want to cross your legs on camera.

If you have a tan, do not get a haircut just before the interview in case your tan line is uncovered. Men with heavy "5 o'clock shadow" should shave just before the crew arrives. Women should not wear too much make-up, especially eye shadow; the right amount for work is normally the right amount for television. Men should not refuse a little powder just before the cameras roll; if a TV technician makes the suggestion it means some perspiration is visible on the TV monitor's view of you—not surprising considering the bright lights and a normal amount of nervousness.

All of the techniques you practiced to help present your position persuasively to print journalists apply to television— only more so. Civil rights leader Jesse Jackson knows that well: "If you had a camera with you I'd be talking differently," he told *Newsweek*'s Lea Donosky.[23] It is critically important that you speak in sound-bite headlines. Make your points short and simple. TV's formula is to use perhaps 100 words from the reporter and a "sound bite" of 10 to 20 words from the speaker.

Keep two facts in mind: First, television is a visual medium, so what the eye sees is more important than what the ear hears. And second, the camera magnifies whatever it sees. It sounds trite, but you should act naturally. Do not smile when it is not appropriate—you will look phony, not friendly. Do not gesture wildly or move suddenly—the camera may lose you altogether. Do not stare upward into space when you are thinking—you will look like you are praying for divine guidance.

If you are being videotaped in your office, you or your media relations person should suggest other attractive areas of your operation for shootings, or provide "already in the can" background footage. Think visually. Television is at its best when it can show something happening. A picture of nothing but a person—a "talking head"—is visually boring. Your chances for coverage will be immeasurably improved if you make it easy for the program's producer to illustrate what you are saying. (That does not mean you should refer to complicated charts and graphs filled with detailed information, since it is unlikely they will be readable on the TV screen.)

Take a look at existing props in your office that may appear on camera if the interview is taped there. Family photographs add a warm touch. But a plaque with two small gold axes presented as an award for an expense-reduction program can give the wrong impression if the interview is on layoffs or a plant closing.

Television is an intimate medium. You will be speaking not to the "general public" but rather to individual people—a family gathered together in the living room, a tired worker dozing in the den, someone catching up with ironing while watching the news. Eric

Sevareid said he tried "to remember always that the public is only people, and people only persons, no two alike."

Jim Scott, assignment editor of WISH-TV affiliate in Indianapolis, offers this advice: "**Talk one-on-one with the reporter**. You are talking to an individual who is interested in what's going on, and thinks you have something of importance to say. Try to ignore the camera—or treat it as just somebody else who is looking on."

Normally the interview will be videotaped and then severely edited before being aired. Many times TV reporters will ask you the same question several times in different ways. They are giving their editors a variety of versions and lengths from which to choose. It may be disconcerting to have the reporter pay more attention to a stopwatch than to your words, and it may seem unnecessarily repetitive to be asked the same question. You should take the opportunity to sharpen your answer. **No matter how often you are asked, you should always include your main point in each answer—right up front—said in different ways, of course.** When the tape is edited, only one response will be left—and you and the reporter both want it to be a clear and concise statement.

Do not be intimidated by a reporter with a microphone during a fast-breaking "spot news" situation. An unnerving interview technique is to thrust the mike at you and then pull it back when the reporter has what he or she wants. You have two options in this situation: Gently take hold of the mike—over the reporter's hand if necessary—or smile and say "I haven't finished answering the last question yet," and go back to making your point.

Regardless of what reporters or TV technicians tell you, **assume you are on the air all the time you are in their presence.** An old ploy is to have the cameraperson tell you a small adjustment has to be made in the equipment: "It will only take a minute. I'll let you know when I'm ready, so just relax and bear with me." Then the reporter leans across and murmurs an "off the record" question with a smile. Remember, you are always *on* the record. Bright lights and a quiet room are no longer needed with the latest video hardware.

Sometimes attempts to be pleasant and polite can backfire. Try to avoid nodding as the reporter talks. It could be viewed on camera as acknowledgment of the premise behind the question. Similarly, be careful about saying "That's a good point" after a negative question. Tight editing could wipe out the rest of your response.

Hints for Radio

A radio interview has some different characteristics from either a phone interview with a print reporter or a televised taping. Unless it is a major news story, the station will use only a very brief segment (10 to 20 seconds) of your interview—although it is likely to rebroadcast the item several times, perhaps using different sound bites each time. So it is even more important that you make your main points succinctly. Also, radio rarely uses the reporter's questions on the air. Before you answer you should pause a moment to be sure the questioner is finished and you are not "stepping on that person's line." You will ensure cleaner edits and warm thoughts from the audio engineer.

You are not seen by anyone, so you can have your key points written out and handy where you can see them—but you must be careful not to rustle the pages because even soft sounds may be heard over the air. This is crucial if you are appearing on a call-in talk show, where the studio's powerful microphones can pick up and amplify even the tiniest noises, including the sound of swallowing when you take a drink of water.

Practice out loud. If you sound awkward or must gasp for breath, shorten your sentences and eliminate difficult phrases. You want to guard against sounding like you are reading a prepared response—on the air you will sound terribly stilted. You should speak in a conversational tone as you would with a friend on the phone.

During the interview you should gesture as you would during a normal conversation; it will help both your voice and your body to relax. As well, smile when you talk; it will make your voice sparkle and also help you to relax.

Be sure to repeat your company or brand name several times during the interview. People listening on the radio have no visuals to remind them who you are and what you are talking about. So your need to paint repeated word pictures for your messages to be remembered.

Hints for News Conferences

When you are participating in a news conference, you have the obligation not only to answer reporters' questions but also to make a few opening remarks giving the purpose of the conference and formally announcing the news that caused it. Answering questions at a news conference is very similar to being interviewed except that you have more than one person asking questions and you are not in the comfortable surroundings of your own office. Making the opening remarks of a conference is much like giving a brief speech. As you look out over the crowd of cameras, lights, microphones and people peering up at you expectantly, you may feel like a mother robin perched on the edge of her nest looking into the hungry, gaping mouths of her babies. Much like the mother bird, your obligation is to feed the media—that is, provide them with news in an interesting way in the shortest period of time. The same techniques you use for interviews and TV appearances will serve you well here.

Several hours before the news conference, come to the room to familiarize yourself with the set-up. Work out signals with your media relations person as cues if you begin speaking too quickly or answering reporters' questions too abruptly. Then leave, and use the time to practice what you intend to say—and perhaps to go for a brisk walk to clear your mind.

Do not show up again until immediately before the news conference is scheduled to start. Do not mingle with reporters ahead of time. Whether you are introduced by your media relations person or open the news conference yourself is up to you. In any case, ignore the many microphones that are placed on the podium. Do not ask if everyone can hear you—it is the responsibility of the audio engineers and your media person to ensure all the mike levels are correct. Just begin your formal remarks, speaking slowly and clearly and following your text closely if it has been included in the press kit materials. Like any attentive participant, the TV camera will be focused on you. But if you become long-winded or the cameraperson's attention wanes, the camera may scan the listeners—particularly that station's reporter—for reaction shots. If things really get dull the little red light will go off as the technician turns the camera off altogether.

After your introductory talk, open the session up to questions. Use an open phrase like "Now I would be happy to answer your questions" or "What are your questions?" rather than the closed construction "Does anyone have any questions?" If you do not know them all, ask the journalists to give their names and publications or stations as they are called on. Do not pace around, or the microphones and TV cameras will have trouble following you.

If there are no questions right away, do not panic. The reporters probably are reviewing their notes on your opening remarks and framing questions that will appeal to their readers or viewers. Simply wait a few minutes (it will seem like hours) and then invite questions again. Or point to a reporter you know and say "Susan, you usually have a good question for me." If there still are none, thank the reporters for coming and say you are available for individual questions if they wish.

More likely, the questions will start popping several at a time. Once you select a reporter to ask a question, keep your eyes on him or her as much as possible while you answer. This will keep other reporters from interrupting and help the reporter's camera crew get both of you on tape if they so desire. Allow one follow-up question from that journalist—but then establish eye contact with another questioner so one person is not able to dominate.

Use the reporter's name in your answer whenever possible. Do not be unnerved if someone moves around with a hand-held camera or even crawls up to the podium on hands and knees to adjust a microphone or test the lighting with a light meter. You probably will be asked several similar questions by TV people, because broadcast editors generally like to show their own reporters on the screen asking questions. So don't hesitate to repeat your key point in answer to each question—again, only one version will appear on each channel—and be sure *not* to say "As I said in response to an earlier question . . ."

If very few journalists have shown up, you should proceed as planned. But if the small turnout is obvious, you may wish to acknowledge it with a light comment such as "Ladies and gentlemen, it looks like you will have an exclusive by coming here today . . ." and conduct the session in a less formal manner.

Equally important is for your media relations person to be prepared with everything from extra chairs to additional press kits in case many more people than expected show up. But if they are nonmedia people, they should politely but firmly be kept out of the news conference room. Journalists do not appreciate an audience, which can create distractions and generate noises picked up by the sensitive TV and radio audio equipment. And you are likely to be nervous enough without having kibitzers present.

Twenty to 30 minutes is the normal length of a news conference in North America—although if questions are still coming you may decide to go a few minutes over the scheduled time. You can end the conference yourself or have your media relations person do so by announcing that you have time for one more question.

Mingle afterwards with reporters in case they want private interviews or individual on-camera shots of you talking with them. But remember that everything you say during these conversations is also on the record. Therefore, you should be no less careful with your comments than you were when you were at the podium.

Hints for On-Line Chats

If an executive or other spokesperson is wary of agreeing to an on-line chat because of his or her lack of familiarity with the technology or inability to type, you should offer alternatives.

One solution is for you to supply a professional typist to input answers in real time that are being dictated by the spokesperson. As well, commercial services are very accommodating to on-line spokespersons—especially celebrity guests—who cannot type or spare the time to sit for hours at a keyboard inputting their own answers. When we were at Prodigy for a book publicity chat, we saw someone typing in actress Jodie Foster's answers. Jodie had received the questions by fax and phoned back her replies, which now were being sent out on the Internet by a Prodigy ghost typist.

Interview No-Nos

Here are some topics to avoid when you are talking with reporters, since they inevitably cause misunderstandings.

- *Do not ask if you can review the story in advance.* Just as the reporter cannot expect to see your annual report or latest product plans until you are ready to make them public, so you cannot have advance access to their reporting of the news.

- *Do not mention how much your organization advertises in the reporter's medium.* No reputable publication or station permits its editorial judgment to be influenced by advertising, and you may unwittingly insult the reporter's personal and professional codes of behavior.

- *Do not tell broadcast reporters you think 30 or 60 seconds is too short a time to tell your story adequately.* They are no more satisfied with the time constraints they work under than you are. Only 21 or 22 minutes of a half-hour network television news program are devoted to news; the rest is commercials. In a column for the *Wall Street Journal,* Dan Rather said that every night at every network good and important stories wind up on the floor because there's not enough time in the broadcast.[24] Walter Cronkite, speaking in support of extending the evening news to an hour, said that "if we had more time, we could do a much better job. We'd make what we're broadcasting far more understandable and be able to give stories that need it greater depth."[25] But it is also true that businesses spend billions of dollars every year telling their stories and selling their products in 10-, 30- and 60-second commercials on TV and radio.

- *Do not tell a reporter you will provide written answers to questions if he or she will send them to you.* The media is not in the business of taking dictation. That type of exchange probably is too time-consuming to meet the news deadlines. In any case, it will make the reporters think you are hiding something because you will not talk face to face.

- *Do not ask a reporter to keep what you say "off the record."* Perhaps the public's perspective was permanently changed by so much talk of "deep background" in the Woodward/Bernstein chronicle, *All the President's Men*. Remember that the sole reason a reporter is interviewing you is literally *for* the record—that is, to write and produce a story for publication or airing. Editors are adamant that their reporters identify their sources in all but the most unusual cases. Presidents and secretaries of state may wish to continue demanding off-the-record status for their remarks, but it is a much safer practice for the rest of us to assume everything we utter will be attributed. Thus, we should not say anything we would not want publicly associated with ourselves or our organization unless we have a long relationship and a special understanding with a particular reporter.

How to Avoid Interviewing Tricks

The vast majority of all interviews are pleasant, nonthreatening experiences. But when the interview has not resulted in any news or interesting quotes, the reporter may reach down into his or her bag of tricks. When that starts to happen, you need to be prepared. Here are some helpful techniques:

Technique: Needling

Example: "Oh, come now. Do you really expect us to buy that?"

Response: Stick by your guns. Don't equivocate or vacillate. Say "Absolutely, [reporter's first name]," then go on to reinforce the positive point just made or make a new positive point.

Technique: False facts (unintentional or deliberate)

Example: "So your profits are seventy-two percent [Actually they were 11 percent, but up 72 percent from the comparable quarter last year]."

Response: Correct graciously and go to your positive point. Begin with "Perhaps I could clarify that for your viewers, [reporter's first name]," fix the error, then go on to make a positive point about how the profits are used, about providing jobs or about investing in research and new product development.

Technique: Reinterpretation of your responses

Example: "So what we have here is a possible epidemic."

Response: Avoid repeating loaded words. Say "[reporter's name], what we're saying is, six of our employees have developed a minor skin rash, which we discovered through our own in-plant medical program." And go on to make a positive point about caring for employees' health and well-being.

Technique: Putting words in your mouth

Example: "So you're still dumping your garbage in the river then, aren't you?"

Response: Recognize that their effort is to get you to use words you would just as soon not say. Don't argue. Instead, say: "Let's see what's at issue here, [reporter's name], if I may," then make your positive point.

Stephen C. Rafe and Walter J. Pfister Jr.
The Executive Televsion Workshop, New York City.

Chapter 7

ETHICS
The Golden Rules
of Media Relations

Faced with a long prison term and financial ruin, Michael Gallagher did what criminals routinely do in such circumstances: he cut a deal with prosecutors, swapping incriminating information against someone else for leniency and a lighter sentence. But Mr. Gallagher was not just another white-color miscreant or small-time hoodlum. He was an investigative reporter who had worked for Cincinnati's dominant newspaper, *The Cincinnati Enquirer.* His decision to reveal the name of a confidential source, along with notes, documents and secretly taped conversations, is echoing through the legal and journalistic communities as a major assault on the revered principle of protecting sources. Mr. Gallagher had promised his source, George F. Ventura, a former lawyer for Chiquita Brands International, that he would go to jail rather than reveal that Mr. Ventura helped him gain access to Chiquita's voice-mail system. . . . But in the end, Mr. Gallagher struck a deal with prosecutors and identified Mr. Ventura. Now it is Mr. Ventura who faces the prospect of going to jail. He is charged with unauthorized access to a computer and violations of Ohio's electronic communication privacy law.[1]

A recent study reported that local news is especially violent. Of the 100 newscasts analyzed on a single day, the average "mayhem index" was 43 percent, meaning that almost half of the news in each program involved violence or disaster.[2]

The board of directors of the PRSA voted to end contact between its board members and Jack O'Dwyer, publisher of PR publications and directories. In a written statement, PRSA said: "We have attempted to provide the newsletter with facts and information which are routinely absent from the newsletter's reporting."[3]

Efforts by the College of the Canyons to resolve quietly a sex-harassment complaint against a professor on its campus were blown wide open Wednesday when a lawyer for the student who had made the charges held a press conference and attended the college trustees' meeting with a camera crew in tow.[4]

These stories, standards and scenarios, repeated often in offices and meeting rooms around the world, demonstrate the constant tension between the media and the rest of the world. Journalists are looking for a story; often the objects of their interest are not. Over the years, the tension has reached unprecedented heights, primarily because of the advent of tabloid journalism which seeks—and finds—the sensational in business, city government, the entertainment world, the small-town community, royal families and even grief-stricken families.

"Freedom of the press" is redefined daily, with proponents seeing little reason not to monitor probes into lives and programs; opponents argue that "freedom" has become a legal way to pry unnecessarily, to peer into people's lives, bedrooms, boardrooms and institutions. The question often becomes: where does ethical behavior begin and end? Ethics is the hot topic of today with a proliferation of professional codes of ethics and numerous allegations of unethical practices. Ethics should be easy to recognize and define. But it is not, especially as the world becomes more homogenous and the ethics of one society are looked upon as ridiculous by another society. Businesses in one region operate under different laws, mores and structures than businesses in another region.

Chester Burger, Accredited Public Relations (APR), public relations executive, suggests that "ethics are nothing but standards of behavior, and who among us is qualified to suggest that his or her standards deserve to be followed by others?"[5] Dr. Albert Schweitzer offered his definition: "Ethics is the name we give to our concern for good behavior. We feel an obligation to consider not only our personal well-being, but also that of others and of human society as a whole." The Ethics Resource Center found that the general public readily understands what ethics are. "More than 86 percent of all people interviewed associated ethics with standards and rules of conduct, morals, right and wrong, values and honesty. The public also understood that if ethics appeared in the headlines the story would tell about the lack of ethics—the doing of wrong as opposed to right."

Ivan Hill of the Ethics Resource Center believes that "Honesty and ethics are basic, working social principles, not just moral guidelines." He adds: "True, ethics involve more than honesty but without honesty there are no ethics. When honesty is left out of ethics, there is a smelly residue of hypocrisy. Such hypocrisy creates a real danger in the efficient functioning and manageability of an open society, especially in business and in government."[6]

And Lee W. Baker says ethics "concerns one's moral values, standards, and choices. Ethical dilemmas confront individuals, not organizations."[7]

Examples of the lack of ethics abound. Most notable, and perhaps the event with the longest reaching impact, was Watergate. Subsequent investigations have shown that throughout Watergate, the emphasis was on forcing the so-called solutions to fit the problem, rather than defining the problem and seeking a solution to it. It appears that at no point did anyone ask, "Why are we doing this? Why are we putting layer upon layer of cover over this problem?"

Ironically, the newspaper that was so instrumental in the Watergate revelations, *The Washington Post*, found itself in the middle of an ethical dilemma when a reporter, Janet Cooke, created a totally fictitious tale of an eight-year-old heroin addict—an article for which she won the Pulitzer Prize for feature writing.

The difference between these two events is in how they were handled when the problem was discovered. After Cooke admitted the story was fiction, the Pulitzer Prize was returned, the newspaper took its share of the responsibility and the journalist and the newspaper agreed to part ways. Whereas both President Nixon and Cooke share ignominy as people who have practiced unethical behavior, in Cooke's case the newspaper emerged as showing and practicing a high regard for ethical behavior.

It appears that one way to create a standard of ethical behavior is to learn not to practice behavior considered by the majority of people to be unethical. Because what constitutes ethical behavior and what does not is debatable, we will attempt only to suggest certain guidelines for preferred behavior when dealing with the media. Even these guidelines will be argued by some, depending on experiences, country of origin, individual philosophies and so forth. However, we have found from our own experiences that these guidelines work the best for us.

Trust Each Other

There is a story told of animal trainer Clyde Beatty, who was asked by a reporter: "Mr. Beatty, even though you deal with lions and tigers as though they were kittens, surely you're afraid of something—spiders or snakes or something. What are you afraid of?" Beatty replied: "Son, I'm afraid of those lions and tigers."[8] Fear and respect are often synonymous. His respect for the power and intelligence of big cats helped Beatty to work with them, not against them.

The same is true with the media. The media are powerful. Because they are powerful, they must be respected. But to fear the media is to put yourself on the defensive. Your true position is that of a professional exchanging information with another professional.

Lou Williams, president of L. C. Williams & Associates in Chicago, has lamented:

> I must admit I'm constantly amazed at the continuing level of distrust between journalists and public relations folks.
>
> Is all of journalism an NBC report playing questionable tricks on GM trucks? Of course not.
>
> Is all PR a search for the big story placement? Of course not.
>
> There are good and bad reporters, just as there are good and bad publicists.[9]

Think of the media as customers. You are selling them a product—a story, news release, interview—and they are going to use it widely and, it is hoped, to your benefit. So trust the representatives of the media. They are performing a job, not staging a lynching.

Lying

Because an adversarial role exists between many organizations and the media, people often think the way to maintain power and control over the media is to lie to the media. There is simply no rationale for such convoluted thinking, but it exists. A lie is a lie is a lie. No good comes of lying; particularly, no good comes from lying to the media. Eventually a lie will come out in print or on television. It will be taken as truth by the public who, when they later discover the real story, will disbelieve anything further that your organization says.

Lanny J. Davis, former White House aide, and George Stephanopoulos, former advisor to President Clinton, describe in their respective books how the White House team routinely delayed getting information to the media or resorted to lying or misleading the media, rather than telling the truth quickly, expeditiously and thoroughly, actions which both men found to be counterproductive.

While both also talk about "spin control," Davis elucidates: "Facts are facts—and no amount of spinning will alter those facts." He defines "good spin" as a way to minimize the damage—by surrounding bad facts with context, with good facts (if there are any) and, if possible, with credible, favorable (or less damaging) interpretation.[10]

"Lie once and you are a liar forever," according to Frank Swoboda, staff reporter for *The Washington Post*. He cited Mitsubishi Motor Manufacturing of America, saying the company lied and threatened reporters in an effort to prevent them from getting details about the EEOC's sexual harassment suit against the company. "It just whetted our appetite," asserted Swoboda, who said the *Post* used the Internet to locate some of the women who said they had been harassed.[11]

Joseph Sullivan, writing in *Business and the Media,* reminds us "that both reporters and the public are sophisticated enough to recognize smokescreens, if not penetrate them. Honesty is the best policy."[12] Adds Judith Lederman, owner of JSL Publicity & Marketing, "Clients come and go, but the media is always there and they don't forget a liar."[13]

Lying to the public is no different from lying in the courtroom under oath. The sentence, however, can be tougher: loss of credibility, loss of respect, loss of customers, loss of trust by the community and by shareowners. There is no such thing as a "half-lie," a "small lie" or a "white lie."

Watergate produced one of the better examples of the attempt at a half-lie: the use of "not at this point in time." This qualifier specifically defines the scope of the statement given, thus producing a built-in defense of the statement later. For example: "Are you negotiating to buy out XYZ Company?" "We are not contemplating buying out XYZ Company *at this point in time*." This response begs the question: Will you contemplate a buyout later? Have you already considered the question? Have you actually bought out the company and are denying only contemplating a buyout?

There are other ways of handling this situation. You could issue a standby statement that you are holding talks with the XYZ Company. Alternatively, you could simply state that as a corporate policy, you never discuss any talks you may be having. Such statements will satisfy the reporter's needs and prevent you from backing yourself into a half-lie corner. Remember, a painful truth will arouse more sympathy if it is given out by the company's leader than by an angry critic or a disgruntled employee.

To Comment or Not to Comment

Few words create more frustration for a reporter than "No comment." A key element in a reporter's job is the process wherein the reporter asks questions and the respondent answers. "No comment" throws a red cape in front of a very large and angry bull.

The problem stems from the connotations of the phrase "No comment." For the person issuing the statement, it is a safeguard against putting one's foot in one's mouth. Saying "No comment" seems safer than saying "I don't know what you are talking about," or "I made a mistake," or "The company regrets that it made a decision 50 years ago which has adverse effects today," or "We prefer not to discuss that topic." Reporters and the general public, on the other hand, have assumed that "No comment" really means "I am guilty as hell but I won't admit it."

According to a survey conducted by New York-based Porter/Novelli, when a company spokesperson declines to comment in a controversial situation, approximately 65 percent of Americans think the company is guilty of wrongdoing.[14]

In support of that finding is one professional's look at the conflict between lawyers and public relations practitioners. He says "Both professions have image problems. But the public's perception of both are actually the opposite of reality. Lawyers appear to want the truth to prevail. Public relations folks are seen as spinners of truth."[15]

In actuality, the safest course to take is to answer the reporter's questions. If you do not know the answer, reply "I don't know but, I'll get that information and get back to you." The more information you can provide, however, the less the reporter can speculate about your activities.

Bill Harlow, director of public affairs for the U.S. Central Intelligence Agency, says his agency "almost never [says] 'no comment.' We'll find some way to say something in a positive way when we can't respond to a question."[16]

One way to gain control of a lazy reporter's "Would you care to comment?" question is to ask the reporter: "Could you be more specific about what you want to know?" Or, you could take the question away by saying: "Yes, I want to comment. I want you to know that our company has been making and selling these products for 37 years with no failures. I will show you the letters from happy customers . . ." You get the idea—take control and don't let a lazy reporter have control of you.

Following is a list of sample situations with examples of ways to avoid "No comment":

1. Rumors of an imminent layoff or plant shutdown. "When we have any such announcement, I will let you know at once. I am sure you understand that our procedure is to let the employees know first so they don't hear the news on the radio, television or Internet."

2. Employee arrest for stealing, drugs, etc., on or affecting your organization's property. Confirm facts like date, time and number involved in the arrest that would be readily available to a reporter at the police station, as well as the employment status of your employee. Then: "We are cooperating fully with the appropriate agencies [name them] in the investigation. Beyond that, it would be best for you to talk with the local police [or whomever] for further information."

3. Employee activity (positive or negative) not affecting your organization. Confirm employment and job title only. Then: "We do not give out any additional information about our employees, because we feel doing so might intrude on their privacy."

4. Sales results, production plans and other proprietary information. "I hope you can understand that answering that question would give our competitors too much valuable information about our sales plans [or manufacturing processes, or marketing strategies, or whatever]."

5. Information from an employee. "That's an individual's opinion. The company's position is . . ."

6. Rumors of imminent dividend action, stock offering, debt issue, merger, etc. "We have nothing to announce at this time. You are well aware that there are clear procedures [prior notification of the stock exchange on which a company's shares are traded, simultaneous release to the financial and business wire services, etc.] for any announcement that could affect our stock price or an investment decision." Or, "As a matter of policy, we never discuss or speculate on rumors in the marketplace."

7. Frivolous charges. Respond with "That's absurd," or "That statement is so ridiculous that I won't dignify it with a response," or even "That's hogwash!"

8. Inappropriate questions. "Our organization has no position on that issue one way or the other" is an appropriate answer to questions about political, social, religious or other issues on which a public position might unnecessarily alienate segments of the public. Also, "We are in the business of telecommunications [or whatever], not religion."

9. Leaks of settlement plans or other bargaining information. "We are negotiating with the union in good faith to resolve the issues that separate us. Certainly we all want to avoid a strike. I shall confine any other remarks to the bargaining table, where I hope they will contribute to the negotiation process."

10. Advance publicity prior to a new product announcement. "The company has made no such announcement," or "We have read those reports with great interest," or "You know you are always among the first to know whenever we are ready to go public with new product plans."

11. Question on a judicial or regulatory ruling. "We will have to study the decision [or ruling, or judgment] before we can discuss it in detail."

When You Have to Say No

As a media relations spokesperson, do not confuse "No comment" with "No, I can't answer that question because . . ." There are legitimate times when information cannot be disclosed; reporters know and respect those times.

In an effort to make sure cases are tried in the courtroom and not in the media, many judges impose restrictions on the parties in the action, which prevents any discussion of the case with the media. Either party found guilty of ignoring this restriction often can be charged with contempt of court. Thus, if a reporter asks about a court case, it is perfectly understandable and permissible to reply: "I'm sorry but we're not allowed to discuss this case under terms agreed to in the court." You are neither commenting on the subject nor are you stonewalling; rather, you are explaining to the journalist why, in this instance, you cannot be of help.

Similarly, if you are asked about talks between your company and another, you can respond: "I'm sorry, but we have agreed to keep our business discussions private." This often will be the case as companies considering major agreements, alliances or acquisitions declare at the outset that no material will be issued to the media unless jointly agreed to by the parties.

Another instance of being able to say no without guilt is when the information sought is specifically proprietary. For example, if your company has been purchasing large quantities of aluminum for its products for more than a decade and then suddenly decreases its purchases of aluminum while increasing its supply of a less costly material, then the competition could assume one of many things: that your company is offering a new product line, that it has found a less expensive way to produce the same product, or that it is having some difficulty as yet to be determined. Whatever the answer, it is the type of thing you would not want to have in the press because it is damaging to your company's welfare.

Some cases of employee privacy also allow the spokesperson to say no to a reporter's request. More and more, employees are seeking to disassociate themselves from their jobs. This separation of person and job can cause some gnashing of teeth when it comes to answering a journalist's legitimate inquiry and simultaneously respecting the employee's right to privacy.

A well-known, but not as well-used, procedure to protect all parties concerned during a photography session is the model release. This paper, when signed by an employee, allows the company to use the employee's photograph in advertising, training or general publicity or for any other causes stated in the release. Such a release is not sought for written material, however, and perhaps it should be. Questions about a job function can be answered without concern for any one person who happens to hold the job.

Questions about the job function as it relates to the person performing the job should be handled differently. For example, a reporter could ask about a specific piece of equipment. After being told that it is an advanced computer for the central communications room, the reporter asks, "How have your employees responded to this equipment?" If you reply, "Not well. The equipment seems to be too tough for them and we've had to put them through training many times," the reporter may ask to speak to one of the employees. This is an obvious dilemma. You have already given the impression that your employees are not capable of being trained on the equipment. To agree to an interview on behalf of the employees would be disastrous. In this case, it is best to ask the employees first, explaining carefully what the interview will be about so they can decide if they want to appear in public.

Obviously, a media spokesperson does not answer any question about employees that is beyond the realm of the spokesperson's responsibility. For instance, a question about an employee's financial status or personal habits must be referred to that employee. You should identify in advance those situations and circumstances in which you will have to say "no."

Making Demands

In many organizations, some upper-level or executive management person reviews the material that is written for internal use, such as the employee newspaper, management newsletter, benefit pieces or internal magazine pieces. The annual report, an external vehicle, is also closely scrutinized by top management before being issued for public consumption, as are advertisements and other public documents. It is easy to understand, then, how executives might assume they have a right to review a reporter's copy. Sadly, this natural desire to make sure the material is accurate, fair and legally defensible often creates a totally different impression on a reporter.

Clearly, it is the responsibility of the media relations spokesperson to educate the management about the differences between a reporter and an in-company staff writer, the different audiences being served by each and the rules under which each operates.

Andy Rooney of *60 Minutes* was once asked if he thought the manner in which the management of a large corporation dealt with him in imposing limitations on the questions to be asked damaged that company in any way. Rooney replied: "It made me suspect they had something to hide. To this extent it damaged them. And because it was difficult to get information from them, I got it from a dozen less sympathetic sources . . . former executives of the company, drivers, pilots and dissidents from within the company itself."[17]

Instead of making demands about an interview, you should make clear the subject matter of the interview, the time allowed for it and what the material will be used for. This is good common sense in establishing interviews, and both you and the reporter will be glad for the understanding. Also while you should not ask to see a story before publication, you can suggest to the reporter that you are available to check quotes, facts and figures at the reporter's convenience. You can also remind your management that the only way to see copy in advance and assure that it says exactly what you want it to, is to buy advertising space and create the ad.

Off the Record

We practice the theory that there is no such thing as "off the record." There is still controversy concerning the use of "off the record," evidenced by the definition of the term given to foreign journalists by the U.S. Foreign Press Center:

> The flat rule is that the material is not for publication, it is solely for the reporter's private knowledge. The off the record interview or briefing is most commonly used by officials to advise reporters of something that is going to happen so that they have the background or information necessary for planning purposes to cover the event when it does occur. For example, an official may explain that the Secretary of State is going to the Far East on a given date and that he will be talking about specific topics. The reporter cannot print that news since it is off the record, but he or she can make plans to follow along on the same trip and to report on the speeches and press conferences that the Secretary of State may hold.[18]

Obviously, there are times when you must give background material to a reporter before he or she fully understands a subject. The same rules apply for background material as they do for current material: you do not give out proprietary information, legally restricted material or material that would jeopardize an employee's privacy. Everything left over, then, should be available for publication. In short, everything left over should be on the record.

Another argument about "off the record" contends that using this ploy will curry favors with reporters. We disagree on several counts:

1. Being an effective media relations spokesperson depends on building trust and credibility, not building a "favors list."

2. Telling a journalist information "off the record" cannot help but imply that there is still more information not yet released or perhaps being told to another reporter.

3. Not all journalists will honor an "off the record" request. Many people know, from bitter experience, what the results of this can be.

Supporting those points is a U.S. Justice Department official who has stated:

> Many Washington reporters today do not want on-the-record comments as much as they want to talk on some sort of background basis . . . I get the strong impression that reporters are being pushed by their editors, who must think that comments made off the record are more truthful than those made on the record . . . All of the spokesmen for the Department of Justice have been told always to speak on the record and to have their names attached to comments they make. This policy makes them accountable for what they say, and it gives the readers assurance about what they are being told.[19]

If you are in doubt about which way to go, then use this guideline: **Never say anything to a reporter you are not willing to see in print or to hear on the evening news.** This guideline should apply at all times, even in social settings, for reporters are creatures of habit and are seeking information from any available source. They are doing their job 24 hours a day, as should you.

Advertising

The temptation to use the media for free advertising is a great one. Resist it mightily. The media are there to report news, not release your organization from a financial obligation to advertise.

If your announcement does not qualify as newsworthy, do not send it out; instead, buy advertising space. For example, if a store is closing for two days to take inventory, it should make that announcement to its customers through advertising. Such a closing is not news because it is not unique, not different, not unusual.

Conversely, do not try to use your advertising might to blackmail the media into thinking your way. It will not work. A disagreement with the media about how a story on your organization was handled should not come down to, "Well, if you don't change that story, we'll pull all our advertising." Such a threat hurts only your organization as you lose a prime way to reach your customers at a time when you possibly need them. (You would not be threatening such a move if the story was favorable, would you?)

Along those same lines, do not assume that because your organization advertises with a certain medium that your releases will always be run with that medium or that resulting stories will always be positive. A news release must be determined on its own merits, not on its association with another department.

One of the most famous examples of confusing the editorial and advertising pages occurred between Mobil Oil Co. and the *Wall Street Journal*. The newspaper ran an article not favorable to the oil company, and Mobil announced it would no longer have "anything to do with the [paper]." Additionally, almost half a million dollars of advertising was pulled from the paper. The company had said the paper was conducting a "vendetta against Mobil."

The managing editor of the *Wall Street Journal* replied, "The fact that we don't always print articles the way [then vice president for public affairs] Herb Schmertz or his staff writes press releases should come as no surprise to anybody. We'll certainly continue to ask Mobil for comment when it is appropriate. It is an important company."

"This is corporate governance by tantrum," stated the managing editor of *Forbes* magazine. "They [Mobil Oil Co.] will not get what they want, which is a better-behaved *Wall Street Journal*."[20]

Eventually the boycott was recalled, but you have to wonder whether it was worth it. The newspaper didn't change its editorial policies, the oil company continued prospering and the readers never heard Mobil's point of view.

The Golden Rule

At this point, you should be realizing that most of what has been discussed really comes down to this: Do unto others as you would have them do unto you. Just as you seek help in performing your job, so does a reporter. The reporter looks to you for assistance, and giving that assistance is your job. Make the situation easier for both of you by remembering that you are not dealing with an enemy, someone you have to defeat. You are dealing with another human being, one who wants to be treated with the same courtesy and respect as you would like to be shown.

Chapter 8

MEDIA EVENTS
How to Make Them
Work for You

- When Volkswagen relaunched its famous Beetle in 1998, events at the Detroit and Los Angeles auto shows resulted in so much positive media coverage that there was near universal awareness and anticipation of the new Bug before any ads broke or the cars were even in dealers' showrooms.[1]

- To publicize its celebrity pet calendars, Ralston Purina hosted a satellite media tour. While a celebrity photographer chatted with reporters about getting famous animals to pose, viewers ordered the calendars via an 800 number and the call center received almost 4,000 orders.[2]

- To attract young people to its new line of instant photography products, Polaroid launched a contest and road show hitting 10 cities. To target children, the colorful traveling display went to children's and science museums. During the day it also visited popular beaches where teens were skateboarding, and in the evenings it stopped at nightclubs to reach 18–24 year olds. The company lent instant cameras to its mobile display visitors, and collected their pictures for a digital photo mosaic.[3]

- A broadcast VNR and Internet news release about the filming of a Qantas Super Bowl TV commercial featuring the Australian Girls' and National Boys' Choirs reached more than twice the 14 million viewers who saw the commercial. It appeared on high-credibility programming such as CNN International and *ABC World News*. And it did so at a small fraction of the cost—$50,000 for the PR campaign compared to more than $6 million to film the commercial.[4]

- Tom Brokaw's *The Greatest Generation* became one of the fastest-selling nonfiction books of the 1990s, thanks in no small part to his constant discussions of it on his own *NBC Nightly News* program and on other NBC-owned media such as MSNBC and CNBC, the network's cable operations, and *MSNBC.com*, its on-line news site.[5]

Your organization may not always have such dramatic new products to attract reporters' attention. And none of us will be fortunate enough to have the vast resources of the many NBC-controlled media outlets at our disposal as Tom Brokaw did. But the basic principles remain the same for all of us, and you too can hold an event to help your organization generate increased sales and positive media coverage.

In addition to new product or service announcements, a plant opening, new CEO, dignitary visit, open house or market expansion all are fine reasons to host a celebration and news conference. These media events are staged occurrences, so you usually control the timing. They are held to promote good news, so you are on the offensive, not the defensive. They tend to have a more casual, party-type atmosphere to encourage person-to-person dialogue between the news media and your organization's executives. Working on media events is fun. The trick is to make it profitable for your organization in terms of increased sales, positive news media coverage, improved public opinion—and maybe also a jump in the stock price.

There are two keys to getting the most effective media relations results from these events. First, clearly enunciate your communications objective and then evaluate every idea by whether or not it helps meet that objective. Remember that when management asks what it is getting for its PR investment, it is asking for evidence that communications activities have supported business goals. Second, keep running lists that track progress and responsibility for all planned and possible activities. You must think constantly in generalities while at the same time living in detail. Michelangelo is said to have counseled a young artist, "Perfection is made up of details." It will be your ability to keep sight of the forest and every single tree that will make the event a success from a media viewpoint—and well worth the expense from your organization's perspective.

Remember Your Target Audiences

Look at your event from the point of view of the reporters you will be inviting. They get invitations almost daily. *Fortune* magazine reported that in 1998 there were 17,000 new grocery products alone introduced into the U.S. marketplace.[6] So your event must be different in some way to attract their attention. It must be *unique*, to differentiate you from the competition. It must be *relevant*, so when the invitation comes in it immediately is noticed. It must be *cost-effective*. And, above all, it needs to *sell*—because that is what we all are here for. As the late advertising legend David Ogilvy counseled his agency, "When I write an advertisement, I don't want you to tell me that you find it 'creative.' I want you to find it so interesting that you buy the product."

Another helpful hint is to consider the personal as well as the business benefit to the media. For example, many journalists have the same complaint as the rest of us—they do not have enough time to spend with their families. Talk about trends: In the United States a few years ago, couch potatoes and homebodies were sneered at in some so-called sophisticated circles. Today home cooking is considered upscale, country music is mainstream, people are spending more money on their homes and gardens than on exotic travel, and family values are a guiding fact of life as yuppies become parents.

These trends probably explain why any events we have hosted where journalists can bring their partners or families have been great successes. For example, in New York a special family outing for advertisers sponsored by *Reader's Digest* magazine—an afternoon at the New York City Ballet's "Nutcracker"—was such a hit the first year that it became an annual holiday tradition. Photo-ops at these events are especially popular, and framed family pictures make great mementos.

If your company's stock is traded publicly, you also will want to coordinate with those colleagues responsible for investor relations. Reporters frequently call financial analysts and market experts for an outside, objective evaluation—and a quotable quote—to include in their story on a major corporate announcement. Thus it is to your advantage to keep financial analysts who follow your company and industry fully informed about your news, preferably on announcement day. You can have copies of the press kit delivered electronically or via fax to key financial analysts. Or you may want to arrange a separate restaging of the news conference for them. (It is normally not wise to invite journalists and financial analysts to the same announcement event. Their interests are different, and they deserve individual attention.)

Also, remember your employees. If you will have a celebrity at the event, try to arrange for that person to visit your offices as well. Or broadcast the event live to employees via the Internet or a video network.

Announcing a New Facility

Announcing the purchase of property and the building of a new facility provides unparalleled opportunities for positive media and community relations. It also serves as a fine example of how to plan a media event. In particular, it will tax your abilities if you find yourself operating in new territory without the benefit of established relationships with local reporters and editors (or even knowledge of the local geography) if the move is an expansion into a state or country in which your organization has not operated.

Integral to your planning should be the knowledge that your plans very likely are not going to be kept secret until announcement day. If the deal is a big one—in terms of size of the property, prestige of the company or number of potential jobs, for example—you should count on the fact that there will be a leak. Real estate agents showing property, local boards approached for zoning regulations, a hotel visited to evaluate conference facilities, a pilot hired for aerial photographs of the site—all these provide ample opportunities for the news to slip out no matter what precautions your organization takes.

You should have approved and ready for immediate use a standby statement in case a reporter calls seeking your comment on rumors. If your plans are so uncertain that you do not even have an announcement date tentatively set, you should probably say nothing more than that your organization is looking at a number of potential sites for possible future expansion, but no plans are firm yet. If you have a timetable in mind, you might want to go further by adding that you will let the reporter know when a decision is made and an announcement is imminent.

You also will want to develop a solid relationship early on with others involved in the project. People from such disciplines as real estate, legal and finance, either on your organization's staff or retained for this job, will become critical resources as announcement time draws near. Your involvement in the planning stages helps build their confidence in you and in your contribution to the project's successful conclusion. It also makes it more likely that you can get their early concurrence on an objective and working strategy—not to mention their personal involvement in the implementation of your information plan.

Develop a Master Checklist

Once you know the announcement is a "go"—even before you have a firm date—you should immediately develop a checklist of all activities which need to be undertaken and write down any related issues that must be considered. This will be your overall master list. It will also spawn a number of more detailed "to-do" lists for many of the entries. Included on your master list should be the following:

1. *Date/time of announcement.* Probability of bad weather? Other conflicting events such as a holiday or an election? Best time for the local news media? Availability of key participants?

2. *Site of announcement.* Your organization's headquarters or at location of new property? On-site or in a hotel or commercial establishment? Cancellation policy if commercial or private club location? Ease of accessibility for guests and news media? Fire and other emergency exit procedures? Facilities for the handicapped? Necessity for on-site medical support? Lighted parking lots if event is at night? Insurance needs?

3. *Main theme.* Expansion of your organization into new territory? New business? Move from older facility?

4. *Guests.* Federal, state and local government officials? Key community and business leaders? Local people helpful in

site selection? News media—local? national? trade? Other VIPs? Employees? Spouses? Financial analysts?

5. *Speakers.* Only your organization's executives? Governor or top state or federal official? Mayor or local official?

6. *Type of occasion.* News conference alone? With lunch or dinner? Reception? Local customs on food and alcohol? Budget restrictions?

7. *Media relations.* Press kit materials? Sound and lighting facilities for electronic media? Transportation to site? Internet broadcast to those who cannot attend?

8. *Invitations.* Written or by phone, fax or e-mail? Special arrangements with typing pool? RSVPs required? Who to handle? Separate for news media? For head table?

9. *Mementos.* Appropriate? Cost? Different ones for media or VIPs? In keeping with theme? Time to engrave or personalize? Place on tables if meal, or distribute as guests leave?

10. *Arrangements if travel involved.* Hotel and travel reservations for your organization's executives? Fruit basket or similar welcome gift in rooms? Other VIPs? Spouses? The media? Pre-registration courtesies? Billing arrangements? Late checkouts?

11. *Staffing.* Enough well-trained, service-oriented staff that guests do not wait in line for anything, from coat checks to beverage bars?

12. *Collateral materials.* Exhibit? Printed program? "Who we are, what we do" brochure on your organization for guests? Place cards at table settings? Name tags? Reserved table signs? "Working news media only" sign outside news conference room?

It is a good idea to ask others who will be involved to review your list to see if you have left anything out or overlooked any local customs. Next you should establish an information objective and budget, assign responsibility for each of the activities, develop an overall timetable, and set specific due dates. Then you must oversee implementation on virtually a day-to-day basis to ensure everything gets done on time.

Guidelines for Media Events

Planning before the Event

1. Make sure the objective and theme for your information effort is supportive of your organization's goals and your overall media relations plan and is agreed to by everyone involved. It should include both your key message and target audience. Before making any decision, evaluate it against that objective. For example, when we were discussing possible speakers for the official opening of AT&T's Network Software Center in Illinois, someone suggested we invite the vice president of the United States "to get publicity" since it was an election year. Our goal was not, however, publicity for the sake of publicity. If it were, we pointed out, we could do something bizarre like have an employee stage a loud demonstration in the middle of the ceremony. Rather, our objective was to get media coverage on AT&T's software expertise and the contributions it will make to new Information Age services. Having the vice president speak—*particularly* because the ceremony would take place only a few months before a national election— could divert attention from our software message and focus it on politics. Thus, it might inhibit rather than support our information objectives. Better to invite the president of Bell Laboratories to join our CEO on stage so the speakers would personify the high-technology partnership that will deliver AT&T's products to the marketplace.

2. It sometimes is good politics as well as good media relations to invite the governor of the state, or the mayor or chief county official, to make a few brief remarks. It is wise to restrict a politician to a five-minute official welcome rather than the keynote address; this way you control the length of the program and the main message the media take away from the event.

3. Choose your speakers and spokespersons very carefully. Then provide them with solid background information and help them practice (see chapter 6).

4. Do not let yourself be distracted by time-consuming tasks. Such duties as travel arrangements or hotel reservations for VIPs can be delegated to others. Conversely, you will want to maintain oversight to the extent that you are comfortable all these details are taken care of.

Implementing the Event

   5. **If a site or facility tour is part of your program, time it with a manageable-size group that can move around easily on the big day, rather than your walking the planned path alone.** Keeping a group of people together (and rounding up stragglers) can throw you off schedule.

   6. **Severely limit the number of officials introduced individually or allowed to speak as part of the news conference or ceremony.** "Obligatory" recognitions are terribly boring to the audience—and normally not required at all. They also distract from the main message your organization wants to deliver. Better to have your emcee or the organization's top speaker use one general statement to thank "all the local people who made us feel so welcome" or commend "the employees whose dedication and talent made this event possible." To have public officials or key executives feel they are getting VIP treatment, you can reserve a special table for them at the luncheon or have your CEO thank them personally after the ceremony.

   7. **Use still photography (black-and-white and color) and film or videotape to document each stage of a new facility—** from architect's drawings through construction and official opening. Such a photographic history will be invaluable not only to meet the needs of the news media but also for your annual report, year-end video program or other external and internal information materials. Make plans early; you don't want to implement the plan only to find construction nearly completed.

   8. **Review and update your checklists often.** The ball takes some funny bounces on occasion, and the only way to track it is to keep it perpetually in sight. Conduct frequent meetings where everyone involved shares progress reports. If your committee is physically separated, issue written or e-mail status reports and have telephone conference calls. Occasionally send brief progress reports to your organization's top executives.

   9. **Keep track of your expenditures** and get approval before making commitments over your budget.

   10. **If you decide to give a memento to the media or to guests, personalize it with your logo so that recipients are reminded of your organization when they use it.** Pens or pocket calculators carrying your logo are useful, and they can be inserted

into the press kit if you want to give them only to reporters. Tote bags or briefcases are especially good giveaways because they are carried and become moving billboards for your brand. At the announcement of a new electronic components plant in Florida, we gave guests a pewter plate engraved with, "AT&T and Orlando— Partners in new telecommunications technology." That theme was picked up in the news conference announcement, luncheon key-note address, lobby exhibit, on the press kit folder and in the pro-gram. To take advantage of the new product's name at AT&T's introduction of the Merlin communications system, we gave report-ers heat-sensitive mugs on which a message "magically" appeared when coffee was poured in.

11. Arrange for photography—still and video or film—of the news conference and announcement ceremony.

12. You can have a first-class press kit folder and also save money by carrying a photograph or drawing of the new facility along with your organization's name on the cover—but *not* including the date of the event. That way you can arrange for pro-duction of the folders before a final date is set to avoid rush-job printing charges, keep your last-minute duties to a minimum, and avoid wasted paper if the date changes at the last minute. You also can use the folders for other occasions such as open houses or background information packages for the media as construction proceeds or new reporters request materials.

13. Target your press kits so that each reporter has the right information for his or her audience—hometown angle for the plant site's local paper, long-term growth for the business and financial media, relationship to industry trends for the trade press, etc.

14. Well in advance, circulate a proposed invitation list to key people who can provide counsel on who should be included. In some communities, for example, the sheriff or chair-man of a local regulatory agency can be as influential as the mayor or county commissioner. Divide the list into categories: business and civic leaders; federal, state and local government officials; peo-ple directly involved in site selection or facility design such as industrial development commissioners, architects and real estate people; community leaders such as educators and clergy; working reporters who will be invited separately to the news conference (as compared to publishers and station owners, who normally are included in the civic or business leaders category).

15. Just before the event, write out a final detailed chronology of every activity related to announcement day. Include arrival and departure times of your organization's executives and other VIPs, limousine arrangements and the agenda timed to the minute. Give copies to everyone involved—including limo drivers, the hotel catering manager and the person at the guest reception table.

16. Supervise all aspects of the news conference personally, from the opening statement to the contents of the press kit. Anything affecting the information effort is your business, regardless of who is responsible. You may be the only person with the complete picture.

17. If there will be a meal after the news conference, put "Reserved for press" cards on tables nearest the podium or head table. Do not assume reporters will stay for the meal just because they are coming to the news conference. Ask them to RSVP to the news conference and luncheon or reception separately.

18. If you are having a meal, review the schedule with the catering person in minute detail. Specify serving times and forbid any clearing off of tables while the speeches are underway. Many a first-class occasion—and potential broadcast coverage—has been ruined by the sound of clattering dishes.

19. If possible, arrange for a separate room for individual private interviews between your CEO and selected reporters after the news conference. Allow time in your schedule for such interviews between the news conference and the meal, perhaps by scheduling a reception between the two. Schedule Internet on-line chats for the next day.

20. Try to have a separate "working room." This is ideal for storage of press kits, mementos, and other office materials such as computers and blank news release paper in case you have to revise the release at the last minute. If your event is taking place at a commercial establishment, get permission from the manager to ship as much of your material as possible to arrive early.

21. Have plenty of copies of your business card to give to the media. Try to find time to chat with any reporters you have not met before. The relationships you begin to develop at the announcement ceremony will serve your organization well as construction proceeds—especially if you face unfortunate events like an accident or a union problem—and if communication will be primarily by telephone because your office is not near the new facility.

22. Understand that the primary focus of local reporters' questions will be on the economic advantages to the community in terms of jobs, taxes and related support services. Anticipate their needs by being prepared to give out general figures and a probable timetable. Be careful not to lock yourself into a potential problem of appearing to renege on a promise a few years hence by being overly specific at announcement time. Use round numbers: "We expect to hire about a thousand people over the next few years" is better than "We plan to hire 1,083 people by next December," unless you are positive your figures will not change. Also, for local taxation purposes be careful about placing a value on your project until your design and construction plans are firm and you have consulted with a tax expert.

23. Make sure the head table and news conference setup photograph well so that you get maximum exposure for your organization's message. The lectern should carry your logo, not the hotel's. If the drapes behind the announcement area have a busy pattern or inappropriate color, put up portable curtains or an attractive sign with your theme or organization's name behind the speakers. All visuals should be simple, with copies included in the press kit. View the staging through a camera's eye—literally if necessary.

24. Provide three or four phones for the media's use. Arrange for at least one line for the exclusive use of your organization's executives, the governor or other top government officials and their key aides.

25. Have a reception table where at least one person stays to direct guests to coatrooms and bathrooms, control access to private phones, take messages and provide other logistics support. Give this person photos of VIPs who should receive special treatment. Alphabetize name tags if you are using them.

26. Set up a separate table with another dedicated person who will help you handle the news media. This includes press kit distribution, requests for private interviews or any other courtesies that should be extended to working journalists.

27. Prepare a separate package of materials for your key executives involved in the program. Include the press kit and detailed agenda—and also private background and Qs and As that could come up, key officials and reporters deserving personal attention (with nicknames and phonetic spelling if their names are difficult to pronounce), potential local concerns such as environmental issues or union problems, and their individualized itinerary and schedule—with a reminder of the times they should be available for separate media interviews. Give a copy of this package to the executive's secretary or chief staff person, along with the private phone number reserved for their use—and keep a few extra copies with you in case they are misplaced.

28. Coordinate the agenda and schedule closely with the press secretary or chief aide of government officials and celebrities who are participating in the program. Inquire about security or other special arrangements you should make. For example, governors and top federal officials often are accompanied by security as well as staff wherever they go, so they need to be included in your meal count. Get on their calendars early because their schedules often are set well in advance.

29. Arrange for setup time and personally inspect all the facilities the night before and the day of the event. Test the sound and lighting arrangements for broadcast needs. If your CEO is flying in, consider meeting the plane and taking advantage of the drive time to the announcement site for a last-minute briefing. Read the local papers and alert your CEO to any noteworthy current issues.

30. Arrange for separate distribution of the press kit to reporters not attending the event, and put it on your Web site. Distribution should take place at the time of or just after your news conference. Only in rare cases should you allow advance distribution, or you will hurt chances of the media's covering the event in person.

Following Up and Evaluating the Event

31. Monitor that evening's television news programs. Arrange for videotapes of TV shows and audiotapes of radio coverage. Get copies of the daily papers. Within 24 or 48 hours provide your organization's top executives with samples of initial news coverage of the event, plus a videotape of the full news conference and ceremony if you made one. Consider a separate, shorter version for showings to your employees and the board.

32. Promptly after the event write thank-you letters for the CEO's signature. These should be sent to key dignitaries who participated in the project and to those who worked with you to make the occasion a success.

33. Set up a system to handle the inevitable queries generated by the news coverage of your announcement. You will receive queries from real estate agents, relocation people, job applicants, banks and other prospective product and service suppliers. Make sure those responsible are prepared to handle them.

34. A month or so after the event, when all the news coverage has been gathered, put together a summary that includes objectives and a brief analysis of how they were met. This can be done in print or on video, may include selected samples of news media coverage, and should be distributed to your organization's officers and board and to all others involved in the event.

35. Consider putting together a formal scrapbook and video program to commemorate the event. After circulation and presentation to your executives and board, copies could be given to the new plant manager and included in your organization's official archives.

36. Conduct a post-event performance review. Get everyone's opinions on what went well and what could be done better as a "lessons learned" for the next time.

37. Put together a complete file including everything connected with the occasion, from your private memos and checklists to the press kits, official announcement speech, and overall evaluation. It will be invaluable not only as a record of an historic event but also as a model for planning future announcements.

When Your Event Is for an International Market

Chapter 9, "Going Global: How to Manage International Media Relations," contains advice on operating beyond our borders that should be helpful when you find yourself working in an unfamiliar country. In addition, here are some tips specifically related to meeting and event planning outside your home country:

1. Consider hiring a destination management company (DMC). They can be very helpful in introducing you to local hotels and caterers, arranging visas, setting up tours, handling local transportation, and selecting appropriate off-site festivities. Before choosing a DMC, check references and determine their billing methodology—per person? flat fee? cost plus?

2. While one site inspection may suffice here at home, you likely will need more in unfamiliar markets. A first-class hotel in the United States is different from one in Europe or in third-world countries. Also, organizers must plan for differences in audiovisual formats and electrical voltage, expectations of meeting rooms and news conference sites, even the size of tables, chairs and beds (many hotel rooms outside North America have twin beds, which can be an issue if spouses are included). You or someone on your event team will have to test all the tours you will be hosting.

3. Exchange rates will have a great effect on your budget and decision making. Portugal has become well known for great value as a site for special events. But currency changes might make more exotic spots in Asia affordable if a country devalues its currency. Be flexible as currencies fluctuate during the planning phase. And talk with your Finance Department colleagues about the pros and cons of hedging your foreign exchange risk.

4. Understand the VAT rules. Value-added taxes range from 3 to 25 percent, so they can have a great effect on your budget. Fortunately, many countries have a system in place to allow at least some of your VAT charges to be refunded. Get local advice on the rules and how you can determine your organization's eligibility.

5. Transportation is a critical factor. Most journalists do not have time for lengthy travel, so you need to consider a site's accessibility to airports.

6. Check the U.S. State Department list before settling on a venue. This security and alert list lets you know what countries and geographic areas it is better to avoid at any given time.

7. Use only well-known, experienced shipping companies—preferably those with whom your organization has a longstanding business relationship. You may need a freight forwarder who is also a licensed customs broker. Check references. There is no second chance when you ship materials to a trade show or special event and they disappear en route.

Helpful Tips

Barbara E. Griswold, director of meetings and special events at The Reader's Digest Association, has had years of experience organizing media events, customer receptions, employee and other special events around the world. She recommends networking with others who have held similar events in the areas you are considering by e-mailing members of Meeting Professionals International. Also, U.S. suppliers often have business relationships with companies in other countries.

> We recently held a Town Hall meeting in Stuttgart, Germany. Via satellite we were able to broadcast it live to destinations in Europe, Canada and the United States with a two-way capability for questions. For our offices in Asia and Australia, where it was impractical to broadcast live because of the late hour, we provided a phone-in audio transcription of the meeting for 36 hours after the actual event. This way those who couldn't "attend" in real time could listen to the content as soon as it was convenient for them. Our video team worked with a vendor in New York City that had a partner company in Berlin to make this happen.

Another tip:

> Have a clear understanding of what you are trying to accomplish and your budget, so you can express your goals to all vendors in clear, easy-to-understand terms. Remember, there are language differences so you have to be very precise regarding your requirements, especially your technical needs.

She finds it useful to take advantage of technology to do her research: "Make use of the Web to search for information—everything from customs problems and protocol to event locations and security issues. You can also use chat rooms to discuss things with other event planners."

Griswold also suggests asking the director of sales or the convention manager at the site you are considering for recommendations on DMCs and the names of other organizations which have held similar events in that city. If your organization has an office in that city or nearby, seek their advice and help. Then arrive early to get set up and rehearse. "Don't try to be a hero and do it all alone," she says. "But also, don't panic. Gratuities always help get things done quickly—in any city or country around the world."

Case Studies and Success Stories

Herrick Memorial Hospital

Far too often publicity efforts surrounding modernization or expansion programs are mostly cosmetic. News coverage and public interest are generated by one big event, but once the decorations have been put away from the last open house everyone goes back to business as usual. In effect, the whole exercise has been "more show than go."

Such was not the case, however, with the public relations program at Herrick Memorial Hospital in Berkeley, California. It had the traditional image-improvement objectives of many PR plans, but it was grounded in solid research. It involved the introduction of ongoing health care information programs, and it was backed by a change in the hospital's name that symbolized an enhanced mission to educate the healthy as well as treat the sick.

The hospital had been a significant force in the San Francisco East Bay Area for the better part of a century. Founded by a man whose interest in medicine had been prompted by the death of his wife, the facility opened in 1904 in an ornate Victorian mansion under the name of Roosevelt Hospital. Later it was renamed Herrick Memorial in honor of its founder.

The construction of a new $14-million, 153-bed wing offered a perfect opportunity to update the hospital's image and to bring its many publics—including the news media—to the hospital to see the new orientation of the staff and facilities. "A community survey and staff interviews showed that Herrick had an unclear or nonexistent reputation with many of its publics," explained Gloria Dunn, then director of community and public relations for the hospital. "The issue was viability. We had to become better known so we could increase usage of our services." Thus the effort met the ultimate test of a good public relations program—it directly supported the organization's overall purpose and profitability.

Dunn developed a broad plan which she presented to the hospital's administration, board of trustees and medical executive board for approval. Heading the list of action items was a recommendation to change the name of the hospital from Herrick Memorial to Herrick Hospital and Health Center. "We needed to remove the death connotation inherent in the word 'memorial' and add the positive philosophy implied by 'health center,' " Dunn said. She sold the decision makers on the name change because it provided advantages for the institution to (a) derive image advantages from a name that conveys a clear statement of purpose; (b) demonstrate the hospital's expansion and change of direction; and (c) offer to those involved with the hospital a reason for association—pride for employees, physicians, trustees and patients; and encouragement to donors and volunteers. The plan also included a new logo with the Herrick "H" extending an embracing arm around an orange sunburst representing life. Like the name, the logo symbolized a new mission: "It is Herrick's purpose to prevent illness whenever possible, and to cure and heal whenever necessary. Herrick embraces life."

Timing was on Dunn's side as she sought and received approval for her plan, since she was able to show how the new wing and new name could work together to build visibility for the hospital if they were supported by a targeted public and media relations effort.

Once the changes were agreed to, new information materials and health-related programs were developed. The *Medical Staff News* became *Vita* (Latin for "life"). Employee newsletters were renamed *Pulse* and *Pulsebeats*. The community magazine *The Herricker* became a new quarterly tabloid called *Life,* with its circulation increased from 15,000 to 160,000 for almost the same cost because of a format change. Coupons in each issue offered a speakers bureau booklet and two new health education packages, the "life preserver" kit and "vial of life." The kit was designed to store practical health information. Actually a binder intended to be updated with new health tips included in each issue of *Life,* it came with telephone stickers, a first-aid fact sheet, Mr. Nasty comic strips to help deter children from household poisons, emergency information cards, personal medical history records and a home fire safety checklist. The "vial of life" was designed for the ill or aged who have more frequent need for an ambulance or other emergency care. A sticker on the person's refrigerator door signaled the existence of a vial in the fridge. Within the vial was a rolled-up sheet of paper on which was written the owner's medical history, blood type, allergies and other relevant information invaluable to ambulance attendants if the person was unconscious.

To celebrate the completion of the new wing and to use the occasion to introduce "the new Herrick" to its many publics, Dunn arranged an eight-day open house. It involved a wide variety of health-related events aimed at internal and external audiences, including the media. News stories under headlines such as "A New Hospital for Berkeley" in that city's *Independent & Gazette*[7] and "Herrick Hospital an Innovator in Health Care" in the *Oakland Post*[8] provided wider exposure for the hospital's expanded health care services. The overall program generated positive feedback and unsolicited donations. It resulted in almost six thousand visitors to the new wing, some of whom had never been in the hospital before. It brought requests for hundreds of "life preserver" kits, "vials of life" and speakers bureau booklets—and a very personal response from one mailing recipient: "Congratulations. This is the best piece of junk mail I have ever received."

Dunn reflected on the role her department played not only in demonstrating their professional skills but also in contributing to the hospital's operations objectives: "I was very proud that the public relations program generated goodwill, greater visibility and employee pride. But more than that, I was able to show the relationship between public and employee perceptions of the hospital and our results. There is nothing more rewarding to a public relations professional than to design and implement a public relations program that effects significant change."

Bestfoods

CPC International Inc.'s name change to Bestfoods is an example of another highly successful, multi-year, new-identity program. It was strongly supported by media events designed to showcase not only the new name but also a new company persona that was innovative, willing to take risks and ready to seize on a market opportunity.

The name change was made in connection with the spin-off of CPC's corn refining business. Bestfoods was chosen because it was a predecessor company of CPC, the name of its North American business, and one of the best known of its brands. Bestfoods replaced an acronym little known outside of Wall Street that did little to enhance the company's world-famous consumer brands such as Skippy peanut butter and Hellmann's mayonnaise.

With the company's new trading symbol becoming BFO, the stock market became an obvious and excellent focal point for the publicity effort. Gale L. Griffin, vice president-corporate communications, and her staff led the team that staged a "running of the bulls" down Wall Street in New York City to commemorate the first day of trading of the new Bestfoods stock. A herd of trained bulls chased seven of Bestfoods' leading brands—as represented by costumed characters—to symbolize the company's "bullish" outlook on its future.

This unique event attracted the attention of the traditional financial media as well as the general news media and provided photo ops that were both humorous and powerful. The effort was highly cost-effective, yielding an advertising equivalency almost five times greater than the investment of less than $100,000. There were 150 television placements in more than 40 major markets, including the CNNfn and FOX networks, where Bestfoods' CEO was featured in in-depth interviews on national financial programs. There also was extensive positive newspaper and radio exposure nationwide, a pickup in *Fortune* magazine, and coverage on 12 sites on the Internet. To build excitement and pride among employees, a videotape of the event was shown to staff worldwide and also featured at sales meetings.

The running of the bulls was such a success to introduce its new name that Bestfoods decided to make it an annual affair and broaden the theme. The second year the company partnered with the New York Stock Exchange to run 10 bulls down Wall Street while Bestfoods' giant branded costume characters called the race and made market predictions based on the outcome.

With the event taking place on January 4, its sponsors claimed that the 10 bulls in the run could predict the year's outcome on Wall Street better than the groundhog can predict the weather. To add substance to the fun, the run was followed by a news conference with some of the leading financial analysts from top brokerage firms giving their market picks for the year. Media coverage the second time around was even more widespread, with the BBC and French television covering the event and the CEO interviewed on every major business TV network in the United States. "We're thrilled with the association of Bestfoods with the New York Stock Exchange," Griffin said. "Dowdy old CPC would never recognize us!"[9]

Nike

How does a company like Nike communicate to diverse audiences with diverse messages and still maintain consistency in its communications? And how does it build long-lasting relationships if those messages are not identical to one another? The answer, according to Lisa Siracuse, vice president of an integrated communications consulting firm in Colorado, is brand personality.

Siracuse points out that Nike has created such a strong identity and presence that people love to connect themselves to the brand and the "Just Do It" slogan, no matter how good or bad an athlete they might be. The Nike persona exists everywhere in the company's communications and marketing efforts from media events and the annual report to sales materials and advertising. She says that this successful positioning effort enables the company to "tweak" its message to diverse company segments without diluting the brand.

One of Nike's important consumer markets is women. As Siracuse observes, instead of marketing to women using superstar athletes with testosterone pumping through their veins, Nike has taken the concept of "Just Do It" and appealed to a deeply emotional issue for women today—not allowing anything to stand in their way and exploring their potential to the fullest. "Women relate so strongly to this message that they wear Nikes as a symbol of their ambition and self-worth," she believes.[10]

Conoco Inc.

In May 1998, DuPont announced that it would sell 25 percent of its subsidiary, Conoco, in what became the largest initial public offering (IPO) in U.S. history. From the start, the IPO faced significant challenges. Investor knowledge about the company—the single most important factor in achieving a successful IPO—was virtually nonexistent. In addition, as the IPO date grew closer, the new issue equities market began to wither and several other companies abruptly canceled their IPOs. Amid a chorus of negative comments and a dramatic plunge in oil prices, Conoco and DuPont decided to move forward, on schedule, shepherding the lone IPO in October 1998.

Strict "quiet period" rules by the Securities and Exchange Commission prohibit major external communications until three weeks after an IPO—a serious block to a widespread media and special events effort. As a result, even after the roadshow presentations, where senior management outlined their vision and plans for the new company to analysts and potential investors, there still was doubt in the financial community and business media. As the *Wall Street Journal* reported, "Some analysts remain highly skeptical of the success of a $3 billion to $4 billion IPO—one of the largest ever—at a time when world financial markets are in turmoil and the appetite for IPOs has all but dried up."

Reflecting the determination of the company's management, vigorous communications efforts encompassed the initial trading day, underscoring the company's 123-year heritage and its position as a global energy leader. Interviews with the CEO were complemented by satellite news feeds from the New York Stock Exchange.

Outside the exchange, Conoco's logo was draped confidently over the building's facade, and people jitterbugged to a swing band while attendants dressed in 1950s-era gasoline attendant uniforms served coffee from replica Conoco gas pumps, further illustrating the company's rich history. These events, including a special television production on the workings of the New York Stock Exchange, were satellite fed to Conoco locations worldwide where celebrations were underway. They also were broadcast on the company's Intranet.

Meanwhile, during the "quiet period" media relations staff queued up nearly 100 news releases about Conoco's growth plans to be released in a "drumbeat" program primed for worldwide distribution. When the quiet period ended, the first item distributed to news media was a brochure detailing company news that had not been allowed to be released during that time. Then the drums rolled, resulting in hundreds of positive news stories around the world. At the same time, an investor "box" of information was mailed to analysts and business reporters. This was followed by the company's first quarterly and annual reports, which featured key messages about Conoco's growth and the most compelling images from the IPO.

Conoco's global communications got results. At a time when extreme market volatility had virtually upended the IPO market, investors purchased 191 million shares of Conoco stock. Some 70 percent of investors who attended the roadshow presentations purchased stock, compared with the average IPO purchase of only 20 to 30 percent. The IPO raised $4.4 billion, making it the largest in U.S. history.

Most important, investor confidence has proved sustainable. Conoco's successful closing of a $4 billion jumbo bond offering was the largest ever in the U.S. industrial sector. At the 1999 annual meeting, the CEO reported that the company's stock price had risen almost 50 percent since the beginning of the year, compared to the company's peer average of 21 percent. Impressive results for an organization that as a subsidiary of DuPont had been virtually unknown to the financial and business world.[11]

Visa USA

Responding to research indicating consumers would be more likely to use their Visa cards if their transactions could benefit a relevant cause, Visa USA embarked on its first fully integrated national cause-related marketing promotion, called "Read me a story."

The special events and direct marketing campaign stressed that consumers should "use your Visa card and help a child learn to read." The theme was designed to increase the program's news value and perform as a consumer "call to action" by leveraging public attention around White House reading initiatives and the well-documented reading crisis in America.

This reading program was an expanded and more targeted version of Visa's "Read me a story" campaign a year earlier. In this case, emphasis was placed on a harder-hitting message—helping children *learn* to read rather than *reading* one million stories to *them*. This shift was based on new research showing 40 percent of the nation's fourth graders were not reading at proficiency levels.

Ketchum Public Relations, Visa USA's agency, fostered a new family-based approach to the reading crisis. It created the first Family Reading Checkup Guide with the American Academy of Pediatrics, who distributed guides through their AAP physician offices nationwide. Ketchum and Visa also embarked on a cross-country Family Reading Checkup campaign to 67 U.S. cities, with three costumed performance troupes of the nation's best-loved storybook characters performing an original "Read me a story" show for children. Six of the nation's top children's book publishers donated storybook character costumes, provided licensed characters to appear in the performance tour, as well as books and collateral materials to give away to children at the events, and materials for the Visa web site. NFL players and TV celebrities participated in various events as well.

During the campaign, five million copies of English and Spanish Reading Checkup Guides were distributed at tour events, retail locations, pediatricians' offices and through Visa's Web site. From a bottom-line perspective, Visa card usage increased 20 percent during the program, while raising more than $1 million for Reading is Fundamental, America's largest children's literacy nonprofit organization.

This campaign far exceeded the previous year's effort. It produced 100 percent more news awareness, 16 percent more card usage volume, and united policy makers, celebrities, educators, physicians, business leaders and consumers on a mission to uniquely address the nation's reading crisis.[12]

The Prudential Insurance Company of America

For decades, the culture of Prudential was one that focused inwardly, treating Prudential's large agency force as if it were the customer, calibrating service by an internal set of measures, and operating without an eye on the marketplace. When a new CEO came in, he wanted to change the way the company approaches the 30 million people who "own a piece of the Rock." He launched an initiative that is changing literally hundreds of processes and measurement systems, as well as the way employees deliver products and services to customers. And he challenged the PR department to create a connection between "customer service" and "Prudential" in the hearts and minds of the American public.

PR commissioned a research survey through Roper Starch to gather information on customer service issues. "How Americans Rate Customer Service" determined people's varying levels of acceptance, patience, anger and what Prudential called "phone rage"—customer reaction to being kept on hold or caught up in an automated system—as well as regional responses to the on-hold issue.

Taking advantage of the survey results, the media relations staff developed a series of news releases and matte service articles detailing the results. They also created a broadcast media campaign around the results, designed to promote Prudential as a leader in financial services customer relations. As well, they produced a satellite media tour and video news release providing guidance to consumers who use service call centers, and showing them how to be proactive in their approach to getting good customer service. And they produced an audio news release that aired on radio and the Internet, providing consumer tips on dealing with call centers. In addition, they arranged interviews with business and trade publications for key Prudential executives discussing customer service.

While Prudential is the first to say that its Customer Connection campaign is a work in progress, the results achieved so far are significant. Its Property & Casualty Insurance claim department call center has been named a "best practices" organization by the American Productivity and Quality Center. Its media campaign resulted in extensive coverage in the consumer and trade press, on TV and radio, and on the Internet. "Customer service" and "Prudential" are beginning to come together in customers' minds, as evidenced by a cover story on their customer service program in the April 1999 issue of the trade publication, *Supervisor's Guide to Improved Customer Service & Retention.*[13]

ALS Awareness Campaign

Amyotrophic lateral sclerosis (ALS), a fatal neuromuscular disorder more commonly known as Lou Gehrig's disease, is not an entirely hopeless illness. But most ALS victims are unaware that their illness can be controlled to a degree, ultimately leading to an improved quality of life. A public awareness program was developed to let people know of these helpful facts, as well as to increase patient and public inquiries on ALS to an 800 telephone number and to educate target audiences about Rilutek, the only product approved by the U.S. Food and Drug Administration for the treatment of this disease.

"Season for Hope" was a media tour of major North American markets that capitalized on ALS's ties to baseball and Yankee Hall of Famer Lou Gehrig, the legendary first baseman who was struck down by the disease that now bears his name. The tour featured ALS patient Mark Reiman, a 44-year-old husband, father and musician who has the disease. As part of the program's mission to deliver the message, "living with ALS, not dying from it," Reiman set out to sing the national anthem at all 30 major league baseball parks in North America in a single season, a feat never accomplished before. He succeeded.

Makovsky & Company, the New York agency hired by Rhone-Poulenc Rorer, manufacturer of Rilutek, to create and implement this program, faced several challenges. They had to convince all 30 teams to schedule a singer with ALS on their anthem roster; balance the interests of all the partners—the drug company, national and local ALS chapters, and major league baseball's 30 teams; ensure that the prime message was not overshadowed by the celebrity status of baseball; and generate media coverage in the crowded categories of health, lifestyles and sports.

The program was launched at a New York Mets home game at Shea Stadium. The event was covered by both national and New York media, including ABC-TV's *Good Morning America*. A 22-city satellite media tour was conducted from New York. Two weeks later Reiman sang before a sellout crowd in the Kingdome in Seattle, his hometown, with local media attending in full force. Performances at all the other ballparks followed. A 90-second "Season for Hope" video was shown on the electronic scoreboard prior to his singing the national anthem.

Meanwhile, first basemen from all major league teams served as "local champions" for the "Season for Hope" tour and were available for media interviews and photo-ops, as were local physicians in game cities. ALS chapters in the cities where Reiman sang sponsored events to provide additional local interest and media coverage. Tailgate parties, barbecues and picnics were held with the drug company representatives and ALS community (patients, families, doctors) who were provided game tickets.

Results were impressive. Rilutek sales jumped 40 percent. National and local ALS chapters reported a dramatic increase in patient enrollment and 800-number calls. As many as 1.2 million people witnessed Mark Reiman's performance and saw firsthand his message of hope and inspiration. Media coverage on all the major U.S. and Canadian TV networks, syndicated shows, radio stations, national newswires, national and local newspapers added up to 172.1 million media impressions during the campaign.[14]

Philips Consumer Communications

Philips Consumer Communications (PCC) was created when Lucent Technologies and Philips Electronics combined their consumer products divisions to form a joint venture. The new enterprise had little or no public identity.

With Spector & Associates, Inc., Philips decided to launch a program called "Let's Connect" that would meet both corporate and public objectives—for PCC, to build brand awareness and generate goodwill among families and educators; and for the general public, to raise awareness of the importance of good family communications, and to provide motivation and tools to parents, children and teachers to help improve family communications. The focus was on pre-teens, roughly 10–13 years old. PCC felt this age group often was overlooked by the media and public officials, with most of the attention going to teenagers (sex, drugs and violence) or younger children. However, research showed that it is during the adolescent years that many behavioral patterns and attitudes are formed, and when distance—or closeness—between children and their parents begins to set.

"Let's Connect" began with the first national survey of middle school students and their parents. Working with Roper Starch, 504 fifth through eighth graders and their parents were interviewed on a variety of family communications issues. The results showed most parents and children say they spend less than an hour a day talking to each other. Only one in five kids said it was very easy to talk to their parents about things that really mattered. More than a quarter said it was somewhat difficult or very difficult to do so.

A Harvard child psychologist and author, Dr. Lawrence Kutner, served as the program's national spokesperson to lend expert advice and offer credibility. He unveiled the survey results at the New York City launch workshop, hosted the "Let's Connect" workshops, developed and wrote the two "Let's Connect" brochures, participated in a seven-month workshop tour and media blitz, and engaged in ongoing media interviews.

Young Nickelodeon stars were hired to help draw media attention and excite the students at workshop schools. Two booklets— one with tips for parents and kids to bridge the communications gap and the other for parents on how to get their young adolescents to open up—were distributed free at workshops, via a post office box and through the "Let's Connect" Web site.

Bringing "Let's Connect" directly to schools, workshops were held at middle schools in Atlanta, Chicago, New York, Philadelphia, Phoenix and Seattle. A highlight of the workshops involved students from the audience getting on stage with the Nick Kids and participating in role-play skits about communications. PCC also worked closely with the education community to integrate "Let's Connect" into their curriculum. To help quantify the impact of "Let's Connect," pre- and post-workshop surveys were conducted with parents and students in Phoenix.

Among the results: Philips' name recognition increased from 37 to 42 percent. Media coverage resulted in nearly 76 million media impressions on a national and regional level, including publications like *USA Today, Chicago Tribune, Atlanta Journal Constitution* and *Seattle Times*; broadcast outlets like ABC, CBS, NBC and FOX television affiliates and Bloomberg and USA radio networks. Through the workshops and distribution of "Let's Connect" booklets, the program has made direct contact with more than 8,000 families, plus teachers, local and state education officials, and civic group leaders.[15]

American Cancer Society

A report by the American Cancer Society (ACS) concluded that African-American women are less likely to survive breast cancer than the general population. There was a need for increased awareness about early detection of the disease among black women, and the ACS wanted to position itself as the primary organization to which African Americans turned for information on cancer.

ACS leaders recognized that its "Tell A Friend" program needed sharper focus. This effort encouraged African Americans in Georgia, North Carolina and South Carolina to get their female loved ones to have mammograms. ACS hired Matlock & Associates, a PR firm specializing in minority issues, to target the campaign more effectively.

The agency conducted interviews with African-American women and ACS personnel and reviewed secondary breast cancer research to evaluate existing outreach programs. Media kits and four PSAs were heavily promoted to daily and weekly newspapers and radio stations with predominantly African-American audiences. Through the media and with the help of prominent black leaders, ACS executed special events such as the first annual "Tell A Friend" Gospel Fest and a play called "Sister Girl" which promoted breast cancer awareness.

The "Tell A Friend" campaign achieved its objectives of gaining the trust of black women age 40 and older, building a solid relationship of trust and credibility with the African-American community, and educating the target audience about breast cancer and early detection. The number of black women calling the ACS hotline increased by 25 percent. The Atlanta NBC affiliate did monthly features on the campaign. Goodwill between black media and ACS was increased by media materials tailored for their particular audience. The ACS was so pleased with the results that they recommended this program be turned into a national campaign.[16]

United Way

United Way is a model of how nonprofit organizations can effectively use local special events to generate positive publicity for their fund-raising efforts. Prominent CEOs always head up their campaigns. Not only does this tactic encourage increased corporate and employee giving, but it also results in greater media attendance at speeches and press conferences as the CEO's prestige heightens the inherent news value.

Internationally, the campaigns are similar but adapted to social and cultural differences. In Hong Kong, for example, small businesses employ more people than large corporations, so special events for the general public are more effective than organizational campaigns. In Japan, sumo wrestlers are the featured celebrities to draw media and public interest, rather than football players as in North America. The media are always provided with tools to make it easy for them to carry United Way news—from photographs and videotaped footage of children who will be helped by contributions to tours of agencies supported by United Way funds.[17]

Schwab Rehabilitation Center

Sometimes involving a celebrity can help promote an event. When Elizabeth Mitchell was publicizing a play, *Disabled Genius*, produced by the Schwab Rehabilitation Center in Illinois, she had two tasks: to raise the profile of the center as well as to promote the idea that disabled persons have many talents.

The play starred actress Barbara Rush and a cast of disabled actors, both amateurs and professionals. Mitchell involved Joyce Sloane of Chicago's Second City comedy troupe as chairwoman of her promotions planning committee. Sloane not only paved the way in the theatrical community but also provided name recognition for the play. Publicity began with the auditions and spread through PSAs, talk show interviews and a feature in the *Chicago Tribune*.[18]

Alternatives to Media Events

There are times when media events are inappropriate. The hyped ceremony or the minor announcement masquerading as a major event reinforce the cynicism of journalists and the public. Follow the advice the Institute for Contemporary Studies offered President Ronald Reagan: use the news media "with selectivity and precision."[19] On occasion you will have the difficult task of talking your organization or client *out* of a major event like a news conference—and demonstrating how a targeted approach will more effectively meet the stated objectives even though it will not result in coverage in the *Wall Street Journal.*

AT&T

David V. Manahan, whose media relations responsibilities for AT&T gave him wide experience in new product introductions, tells the story of the coal mine phone to illustrate this point. Bell Labs had developed an explosion-proof telephone for use in coal mines. It was the job of AT&T's marketing department to sell it, of course, so the product manager called a meeting to plan a marketing strategy and promotions program. He informed Manahan that he wanted to hold a news conference in New York City and would invite *The New York Times, Wall Street Journal, Business Week* and the three major or television networks.

Manahan asked who the customers were for this new system. The answer was coal mine superintendents. Coincidentally, Manahan had two sons in West Virginia and thus some acquaintances in the coal mining industry. He knew their work left little energy at the end of a long day for *The New York Times* and *Business Week.* Working with the product manager, he researched what they *did* read, and came up with a list of industry-specific publications like *Coal Age, Mining/Processing Equipment* and *Coal Industry News.* Manahan and his co-workers then took a map and some charts from a geography book to create a plastic overlay showing where coal mines were located in the United States. They came up with an eastern pocket including Virginia, West Virginia, Pennsylvania and Kentucky.

The next step was to check trade show schedules for coal mine expositions, and they discovered one planned for Charleston, West Virginia. Space was quickly purchased and an exhibit constructed to display not only the coal mine phone but also other communications systems useful in the mining industry. Manahan booked the product manager on a press tour around West Virginia about a week before the trade show. "The coal mine phone is heavily insulated in a bright orange cover," Manahan explained. "It looked like a big lunch box and it was very photogenic. During the interviews, we had the product manager stress the safety and productivity advantages of the phone, and show how its Touch-Tone dialing capability gave miners direct access to the outside world. No longer were they dependent on a switchboard operator who may or may not be there, depending on the shift."

The *Wall Street Journal* did not even know of this media activity, of course. But the personal demonstrations and the safety message resulted in wide coverage in newspapers and on television in the small communities of West Virginia. When the coal mining exposition was over, the product manager had one firm sale, dozens of leads and news stories in the all-important trade press. "Some media relations purists view marketing promotions as hucksterism," Manahan said. "But product promotion can be as newsworthy as building a modern office complex or electing a new president—as long as you direct your messages to the right media. One of our responsibilities as media relations people must be to peddle our professionalism—and teach our associates what works and what does not work with the news media."

JI Case

Creativity, like targeting, may provide an alternative to the big news conference. For example, an unusual giveaway can do as much for your program as a news conference if you are clever enough to think of one that is both unique and cost-effective. To promote the silver anniversary of its loader/backhoe, JI Case put together a breakfast press kit containing all the utensils and ingredients for a continental breakfast for two. The kit was delivered to reporters at 140 business and construction trade publications throughout the United States and Canada in a cardboard box marked "urgent." Included was a small cassette player providing a four-minute message from Case's president. The cost of producing and sending these kits was one-third what it would have cost to hold a news conference for 140 media people, according to David Brukardt, manager of communications and public affairs at JI Case. Of the 140 publications receiving the kit, 38 responded with news coverage or personal letters to the company, and clips were still coming in 10 months after the event. Further, Brukardt thinks that the unusual and more personal nature of this promotion will help keep his company in journalists' minds longer than a normal news conference would.[20]

Ingredients for Press Kit at a Special News Event

Even with our dependence on the Internet, there still are many reporters who find printed press kits useful. Here are the basic pieces that should be included in the package of special materials you give the news media, both in the press kit and on your organization's Web site:

1. Main news release.
2. Other related feature or "sidebar" stories.
3. Black-and-white photographs or drawings, with cutlines attached or taped to the back in print versions. Include color slides for TV, color prints for magazines and newspapers with four-color capability, and offer network-quality videotape or film to TV stations as background footage if you have it.
4. List of names, titles and affiliations of all people on the stage, at the head table or otherwise participating in the event.
5. Photos and biographies of keynote speakers.
6. Basic fact sheet on your organization.
7. Annual report, brochure and other information on your organization.
8. Name and number (day and night) of person to contact for additional information.

It also is critical that each of the pieces in the press kit be dated, since they undoubtedly will be separated and probably will be filed in the publication or station's morgue for future use by any reporter writing a story on your organization.

The High Price of News Leaks

Frequently, employees are a major cause of news leaks. Sometimes they are salespeople hoping to impress customers by offering advance information about a new product, forgetting that they may be flirting with an antitrust violation by pre-announcing a product. Or they are staff managers carelessly chattering about their work. Indeed, *Business Week* explained how a major article on personal computers came to be written by quoting a reporter as saying, "I heard intimations at a lunch, at a cocktail party, and again from a research expert while I was in a grocery store about a major product announcement coming." Said publisher James R. Pierce candidly: "Using these bits of information as a wedge, [we] got interviews with [the company's] executives."[21]

There is a very basic reason to keep a tight lid on new product information until the announcement day: You likely cannot afford to alienate the news media and lose the free—and probably positive—publicity they will give you. Except in rare cases, journalists will not cover the announcement of a new product as a major news event if the story has leaked out in dribs and drabs. They understand the necessity for a trial location or two. But any more widespread knowledge and reporters tend to say too many of their readers or viewers already know the story to make it news, and they send you off to the very expensive advertising section. As the old saying goes, "Loose lips sink ships," or make it very expensive to float them again.

Editors also frequently refuse to carry a story on a new product on their news pages or programs if your company has a paid ad running. Their feeling is that if your company had time to produce and place an advertisement, the product is no longer "hard news" to their readers and viewers and the publication is being used to provide free advertising. It is thus an important part of the media relations person's responsibility to ensure your news conference precedes any advertising by at least a day or two. (See pages 181 to 184 for a planning model and timeline for major new product or service announcements.)

Integrated Marketing Communications—Powerful Tool for Product Publicity and Brand Enhancement

The poster ads for the new Volkswagen Beetle will go down in advertising history: "Less flower, more power," and "If you sold your soul in the '80s, here's your chance to buy it back." But it was not advertising that launched the new Love Bug. Rather, it was public relations, according to *PR Week*.

The Beetle was introduced at the North American Auto Show in January 1999 with a satellite media tour. Volkswagen and Ruder Finn generated more than 900 national and local television segments about the Beetle in the first week alone. The publicity kept rolling in when the new Beetle was delivered. It made news by stopping traffic whenever it appeared, and customers responded by heading for their car dealers to buy. Said Rudder Finn creative director Michael Schubert, "We arranged it so that the car was seen in high-profile, high-traffic situations like Times Square in New York and Rodeo Drive in L.A."

By the time the advertising started in April, there was 65 percent awareness among the general public. And when a wiring problem caused VW to recall all 10,000 Beetles it had sold, owners who took their cars in for repairs got a loaner or a free taxi, a car wash, a tank of gas and a bouquet of flowers for their trouble. As *PR Week* put it, "Nice PR touches that embellished the Beetle's image and defused a potential crisis. . . . The launch of the Beetle is just the latest in the growing line of companies and brands where PR has become central to the marketing program."[22] In fact, in an editorial titled, "Packaged PR is key to branding," *PR Week* opined: "The success of strongly branded operations like Starbucks, Amazon.com, Virgin and The Body Shop all [are] predicated on public relations and not advertising. . . ."[23]

The softening of the traditional boundaries between marketing, advertising and PR is a natural response to the economic and competitive imperatives facing companies and clients. Organizational silos are out and teamwork is in. CEOs have little interest in what function traditionally had responsibility for a given task. Rather, they want the brightest and most creative minds addressing business challenges no matter where they reside in the organizational chart. Communicating priority messages cost-effectively to journalists, customers, shareholders, employees and other target publics is necessary to an organization's survival. Integrated marketing communications is an effective way to do that.

Said Thomas L. Harris, author, consultant and a professor in the Integrated Marketing Communications division at Northwestern University's Medill School of Journalism: "It is this need to get more bang for their bucks that has driven the growth of marketing public relations and the move to integrated marketing. The leave-it-all-to-advertising mindset is giving way to more targeted, more diverse ways to sell goods and services, maintain customer confidence and build brand equity."[24]

To create an effective integrated marketing communications program and avoid a cheerleading approach to promotions, get all the key functions together to decide on your priority messages and key selling points. Step back and look at the new product or service as a journalist would. Forget ego. Ask, what really is *news*? What is *new* or *unique*? What aspect of the product or service would have the most interest for the media's readers, viewers or listeners? Look for a human side as well as a business side to the story. Your role as a strategist and counselor means thinking through and guiding the entire publicity program, not just writing a news release.

In fact, Harris sees a long list of ways PR adds value to integrated marketing communications programs, including reinforcing brand position, building marketplace excitement before advertising breaks, making advertising news where there is no product news, reviving brand excitement, and building personal relationships with customers. "The opportunity is there if the talent is there to make it happen," in Harris' view.[25]

Sophisticated Sequencing Maximizes Results

Too often great effort is expended on what will be said, with little attention paid as to when. Yet sophisticated sequencing is crucial to maximizing your results.

Experienced CEOs and CFOs plan asset sales and expansion activities to keep earnings rising smoothly and consistently. Similarly, all departments involved in marketing communications should plan so that there is a consistent stream of good news coming out of the company during the year, rather than a large number of new product and service announcements bunched together.

Announcement dates should be set for those strategic moments in time when they will generate the most attention—for example, before a major financial analysts meeting or at an important trade show—rather than at the whim of one person or department. Get all involved parties together and agree upon an announcement calendar for the next year or two that benefits both the individual product managers and business units involved, as well as the overall organization.

Here is a planning model and timeline for major new product or service announcements. It can be a tool to help you and your colleagues in your planning, especially for significant announcements of interest to a wide number of your priority audiences. Of course, all these activities are not appropriate for all products and services, and the one you choose will depend on your organization, its culture, the marketplace, and the nature of the product or service being announced.

Announcement Day Minus Six Months

- Interdepartmental planning committee formed, chaired by marketing or product manager responsible for the new product or service. Consider including representatives from all sales and marketing functions involved, engineering, manufacturing, R&D, distribution channels, training, PR, advertising, promotions, investor relations, legal and customer service.
- Roles and responsibilities for all committee members defined, tentative meetings schedule and announcement timetable agreed to.
- Research, product and marketing plans shared with committee members.

Announcement Day Minus Five to Two Months

- Beta tests with key customers as appropriate to get operational feedback (signed written confidentiality and nondisclosure agreements required).
- Agreement on priority messages, target audiences, key selling/positioning/copy points (consistent with overall brand strategies).
- Agreement on overall theme and visuals for all media and marketing communications materials as well as advertising, and new logo if any (consistent with overall corporate identification program).
- Announcement date agreed to, cleared on everyone's calendars.
- Site selected and agreed to, hotel and travel reservations made if necessary.
- Technical arrangements made for live Internet or video hookup for those who cannot attend.
- Master to-do list agreed to, with responsibilities for each item and issue.
- Standby statements and Qs and As distributed to PR and

sales staff as well as customer service reps to respond to rumors and prevent pre-announcement leaks.

- Shelter magazines, quarterlies and/or other long lead-time publications given photos and general information if appropriate (signed written confidentiality agreement required).

Announcement Day Minus One Month

- Draft announcement materials (including scripts and background-only Qs and As), circulated for comments, clearance and buy-in.
- Demonstration products loaned to two or three key reporters (signed, written confidentiality agreement required).
- Final timetable and responsibilities reviewed and agreed to.
- Board of directors, senior management alerted to plans and schedule on confidential basis.
- Spokesperson training for speakers at news conference, analyst briefing, customer seminars, etc.

Announcement Day Minus One Week to One Day

- Journalists invited to news conference, analysts invited to briefing, customers/distributors invited to reception relating to "important new product/service" (no specifics).
- Rehearsals for news conference and analyst briefing, at announcement site whenever possible.
- Announcement materials on disks or printed, "ready to go" at key staging areas.
- Advance copies distributed to board of directors and senior management.

Announcement Day

- Stock market alerted if publicly traded company and new product/service is material.
- Wire services notified, news conference held, press kits distributed, materials put on your organization's Web site.
- Financial analyst briefing.
- Announcement materials distributed to all employees, with news conference available via Intranet or video.

- Notification of key customers via phone, electronic mail, letter, reception, other special events.
- Notification of legislators, community leaders, suppliers, other VIPs as appropriate.

Announcement Day Plus One Day to One Week

- Advertising begins.
- Customer/dealer/distributor seminars and executive briefings as appropriate.
- Sampling of news media coverage circulated to board of directors, employees as appropriate.

Announcement Day Plus First Few Months

- Messages and materials adapted based on monitoring media and customer feedback.
- Products, announcement theme and visuals appear in trade show exhibits, product fairs, plant and factory tours, open houses—plus related handouts and decorations (banners, balloons, etc.).
- Announcement theme and visuals appear on all collateral sales materials including brochures, direct mail, Internet sites, point-of-purchase materials, billboards, giveaways, product training materials.
- Customer testimonials distributed as news release to business, consumer and/or trade press and posted on Web site.
- Customer testimonials, sampling of positive news media coverage and announcement advertising distributed to distributors, key customer prospects, financial analysts and employees.
- Internet opportunities such as on-line chats, bulletin boards.
- Audio or video satellite media tours to save spokespersons' travel time.
- Speeches at appropriate forums such as trade shows, industry groups, chambers of commerce, Rotary, etc., with reprints distributed as appropriate.
- Employee media features on customer reaction, sales results and staff who "made the product and sales happen."
- Product placements with media personalities (local celebrities

can be as powerful as Oprah and Rosie).

• Product contributions to selected charity events as appropriate.

Announcement Day Plus One Year

• Seasonal publicity pushes at Christmas, Mother's Day, Father's Day, summer vacation time, etc., as appropriate.

• First anniversary update to news media, analysts, board of directors, employees, key customers.

Helpful Hints from Journalists

At the 14th annual spring seminar of the Arthur Page Society in New York in April 1999, two panels of journalists offered tips on how reporters and media relations professionals can best work together. Here are some hints relating to major announcements and media events:

Have video available. You have a major merger or some big news, and we have to go scrambling for video. Our job is, "We want this on the air." So the best thing you can do is have a lot of in-house video and have it broadcast-ready on either beta or 3/4 inch that we can use. That's really important. Another thing is that on the day of an announcement sometimes what happens is that you just want to talk to the print media, and you want to do broadcast another day. We don't really like that, but if you are going to do that, at least talk to us so that we can hit the road running the next day.

—**Susie Gharib**
"Nightly Business Report"

Every time I pitch a story, every time I talk to our executive producers at CNBC about something that I want to report on, the main question they ask me is, "What's the value-added for shareholders, for investors? What are they going to get out of this?" In order to achieve that goal together, we need to be able to bring them the most up-to-date information. . . . We are there to help you communicate your messages in order to provide shareholders with the information that they need. We're constantly being tested in new ways, trying to keep those lines of communications open. But all of the media outlets are 24-hour-a-day operations now.

—**Martha McCallum**
CNBC Business News

The suggestion I have for all of you is, with this 24-hour news cycle that we increasingly are facing, don't worry if you miss the first stop. Get on the train. If you don't get the first deadline, get on another one because things really have a way of feeding on themselves. Stories that we do [at the *Wall Street Journal*] are picked up by CNBC, with whom we have a joint venture, and on our Internet edition. Then it can really snowball. I think even on a daily basis, if you miss our first deadline for a comment or a perspective, give us a shout. Let us know because we are more than happy to change the cast of the story late in the evening if we get some perspective that's going to matter. Because to me the process, if it clicks, means everybody wins.

—**Michael Siconolfi**
Wall Street Journal

There's one company, a very aggressive PR company, and whenever a press release goes out on the wires, the person there will always call my voice mail and say, "Hey, just a heads-up. We're sending this out." While we monitor wires all day long, there are hundreds of press releases from companies. It's very helpful when I get a call like that.

—**Rhonda Schaffler**
CNN Financial News

All of our stories, all of the bylines are hyperlinked to the reporter's e-mail. So if you read a story about a company that's in your industry, you can just instantly e-mail the reporters and introduce yourself. And that can be a good way of getting a relationship going.

—**Jamie Heller**
TheStreet.com

GOING GLOBAL
How to Manage International
Media Relations

Many firms—not only giant corporations but also smaller businesses—are adapting to become global enterprises because of the huge opportunities for increased sales and profits in new markets and the cost-savings inherent in sharing resources worldwide. In fact, more than three-quarters of U.S. CEOs surveyed in 1995 by *Chief Executive* magazine said their companies have developed aggressive strategies for international expansion.

While the opportunities are great, so too is the risk of failure. It takes savvy and sensitivity to succeed.

If your company or client is "going global," you have expanded opportunities to make unique contributions on a larger scale than ever before. Media relations professionals can be vital resources in efforts to enter new markets; establish corporate reputation and brand identity; launch new products; and attract the respect of journalists, customers, investors, potential employees, suppliers and other opinion leaders.

Key to being successful in each new market will be finding the right balance between universal interests and local customs, taking advantage of global scale while also adapting to local conditions. "One size fits all" does not work.

Even the much heralded European Community did not result in one homogenized market in 1992. Nor did the introduction of the euro in 1999 automatically eliminate cultural differences. Europeans have sharply contrasting outlooks, tastes and resources. Three hundred forty-two million people speaking 10 languages in 12 countries—yes, they have common interests, but they also have distinct individual identities. The Dutch will remain Dutch. The French will remain French. And the Germans will remain German.

In fact, as trade barriers come down sometimes sensitivities go up. Witness conflicts relating to the 1994 North American Free Trade Agreement about which countries are losing or gaining jobs. That's what makes "going global" so interesting—and doing business in international markets so dangerous if you do not keep your cross-cultural wits about you.

Little Mistakes Can Cost Millions

Even little things can mean a great deal. For example, entertaining effectively often is very important to doing business successfully. In China, there is no such thing as "fashionably late." In all of Asia especially, and also in other countries, protocol must be observed at banquets because rank and status are serious matters. Very big partnerships have gone bad because North American executives who did not understand local customs and courtesies committed apparently small *faux pas* that cost their companies millions of dollars in lost deals and opportunities. And what about EuroDisney refusing to serve wine in the new park outside Paris until customer animosity and staff defections forced them to "do it the French way"?

Much better to follow the example of a global company like Coca-Cola, operating in nearly 200 countries. At Coke, each brand of soft drink has a carefully defined identity that remains consistent around the world, even though advertising and marketing varies by country. As former CEO Roberto Goizueta put it, "As long as what they do with Sprite in Country X falls within the brand personality of Sprite, the country manager has a great deal of latitude."[1]

Another example: Here's how Bestfoods' executive Nina Henderson answered the question of whether the company's mayonnaise tastes different in Chile than it does in China: "Absolutely. You know, everybody's got very specific opinions about food, sex and money. And every culture has its own point of view, its own cooking techniques, its own savings techniques, and so forth. Subsequently, we *translate*, we don't *transfer*. Because if we transferred we'd have many cultures that would simply ignore our products."[2]

The global trend is even more pronounced in terms of profit sources. Coke earns more than 80 percent of its profits outside of the United States.[3] McDonald's expects 60 percent of its profits to come from international markets by the year 2000.[4] The prediction made by *Fortune* magazine that "in the 1990s globalization will mature from a buzzword to a pervasive reality" has proven true.[5]

It is not a superficial shift. It is not business as usual. It is a major strategic refocus. As a result, media relations professionals have new opportunities to broaden our perspectives and learn a great deal about cultures and traditions other than our own.

Business Week has said that companies today are so untethered from their home countries that they have become almost "stateless corporations"; their managers work out of "borderless offices."[6] With the technological advantages of the Internet, e-mail, faxes, voice mail, satellite hookups, and global networks, you can brainstorm magazine publicity strategy in Sydney and host a news conference in Stockholm while still keeping up with the work in your office.

Cyberspace Lessens Importance of Geography

In fact, *Marketing High Technology* author William Davidow believes that in the information age, with citizens who live increasingly in cyberspace, "geography loses much of its importance as a defining element of history. Distance and physical barriers are spanned by the transfer of data over networks, not by the movement of people and goods over roads and bridges. Intangible assets such as intellectual property become more important than physical assets."[7]

John Gilfeather, a managing partner of Yankelovich Partners, Inc., reinforced this point in a speech to the New York chapter of the International Association of Business Communicators: "In the mobile, electronic world, place is literally meaningless."[8]

These trends have massive implications for media relations people. If your company is "going global," you should be at the forefront of its efforts to position itself in the worldwide marketplace. Organizations with a global business strategy also need a global media relations strategy—with agreement on objectives, priority messages, target publics and product promotion plans from New York to New Zealand. Each country's media relations activities should not only support local operations but also reinforce the corporation's global plan.

The Reader's Digest Association, for example, employs almost six thousand employees worldwide in more than 50 locations. Each of the international companies prepares a public relations and media relations plan as part of its annual business plan. The individual PR plans are based on local issues, local markets and local products—but collectively they all bear a remarkable similarity to each other because they also are based on the company's global communications strategy. As Colgate-Palmolive Chief Executive Officer Reuben Mark put it, "It's essential to push one vision globally rather than trying to drive home different messages in different cultures."9

Alert to Issues In All Markets

Such a role requires more than cleverly crafting messages. You also must be alert to emerging issues in all the markets where your company does business, not just in your home country.

Professionals headquartered in the United States and Canada need to remember that major issues do not always surface in North America. Although most would probably agree consumer activism began in the United States, the consumerist movement today could well be considered more proactive, for example, in Europe, particularly with economic boundaries falling and harmonization from European Community laws. Environmentalists in the United States often are not as politically involved as the "green" movement is in other parts of the world. For example, in Australia and Germany, conservationists have been elected and are making their mark on national policy and lawmaking. In England, environmentally conscious investors can check how "green" their investments are through a society that "grades" companies against certain criteria. Your antennae must be up whenever your organization does business.

When you *plan* on a global basis, you also need to *think* on a global basis. All the *"we"*s and *"they"*s need to disappear from your vocabulary, with each decision based on what's best for the total organization—and your *customers.* Ideas need to be given equal consideration whether they come from corporate headquarters or a field office, from San Francisco or Singapore. Wisdom flows in all directions.

"Think Global. Act Local."

Key to being successful in the global marketplace is to find the right balance between local customs and universal interests and practices. The Bates advertising agency's theme sums it up well: "Think global. Act local."

In mounting media relations programs in other countries, it is essential to understand and respect others' cultures. Some differences should be noted in order not to offend or not to position your company in a negative situation. For example: Do not give clocks as gifts in China as they are seen as symbols of bad luck. Avoid bringing food and gifts in the Middle East lest you imply your host cannot afford them. Handle graphics carefully because symbolic abstractions in one country can be hex signs in another.

These are useful guidelines, but as we travel around the world, we find more similarities than differences. Thus, many media relations techniques that are successful in North America will also achieve your objectives in most other countries around the world, with modifications.

Practical Hints for Global Media Relations

A basic rule of thumb for the media relations professional entering the global arena might be: Stop, look and listen. The practice of public relations and all its related fields including media relations differs throughout the world. Before you develop a media plan to introduce a new product in a different country, take the following steps:

First, STOP and read a bit about the country itself. Get past the travel brochures and read material that gives an overview of the history, religion, culture, government and business of the country. This basic knowledge will help prevent you from asking questions which should have been researched before that important planning meeting.

Next, LOOK at the material already prepared by the marketing people. They have probably taken advantage of extensive studies, white papers, research and on-site visits before coming up with their marketing plan. Reviewing that material will give you an understanding of the differences between marketing in North America and elsewhere.

And, always, LISTEN to what the marketing people and others with in-country experience tell you about operating in the selected country. Sometimes there is a tendency to discount advice and information given by a person who has lived in-country or worked there. This no doubt is a natural outgrowth of the too-typical North American feeling of, "The whole world should operate as we do back home." This attitude disappears once you get to a country and conduct business there; however, valuable time can be lost by not believing words of wisdom from those who have been there before.

Here are some additional tips for media relations in international markets:

Don't start thinking about communication issues until you have studied and understood the local business issues in each market. Take the European Community, for example. Just as U.S. or Canadian federal law has great impact on your business even if you operate in only a few states or provinces, so does EC law affect you even if you do business in only a few European countries.

As various directives are being discussed by the European Parliament, it is crucial that your business gets its views across to the decision makers *before* new laws are enacted. Yet in many European countries corporate lobbying is not accepted. Governments want to hear from trade associations rather than individual corporations. The prevailing view seems to be, "Do your lobbying within your association and then come to us with a composite industry view."

Do your homework—twice. Business and marketing plans are essential background to a media relations person's helping to introduce a product, service or operation in another country. These plans will highlight government relations, trade concerns, technology transfer issues, key competitors in the locale and other items that will be very helpful as you develop a media plan.

If you have no contacts in the new market, go on the Internet to find up-to-date information. Or, try the *World Press Encyclopedia*, a two-volume reference work that discusses history, press laws, editorial policy and readership of more than 170 countries. Other sources include professional organizations such as the International Public Relations Association or the International Association of Business Communicators, each of which may be able to give you names of contacts in your countries. Additionally, in-country public relations agencies will be able to pinpoint for you the contacts and media you need.

Get local advice. Seek out an in-country public relations firm or agency that has done work in an area similar to your present needs.

The best agencies we have found are those with strong North American or British ties and a combination of local and expatriate public relations pros on staff. That way you get a good balance— the professionalism you are expecting combined with local knowledge and contacts. An important caution: Make sure that the agency specializes in media relations, not advertising or political affairs. Many political has-beens are out of work or freelancing. Be careful. Unless it really is a public affairs expert that you need, demand media relations skills and experience.

It's well worth the money to get an in-depth briefing from these local experts on how media relations—especially media relations vis-à-vis marketing—works in that locale. You'll also want local expertise to help you adapt to each market's customs while maintaining your corporate and personal ethical standards and, not incidentally, obeying your own country's and local laws. For example, "pay for press" is a common practice among many non-U.S. media operations. In one form, this means paying the publication a "publishing fee" to have your release printed. In another, it can involve picking up the costs for a journalist to travel to news conferences or come to the United States for tours and interviews. These are not bribes. They can be an economic fact of life in many countries where local media budgets are sparse.

In Japan press clubs control access to government officials, early looks at vital corporate data and most news briefings—and

membership is denied to foreigners. But *The New York Times* has
reported a possible weakening in this ban. More than access to
newsmakers is at stake. The Bloomberg News Service has long
argued that Japanese news services and their subscribers have an
unfair edge because they hear corporate earnings and other mar-
ket-related information first.[10]

In many countries the journalist you deal with may be a lawyer
or engineer first and a journalist second. This often means the difference between a general information interview and an in-depth,
detailed interview. Here again, listen to what these people say and
do not scoff at a public relations practice that would not work in
North America but is essential somewhere else.

Study a globe. Whenever you are heading to a new country,
look at a globe. A globe is better than a map because it overcomes
what we call the "Mercator effect"—the fact that North Americans
were raised with school maps using the Mercator projection, which
makes North America look bigger and more important than it is in
the worldwide scheme of things.

Had companies expanding into former Soviet Union-domi-
nated countries taken a moment to look at a globe, they might
understand, for example, why people in the Czech Republic resent
being called Eastern Europeans. Czechs think of themselves as
Central Europeans, and if you make that mistake while you are
there someone might point out that Prague is farther west than
Vienna.

Read some history. It also is useful to read up on the history
of each market that is new to you. That sounds obvious—but it is
surprising how rarely it is done. A little history can help avoid
offending local hosts. For example, in Warsaw a prominent U.S.-
based company was criticized for running an ad produced in New
York announcing they were "expanding into the emerging Polish
market." The offended Pole was a professor at the Jagiellonian University in Krakow which, at the end of the fifteenth century, already
was famous for mathematics, astronomy and graduates like
Copernicus.

Similarly, Westerners view the People's Republic of China as
an emerging market. From a Western marketing perspective it is.
Yet the Chinese were making glorious silk in 1750 B.C. and their
ancient paintings and sculpture are among the most beautiful in
the world.

So sensitivity to local nuances and a keen respect for the richness of other people's heritage are essential to starting off on the right foot in a new market. You don't need dull history textbooks to get that knowledge. It is available on the Internet, in travel guides, biographies, newspapers and magazines, popular fiction and movies.

Meet the people. When you get there, take time to get out of the cities. John le Carre said that "a desk is a dangerous place from whence to watch the world." Cities can be as well. Ride the trains and buses to see how regular folk live.

Talk with people in the countryside and smaller towns. Your local colleagues should be able to arrange such dialogues. Community leaders, school teachers and others frequently are willing to answer questions and give you their opinions over lunch or a few drinks because it is a great way for them to practice their English and learn about North America in return.

It often can be the subtle cultural differences that trip visitors up. Gary Wederspahn, a senior consultant with Prudential Intercultural Services in Boulder, Colorado, says that business people new to a country often mistake surface familiarities—the suit and tie, the handshake, the McDonald's across the street—for cultural similarity. "In international business, culture is like an iceberg, and companies coming into a market are like the Titanic. It isn't the visible, tangible part of the iceberg that causes the problem. It's all the things underneath—values, beliefs, customs, attitude, assumptions, perceptions." James E. Copeland, Jr., managing partner at Deloitte & Touche, reinforced that point. "Go find out what it's like on the ground," he advises. "Meet the people involved. Understand whether your business can fit into that culture. See how products are delivered, and understand firsthand what it means when the streets are not big enough to move a truck."[11]

Learn about your targets. Whether your intended media targets are newspapers, trade publications or newly issued newsletters, become familiar with them. Read them (in translation, if necessary) as you would a new publication in your home market to find out the slant of the publication, key writers and columnists, use of photographs and type of advertising. Do not get hung up on the circulation of a publication as a key indicator of its importance. A publication with what would be a small circulation for North

American practitioners could be the most significant publication for another country or region.

Be sure to check with local offices of international business or trade publications. They can save you frustrating attempts to get copies of in-country publications. Also, both the editorial and advertising offices can provide excellent overviews of national, regional or global media and their audiences.

Read international papers regularly. Many, like *The Independent*, the *International Herald Tribune*, and *The Economist* are accessible on the Internet. *BBC World News* also is available on-line and on Public Radio International.

In 1998 the Delahaye Group analyzed more than 61,000 news stories on 450 companies in more than 3,100 media outlets in 29 regions of the world. Of those stories, 74 percent were balanced. That marks a 7 percent drop from 1997. At the same time, the percentage of positive articles that left readers more likely to do business with a company increased to 21 percent from 16 percent. Negative coverage increased to 5 percent from 3 percent.

For many companies, particularly those that do business in China, Belgium, Hong Kong and the Netherlands, increasingly subjective reporting actually helps out, according to the Delahaye study. Companies with international interests produced more than 50 percent positive coverage among all stories about their firms, with 28 percent of the stories taking a neutral tone. The United States still leads most of the world in objective journalism, the study showed, although balance in reporting declined in 1998 for the second year in a row.[12]

Electronic media require extra study. Electronic media in other countries may not be as prolific or as sophisticated as in North America, but they often can be of enormous assistance to a media relations and marketing campaign. Learn the differing styles of government-owned or directed television, and also keep in mind their similarity—a need to fill air time. There are programs about educational, business and government issues that can greatly benefit your media relations program. Often they are pleased to receive background video footage—sometimes even complete programs about your company.

Two important technical notes affecting worldwide video usage: First, there are three standard video formats in the world— NTSC, PAL and Secam. Unless a tri-standard monitor and a VCR that plays all three formats are available, you will have to provide your video in the right format for the local market. Second, when creating a video for worldwide distribution to the news media, provide a timed script and put the English-language soundtrack on a track separate from the music and natural sound. Then the countries that need to translate the message can replace the English by recording the narration in the local language.

Don't overlook the North American community "over there." In most countries there are embassies and chambers of commerce with staffs willing and able to help you get started. Not only can they provide a platform for introducing your company and its products or services, but also the staff can offer excellent advice for the novice coming in.

Remember the foreign press corps in other countries. Just as there is a huge group of foreign reporters in Washington, D.C., from Jakarta to Johannesburg and from Montevideo to Mexico City, so too are there U.S. and Canadian journalists from television and radio networks, major magazines and leading newspapers in most international capitals and other big cities around the world. Make sure they get special treatment such as private interviews if you want coverage of your news in your home country as well as the new market.

Local press clubs are invaluable resources for both learning about the country and making key media contacts. Membership often is broad enough to include public relations agencies and corporate professionals.

Work those trade shows. Trade shows offer one of the best ways to get to know the news media from another country or several countries. If your company is exhibiting at a trade show, make sure local and visiting journalists know you are there by issuing personal invitations for a visit to your exhibit booth. Host a reception for trade journalists to meet the key company officers.

Also, get away from your exhibit and visit all the trade publications' booths. Although you might meet only members of the advertising staff, at the minimum you can get copies of key publications, leave your business card to be passed along to the editorial staff and—most important—start building relationships. Business cards vary in size from the format used in the United States to larger, 3" x 5" cards. Most include business and home addresses and telephone numbers, as well as e-mail and fax numbers. In some markets, especially in Asia, information will be in the local language on one side of the card and English on the other.

Serve as a "warning bell" to your marketing counterparts. Just as you are trying to learn new ways of conducting media relations in other countries, so are your marketing people trying to cope with methods new to them. Sometimes you both may forget that you are not operating under North American rules. When that happens, and your marketing colleagues come up with a "great publicity idea" that just won't work outside the United States, explain why the idea is still great, it's just the wrong country for implementation. In return, perhaps they will be just as tolerant of your "great marketing idea."

Know your place. After reading business and marketing plans, you may find that a media relations campaign isn't needed, at least in the early stages. Perhaps the public or government affairs department should be the key player with a behind-the-scenes strategy that does not involve the news media. If that occurs, be mature enough to step out of the picture temporarily and turn leadership over to someone else

Watch your language. It is amazing how often words can trip you up when you least expect it. At The Reader's Digest Association, after half a century of *international* growth, we made a major strategic shift in the early 1990s to become a *global* organization. In our U.S. offices we went so far as to avoid words like "domestic," "foreign," "overseas," "offshore" and "abroad." It is more than semantics. It can be an unintentional sign of arrogance that it is best not to send.

It also can be confusing to your listeners or readers, who must do geographical gymnastics in their minds to follow your meaning. After all, what is "foreign" here is "domestic" there. A journalist in Paris being briefed by a U.S. executive who uses the term "domestic sales" is likely to think the numbers relate to French sales when the speaker might have meant U.S. sales. Or a South African hearing about an "overseas expansion" is likely to think about the United Kingdom while a North American listening to the same briefing would think Europe or Asia.

Similarly, when you are preparing materials about activities around the world, be careful not to write from a U.S. perspective. When you are compiling a worldwide list, for example, do not always start with the United States. Rather, alphabetize the list, thus placing the U.S. information at or near the end, or name the countries in random order.

Announcement dates and times should be selected with the same care as in North America but not necessarily with the same criteria. In North America you would likely avoid breaking news on Fridays lest it get buried in least-read Saturday papers or reporters think you are hiding something. Yet Fridays may be great days for announcements in other countries. Holidays are different so that July 4 is perfectly acceptable in the Middle East but the days of Ramadan are not. Be alert to numerous religious observance days as well as local celebrations that might detract from your announcement.

Also, remember the time zones when setting global announcement times. U.S. publicly owned companies must release all material news before the stock market opens or after it closes. It usually is best for global companies to set announcement times in the very early morning, before the market opens, so the fewest possible journalists, financial analysts, staff and other key members of your global audiences are asleep when the news first comes out. Seven A.M. eastern time works well for U.S. companies because when it is 7 A.M. in New York it is 8 P.M. in Hong Kong and 10 P.M. in Sydney. Take advantage of international electronic news distribution services like Business Wire Global (e-mail: *global@bizwire.com*), which has a satellite reach of 100 countries around the world.

Translate your materials. While the majority of international journalists speak English fluently, they often prefer written material to be in their local language. This is important to remember when sending out media kits or preparing for international trade shows.

Berlitz Translation Service has made available general guidelines to writers working on projects for translation. They advise you to scan the copy for ambiguous word clusters of the type "modifier+noun+noun" (e.g. "plastic widgets and fasteners"). These are commonplace for English, but for languages like Spanish and French, where modifiers must follow their nouns, it is critical that the translator know whether "plastic" refers to both the widgets and the fasteners, or only to the widgets. Also, when you send photo captions for translation include the photo itself. Without seeing the visual, a translator does not know whether "widget assembly" means "widget unit" or "widget being assembled." In Spanish, for example, widget would be translated as *coniunto* in the first case but *ensamblaje* in the second.

Also, remember that most translations "grow." The translated version may take anywhere from 125 to 150 percent of the space of an English version. Indonesian can take as much as 200 percent. Chinese, on the other hand, with a writing system in which nearly every character represents a complete word, will frequently be shorter than the English.

Watch those words! There are classic examples of embarrassing mistakes and product names that just didn't make it when translated into another language. There's the story that when Chevrolet marketed its Nova car in Latin America, it didn't sell. In English, *nova* is associated with the Latin word for new, but in Spanish *no va* means "it doesn't go." Another time Pepsi tried to use its slogan "Come alive" in Taiwan which translated literally means "makes your ancestors rise from the dead."[13]

Check, re-check and then check a third time before introducing a name into a country. These multiple checks can save embarrassment—not to mention lost sales and wasted advertising and promotion efforts.

Be respectful of the local culture and customs. Training companies that specialize in helping expatriates cope with new cultures are becoming a fast-growing new industry[14]—for good reason. Being respectful of local culture and observant of local customs are good business practices as well as good manners. Business customs differ worldwide. North Americans and Britons tend to be impatient to get down to business, while other cultures— notably Asian—prefer to get to know you first. Only in big cities like New York are "power breakfasts" an accepted fact of life. When "early birds" phone Mexico, Spain or Portugal, for example, in the early morning or early afternoon and find only empty offices, they need to remember that the locals will make up for the late start and long lunch by working well into the evening.

Retrain your speakers. While you've probably already put your key spokespersons through good public speaking and media interview training, they will need special training for interviews in non-English speaking countries. For many reporters, English will be a second language. That means that the easy-going banter of U.S. news conferences probably won't come off elsewhere.

Industry or technical jargon, business or government acronyms and non-English English ("actualizing your parameters" probably won't translate anywhere!) cause great confusion.

One of the easiest ways to retrain a spokesperson is to set up a mock interview with a "reporter" who does not speak English and must use an interpreter. The interpreter, only school-trained in English, will interrupt constantly to ask the spokesperson to explain jargon or the meaning of such words as "reprioritization." It's a disconcerting experience for a spokesperson—and also a dramatic way to learn to state your case simply and clearly.

Check for local taboos before coming up with giveaway items for trade shows, news conferences or other events. A small digital clock might be perfect in the United Kingdom but received with dismay in Asia. Colors could have religious connotations in several countries. Key chains are of little use in lesser-developed countries.

Two good resources for advice are in-country public relations agencies and protocol officers at your embassy.

A Case Study from Russia, and Eastern and Central Europe

During the 1990s, The Reader's Digest Association established new companies and launched local editions of *Reader's Digest* in Russia, Hungary, the Czech Republic and Poland while the communist empire was disintegrating and capitalism was beginning to flourish.

We learned many lessons as we planned and implemented our media relations and publicity for these launches. These lessons provide useful hints for others moving into the Eastern and Central European marketplace:

A "back to basics" approach is essential to success. People may have little or no knowledge of your brand—or your company.

Take time up front to work with your operations colleagues to develop detailed business, marketing and communications plans. Do market research early so you have time to recover from surprises.

You cannot assume your target audience even knows what you are trying to sell. In Eastern Europe, for example, consumers thought the Energizer Bunny commercials were selling little pink toy bunnies for children. A shampoo company drew blank stares and weak sales from ads for two-for-one shampoo. In North America the ads would have sold on emotions—like having sexier hair. In new markets the pitch must be more basic and factual—in this case, explaining that having the conditioner in the shampoo results in fluffier hair.

Study the competition. As companies do business around the world, it can be very useful to communications and marketing strategies to understand how your organization is perceived relative to your competitors in each country. It also is helpful to know how your company's corporate image differs in various countries and what strengths are perceived to be more important to consumers in different markets.

The Wirthlin Worldwide Monitor omnibus global tracking study has shown that the importance of these attributes is surprisingly consistent on an international scale. As an example, "providing the very best products and services" is rated as the most important characteristic of a company in eight of the 13 countries in the study. But there are some exceptions. Respondents in Japan place more importance on "caring about the country's social and environmental needs." In Germany and Thailand, "anticipating and responding to customer needs" is rated highest. In Italy, "well run and managed" rates as the most important. And in Mexico, people place the highest importance in general on "being a stable and profitable company."[15]

Make sure your positioning is right. The basic positioning questions that are so key to success in your home market are even more crucial when you launch in new markets. First, is your product or service clearly defined? Second, is it differentiated from that of your competitors? Third, does its performance match the promise? And fourth, can you play up the emotional benefits? The world's greatest marketers sell on emotions. Disney sells magic, not its theme parks. Kodak sells memories, not film. And Nike sells performance, not sneakers.

Think through your positioning carefully. Then pick one or two simple messages and repeat them over and over again.

Ours was *"Reader's Digest Válogatás*: World's most widely read magazine now on sale in Hungary" (and the same in Russia, the Czech Republic and Poland with the local magazine's name). You saw the brand name and this phrase in everything we produced—our ads, news materials, promotional and point-of-sale pieces, VIP mailings, billboards—everywhere. Media coverage adopted the same emphasis.

Never miss an opportunity to picture your product and your logo. Frequency, focus and consistency are key to making them familiar to your potential consumers

Even more than you do in your home country, pay relentless attention to details. The guidelines and checklists in the "Media Events" chapter are useful tools. You also will have added complications because you are operating somewhere other than on familiar ground—and frequently in a foreign language.

You'll need to make sure the translations of your news releases, media kits, speeches and other materials are impeccably accurate. Choose translators or interpreters with experience—and an understanding of the local idiom. Hire several if they will be working long hours—tired people may overlook possible misinterpretations that can cause embarrassment and inaccuracies. Provide them copies of your presenters' speeches in advance so they can familiarize themselves with the content, then warn speakers not to ad lib.

Be aware that some *translators* translate literally, which can result in crazy wording. *Interpreters*, on the other hand, work to put your key message in appropriate language or symbols so that it will be received the way you intend it to be. Make sure you know which skill you're buying. We've had the greatest success hiring interpreters with experience in high-level government events where nuances matter a great deal. Surprisingly, refugees returning home after living many years outside their home countries may not be the best translators if they are out of date on some of the current usage and phraseology.

Hold your news conferences at business centers with experience in and equipment for simultaneous translations. Make sure your video plays in the host country's technical format. Print captions in both English and the local language at the bottom or on the back of your press photographs.

Watch for misunderstandings if you are not used to working in the metric system. Get advice from local experts on the correct protocol for invitations, seating and toasts at banquets. Pay even more attention to money and bills than usual. To protect yourself from inflation and currency devaluations, try to negotiate so your bills are paid in local currency. In some cases we have found it cost-efficient to prepay local agencies the amount of their budget so they can buy space and purchase other services as the dollar fluctuates. Check the local country's laws if there is a value added tax (VAT); ordering and paying your bills through your local subsidiary can result in large savings. Don't be surprised if there is an ulterior motive to generate hard currency when some of your suppliers or partners make recommendations.

Most media relations techniques that work at home will also work well in other countries as their business practices become more universal—and more Western. You may well be asked to advertise or get involved in a business venture by journalists. In some countries there is no clear separation between business and editorial, and it is common to pay a "publishing fee" to get your news release printed. But most professional news media relations techniques work around the world—when they are based on real news announcements and practiced with respect for journalists' needs as well as your own organization's objectives. In fact, in Mexico the local Reader's Digest office helped get the "pay for press" practice stopped by refusing to participate. They supplied real news and they got it treated like real news.

Even universal media tools often require local touches to be successful. We hosted news conferences for all the *Reader's Digest* magazine launches. The Eastern and Central European events followed our Western format fairly closely. In Moscow, how-ever, presentations are expected to be significantly longer—40 to 60 minutes rather than our more normal 20 to 30—and if you can incorporate a historical perspective about your company and prod-uct, so much the better. In Poland they like numerical research from a reputable outside firm to support product and consumer claims. Most reporters ask their best questions at the news confer-ence, not waiting to do so in private after the general Q and A ses-sion, as is true in North America. On the contrary, as soon as the news conference is over, everyone rushes to the food—traditionally a full meal consumed at record speed. Russian journalists have learned from experience that if they don't get to the meal quickly, it will be gone. Food also is a major enticement to attend a news conference in other Eastern and Central European countries.

Giveaways are eagerly received, and it is worth your while to make them special. Knowing the long lines that Russian citizens have endured, we gave each journalist a very large tote with a shoulder strap—featuring our new magazine's logo in English and Russian. Inside was a "traveling office" with a wide variety of office supplies in a leather case, also featuring our logo—just the items that were so hard to get in Moscow. In Hungary our giveaways also matched the market: another tote, with our logo in Hungarian and English—plus a business card holder, again featuring our bilingual logo. We were told executives are now getting and giving business cards for the first time and have nowhere to keep them. These giveaways were popular because they were so useful. The totes became very visible "moving billboards" for our brand long after the news conferences were over.

Our bilingual invitations to the news conference were also special. We engraved them, pictured both countries' flags and individually wrote in the reporter's name in fancy script. We were told these touches made our event stand out in journalists' minds.

To attract media and consumer attention, we used large hot-air balloons and billboards. The balloons drew a crowd, and the one in Moscow made the front page of *Advertising Age*. Our Moscow billboards were unusual enough that Tom Brokaw mentioned them on the *NBC Nightly News.* He'd seen them on his way from the airport into Moscow while covering the Bush-Gorbachev summit the week after our launch. It was great timing and gave us a second round of media coverage.

Direct mail also can be effective if you can purchase accurate lists. But in formerly communist countries, you might initially face suspicion and concern. Privacy is a major issue in countries like Poland. "Where did you get my name?" consumers want to know. After all, for years they lived in a police state where anonymity was the best way to survive.

Always remember your objective and your primary audience. In Moscow we got great pressure from suppliers to invite government officials and others to the news conference. We refused, saying the news conference was strictly for working journalists and its objective was solely to generate media coverage about our new magazine. In most markets you lose focus when you begin to mix messages and target audiences. The one hundred-plus journalists who attended seemed to appreciate our concentrating on them alone—and the extensive positive coverage about the new magazine and our company around the world reinforced our belief that we'd made the right decision. In fact, media coverage was so extensive and our magazine so popular in the republics of Russia, Ukraine and Belarus that we sold out within days. So we scaled back plans for significant additional promotions, relying primarily on mailings of each issue of the magazine to key journalists every month.

In Asia, however, the situation is different. There they expect many local dignitaries to be on the stage with your company's presenters. The more VIPs there, the more important your organization must be.

Choose your speakers based on your business and marketing strategies. The balance between global and local speakers and content should depend on your organization's business strategy and organizational structure.

Multinational companies with autonomous subsidiaries and independent strategies in each market likely would want to concentrate their messages on local plans, products, people, customers and competitors. They also would want to feature local executives as spokespersons and downplay the connection to the corporate parent.

Global companies, on the other hand, operate as an integrated system in which headquarters and all the subsidiaries are interdependent in terms of strategies and operations. Every decision—from where it is most cost-effective to manufacture each product and buy supplies to pricing policies and profit goals—takes into account the entire worldwide system. The sum of the parts is a whole lot more valuable than the pieces themselves. In these cases you would probably want to showcase both global and local spokespersons at your news conferences and other announcement events.

Allow much more time to accomplish each activity than you would at home—and be realistic in your expectations. For generations people in the former Soviet bloc countries were denied access to the rest of the world, penalized for showing initiative or making a profit, and taught that capitalism and private ownership were evil. Indifference replaced initiative because that was the best way to survive.

You will experience problems with bureaucratic inefficiency, shortage of phone lines and high-tech equipment, manual systems and lack of experience. Cultural obstacles—legacies of the communist rule—will work against you. For years people waited for orders and responded to the demands of a grandiose central plan. There were no choices—Moscow did the thinking for everyone. Overcoming that numbness and encouraging individual initiative may take generations, as will attention to deadlines, the ability to be flexible and adaptable, and the desire to work around obstacles that come up in any major project as a matter of course.

At a recent public relations seminar, a Swiss executive talked about his company's entry into Eastern Europe. He said it would be many years before one could assume local people would understand the professional standards we take for granted. He also suggested spending more time doing the work yourself than you would think you needed to do. In Budapest, for example, all the proposed news conference sites initially shown for our approval were much too small and had no provision for translators or television. You cannot manage a project like this from a desk in your home country. Nothing beats on-site knowledge.

English is the universal language of global business. But, be careful! Don't underestimate the language barrier. Most of the people you are dealing with will be listening and speaking in a second language, so each conversation takes place on two planes. You are thinking and speaking in English, but your colleagues probably have to do the translation in their heads before they can comprehend and respond.

Perhaps people sometimes pretend to understand, not wanting to interrupt the flow of the conversation for clarification. Maybe they think they do understand, but subtleties are lost. It's important to state things as simply as possible and be crystal clear in your communications. Get agreements in writing to see if your expectations match theirs. Interact frequently to be sure there's an easy avenue for questions. Get on a plane, make yourself available and find out firsthand what's going on. It's called "management by traveling around."

On the other hand, be wary of business people who have traveled in the United Kingdom or the United States saying they speak no English. Even if they require a translator, they may understand more English than they let on, and you should be careful not to discuss your negotiating strategy with colleagues in asides, thinking no one else understands.

So keep pushing—but try to be tolerant. Also, remember that as you work to fix the problems, you should have a tremendous sense of satisfaction that in some small way you are helping to build a knowledge infrastructure and put in place systems that are helping those countries develop a free market economy.

Take advantage of local resources to help you achieve your objectives and avoid cultural gaffes. Several well-known public relations firms have set up offices in the former Soviet Union and Eastern and Central Europe. Look for those with proven experience and knowledge of local media—plus a staff that speaks the local language and understands the local culture.

You need someone who will catch you if your ad looks like it was created from a North American perspective, like the Coke print ads showing a glass filled with ice, when every North American who travels to Europe knows that Europeans don't use ice in their drinks; to alert you that Ukrainians want their new country to be called Ukraine, not *the* Ukraine; or to remind you that in Hungary last names come before first and in Russia people wear their wedding rings on their right hand. That was important to a U.S. baby-care company that offended consumers when it pictured a young girl with a baby in their product promotions; scandalized viewers thought she was an unwed mother because she wore no ring on her right hand.

Another valuable contact is the U.S. Embassy—especially the press attaché at U.S. Information Service offices around the world. They have daily dealings with journalists and are pleased to give you advice and practical counsel on how to conduct business in their countries.

Case Study—Taking Advantage of Technology

Regardless of the country, the language or the politics, media will always be interested in the latest technology. So, too, are customers who want to be the first to learn of technologies yet to come.

AT&T Bell Laboratories took this premise to its full conclusion by sponsoring in South Korea a one-day seminar for customers on "Technology Trends Toward 2010." To help ensure local support, AT&T partnered with Korea Telecom, DACOM, the Korea Institute of Science and Technology and the Engineering and Technical Research Institute for co-sponsorship.

A group of five AT&T scientists presented state-of-the-art technologies in photonics, global networking, speech image processing and managed data network services. Additionally, the customers were given a communications and computing overview of the latest technology and predictions into the next century.

The local AT&T public relations team combined the visit of the AT&T scientists with numerous interviews given to Korean daily and business press; Korean television and radio; computer, electronic and data trade publications; and regional trade publications. The number of total impressions generated by print and broadcast media was estimated at approximately 15 million.

Unassociated with the seminar but clearly influenced by it, a Korean TV crew visited AT&T Bell Labs in the United States, and the resulting show on KBS-TV (Korea) featured AT&T's speech recognition system for 17 minutes in "Science 2001," a prime-viewing program.

The results from this initial program were overwhelmingly successful, enough so that AT&T conducted similar additional seminars in Korea.

Advice from PR Pros on
How to Succeed in Their Markets

Here are some suggestions passed on by PR professionals, editors and business executives, all of whom are practicing PR in their local markets, to help you get the best possible results from your efforts as you "go global":

Asia

A major difference is the way news conferences are handled in Asia. For example, in Hong Kong and Taiwan it is a real show with all the key people sitting at the head table wearing corsages. The more senior people you have on stage, the more important the event. The setup is also very different. Theatre style is not very popular. Small tables for four where journalists can lean on something and have tea or coffee (obviously not served during the program) works very well, particularly in Taiwan. Because of their culture, Chinese journalists will rarely ask questions as a group, preferring to talk one-on-one with the speakers before or afterward. In Thailand a product launch involves two separate functions in one day, one for VIP guests with lunch, followed by the news conference. The odd thing is that all the journalists gather in a separate room at the same time as the VIP guests arrive and seem to enjoy themselves immensely at this informal gathering before the news conference. Again, the more keynote speakers the better. It may also be useful to know that the media here say they far and away prefer dealing with a company PR manager than an agency in most cases, because they feel they are getting directly to the source.

—Liz Dingwall Mueller, Hong Kong

Australia

Even though Australia and the U.S. may appear to be very similar in terms of culture, there are some key differences. Aussies are not as intense when it comes to business presentations and face-to-face contact. That doesn't mean we're not serious about doing a great job. But we find some of the "show" associated with U.S. fanfare rather false instead of involving. So despite the fact that we follow the U.S. very closely in many trends, we tend to look to our English heritage for what is stylish, frowning upon flashy trappings. Also, American business people are much more direct about what they want and what they expect. Aussies, on the other hand, don't like to be seen as too bossy and we like to be friends with our business suppliers. So what we don't say may be as critical as what we say. We'll just not use your services again if we are unhappy rather than complain and cause a fuss. So you need to find the proper balance between not frightening us but also giving and getting useful feedback. As well, while Americans tend to idolize heroes, Aussies are known to "cut down tall poppies." So, for example, when Bill Gates was here there was as much talk about his being a boring speaker as there was about his brilliance in making Microsoft a worldwide brand name.

—Jo Roper, Sydney

Canada

Consider whether your PR program or campaign is national or regional. We have a huge country and your approach would be different for each region. Nationally, you would aim at the larger media outlets (the networks and syndicated press) which are predominantly centered in Toronto. If you are looking at effectively reaching the entire country, you'll want someone with regional contacts to do the legwork for you. Use your professional network—the International Association of Business Communicators or Public Relations Society of America—to help you find them. Is it a national campaign to the English-speaking public only, or to the French as well? If so, you will have additional costs for translation, a francophone spokesperson, and perhaps an agency that has experience in providing services for both the English- and French-speaking markets. The cultural tastes of Quebeckers, for example, are very different from the rest of the country and, as a result, the way you communicate with this group might be quite different from how you present your story in the west. Also, Canada in recent years has become a nation of nations, with a great many people now speaking a Chinese dialect or Hindi.

—Bonnie Venton-Ross, Toronto

France

If you want more media coverage in France about your company, provide journalists with background information on the history of your company and also how you are sharing the good results of your business not only with shareholders but also with employees and society. Journalists here are very interested in cultural as well as economic success. So it is a good idea to brief them on how the company was built and what it is contributing to society overall—for example, establishing a foundation to support young artists.

—Henri Capdeville, Paris

The language of PR is highly culturally dependent. Any American operating here would have to be competent enough to read and write in French—or hire it done locally. Industry and government rules are quite different from the American scene, and for broadcast in particular the regulatory environment is very different. As a result, the rules and recipes valid in America have to be drastically adapted to fit the context here. Rules governing social and personal relations in France also are different from what an American is accustomed to. For instance, giving out one's home address or phone number would be misunderstood and it is not information expected on a news release. PR people here have many virtues but suffer from a lack of professionalism compared to their American colleagues. So as long as you adapt to "the French way," your ideas and talents would be welcomed and very useful here.

—**Benedicte Barre, Paris**

Hungary

It is important for PR professionals to gather and weigh all advice from their clients and local colleagues—but then take care not to be overly influenced by such advice. The locals often try to manipulate journalists from behind the scenes rather than invest the time, energy and money that a professional campaign requires. Their results understandably often are mixed at best. U.S. PR professionals should make sure they are aware of relevant local laws, customs and attitudes but make their own decisions according to their best professional judgment.

—**Peter Keresztes, Budapest**

Mexico

Before contacting the media, learn how it works in Mexico. It is very different than in the U.S. or Europe—much more personal interaction and less technology and specialized services, for example. If you cannot afford the time for this relationship-building, get local help. Try not to go on your own "the American way." Also, always say no to media people who ask you to pay to get your news release published. It is much less common than it was, but it still exists—and if you do it once you'll have to do it forever.

—**Ligia Fernandez, Mexico City**

South Africa

Firstly, it is absolutely imperative to join forces with a local PR firm experienced in the kind of campaign you are wanting. Contact an ad agency, your local attorney, the local office of a multinational company, even the editor of a major newspaper here to ask for their recommendations. Bigger is not always better. Small consultancies are known to go the extra mile. Secondly, in South Africa contacts are vital to getting your story in print. The media respond to relationships, which is all the more reason for collaboration with a local firm. Whereas in the U.S. journalists would be offended by gifts and junkets, here "social contact" definitely helps. If you are pitching a really big story that will take more than a few minutes in the telling, a lunch or coffee with a key journalist often works. The gift should be relevant to the story. Thirdly, when companies first started reinvesting in the post-sanctions era, any foreign company looking for a little coverage was pretty well guaranteed it. Now the story has to be sold as relevant to the local audience. It is also important to bear in mind that a significant percentage of the consumer market is functionally illiterate. However, smaller papers and especially free issues to local communities are widely read. South Africa as a fledgling democracy takes itself very seriously. All the mainstream papers and TV networks cover mainly politics, crime, the economy and any scandal involving famous people. There is not much space left for "soft" news. Here the sponsorship/advertising dilemma creeps in. Your story may be topical, but you will likely only get your brand mentioned if you are a sponsor or if your story is a must and there is absolutely no way they can cover it without mentioning who you are! But the papers are more sympathetic to publicizing events of non-profit organizations. The news media directory is usually out of date by the time it is printed and, in any case, caters mainly to advertisers. Local PR professionals usually keep their lists updated the hard way—by painstakingly phoning around on a regular basis.

—Fay Davids, Cape Town

Sweden

Find the real decision maker when you have a PR proposal. Many companies have an "information secretary," but that may not be the right person to approach. It could be the managing director or the marketing director. Send a written proposal first—if you phone directly you may be considered too brash. Create a win-win situation with your proposal. Swedish companies have very tight PR budgets and will not go for any PR proposals that they cannot see a clear gain from. Come well prepared and act professional. After all, Sweden has always looked to the U.S. for role models in PR, management and advertising.

—Ullastina Ostberg, Stockholm

Switzerland

Although it may sound simplistic, the best tip I can pass on to Americans coming to Switzerland to do PR is to contact a local PR agency skilled in collaborating with American companies. In Europe the best PR approach will differ from country to country. In Switzerland, for example, you will benefit from the local know-how you can get only from a local partner and adviser. Also, language is very important. Although business and media people generally speak English, an effective PR approach in Switzerland could well depend on a competence in French and German.

—Hans Bosshard, Zurich

United Kingdom

> Be sure to involve local people in the creative process. When you come over from headquarters and talk about rolling *out* a product or a campaign, the local people feel rolled *over*—like they've been hit by a steamroller rather than involved in a communications partnership.

> **—Russell Twisk, London**

Personal and Professional Growth

Your company or client probably is "going global" because expansion into international markets represents the only way to achieve long-term growth objectives. Yet resources can be scarce in many organizations. So your company's future in the global marketplace is up to the vision and skills of people like you.

Opportunities can be endless—not only for your firm's growth but also for your own. Immersing yourself in other cultures is a real learning experience. It also is a little like going through Alice's looking glass: You will never see yourself and your own country in quite the same way.

Long ago, at the beginning of the age of exploration, there was a special warning on early maps that guided navigators heading off to new worlds. They marked unknown portions of the oceans with the warning, "Here there be monsters." Such "monsters" provide opportunities for learning, adventure and heroes. That certainly is true for media relations specialists whose companies or clients are expanding around the world. With patience, a broad perspective, a willingness to learn, and a healthy dose of can-do spirit, you can contribute to your organization's success at the same time you are traveling the world and expanding your professional skills.

Chapter 10

CRISIS PLANNING
How to Anticipate and Manage
Emergency Situations

It is 3 A.M. on Saturday in New York. News about your organization just broke in Tokyo, half a world away. There has been an explosion at one of your facilities and several people have died. You know that the Internet can disseminate such breaking news around the world in milliseconds. Your phone could be ringing within minutes with reporters wanting information on what has happened and what will be done about it. E-mail will get the word out to your organization's competitors and employees almost as quickly.

"Disasters do not produce poor corporate communications. They just expose it." That was the headline of a PR Newswire print advertisement explaining the value of services its bureaus provided clients during Hurricane Andrew in Florida. It is also an appropriate alert to media relations professionals to be sure you have plans blessed by management and in place to handle any crisis that might befall your organization.

Indeed, because of the value of crisis planning and emergency preparedness, an important function called issues management has emerged in the field of public relations. It has come into being as a result of headlines that scream such emotional news as "Woman Files Sexual Harassment Case," "Workers Endangered By Unsafe Conditions" or "Buried PCBs Found in Landfill." Coverage like this appears regularly in newspapers, TV and radio broadcasts, and on the Internet. Although the copy in the full story often contains significantly less sensational language, those familiar with the issues might be forgiven if they—like the judge who admonished a garrulous witness—long for a little less heat and a lot more light.

Reporters often provide only superficial, and sometimes emotional, coverage in disaster situations—as television broadcaster Robert MacNeil put it, "confident that the pundits or historians would sort out the context."[1] In turn, your objective in such "bad news" situations usually is clearly enunciated by the top management of your company or client: Make it go away.

The question is how. Your role is to convince them that often the best way is to initiate contact with reporters—or at least to respond promptly to questions—so your story is told once and for all. Bad news will not go away if you refuse to comment on it. In fact, lack of cooperation with the media and delay in responding to consumer concerns usually will expand the story and make it last longer than if you address the crisis immediately.

Good Planning Helps Avoid Crises

Issues management is not a science. After you strip away the fancy jargon you will find that much of what is called issues management is not really new at all. Until recently most public relations people—indeed, most managers—simply considered issues management to be a natural extension of good planning. Although there are times when we feel some personal inadequacy when events swirl beyond our reach, the feeling is not a modern phenomenon. Even Abraham Lincoln despaired. "I claim not to have controlled events, but confess plainly that events have controlled me," he wrote a year before the end of the American Civil War.[2]

Still, thoughtful planning can help us *not* to be running around stamping out ants without seeing the elephants that are coming. Planning helps us meet scenarios that could turn into first-class media relations disasters with speed, professionalism and at least the outward appearance of calm.

This chapter will cover crisis planning and media relations strategy as they relate to environmental affairs, equal opportunity, sexual harassment, employee layoffs, accidents, strikes, product recalls and other situations that could develop into crises if not properly handled. We will cite case studies to show how media relations people actually managed critical issues communications, sometimes very professionally and sometimes not so well at all.

There is a danger in glamorizing examples in that they tend to mask the noteworthy nature of our routine, day-to-day activities; what professionals see as basic or even trivial situations can be considered extraordinary by a beginner. However, these case histories can help us learn to apply the tools of our trade covered in earlier chapters. The principles, of course, are transferable to almost any subject—with some modification depending on whether the issue fundamentally concerns people, economics or technology.

We will talk about how to plan so that crises do *not* happen. We will discuss how to handle crises when they *do* happen. (They will, in spite of the best planning, because you cannot control the elements, human nature or the outside world. The secret is to know what to do—to paraphrase Rudyard Kipling, "How to keep your head when all about you are losing theirs.") We will also look at ways to get positive news into the media about your organization's efforts to deal with a critical issue or event.

Media relations people should be aware that news organizations also have crisis plans. For instance, CBS network news crews taped downtown and landmark scenes in Los Angeles to update file video footage stored in New York that would be used in covering a major California earthquake. At least two of the television networks maintain lists of southern California amateur radio operators to contact if phone communications with their Los Angeles bureaus are cut off.[3]

Another example: The Oklahoma City Fire Department has a lengthy written policy detailing how it will establish and maintain a positive operating relationship with the news media. As well, Jon A. Hansen, assistant fire chief, prepared a News Media Guide to give reporters background on the fire department organization, services, radio codes, emergency operations and sources of information. This advance planning and emergency preparedness no doubt helped immensely in April 1995 when the Alfred P. Murrah federal building was bombed and 168 people were killed in the most deadly terrorist attack ever on U.S. soil.[4]

Environmental Issues as Crises and Opportunities

Thoughtful planning is critical to all aspects of the media relations job, as we have pointed out previously, but nowhere is it more necessary than in the area of environmental affairs. Most of us will never find ourselves participating in the nightmare that faced the Hooker Chemical Company and its constituents at Love Canal, a landfill in Niagara Falls, New York, where leaks from a chemical waste dump prompted the evacuation of citizens' homes and their eventual purchase by the state.[5] However, a few barrels of waste shipped decades ago to a now-forgotten subcontractor running a disposal company can suddenly project you and your organization onto the Internet, the front pages of the local newspaper and lead item on the six o'clock news—usually in a very negative context.

In the case of environmental issues, planning begins with good teamwork and good communications among the public relations, engineering and legal people in your company or organization. If we restrict our thinking to stereotypical terms, the prospect of being a partner in a union of such diverse professions might prompt visions of discord, with the engineer insisting on a narrow, excessively logical approach; the lawyer intent on slotting acts into the black-and-white world of innocence or guilt; and the public relations person hiding the organization's sins behind a shield of "No comment." These stereotypes—if indeed they ever were built on the truths of some bygone era—do not exist in today's reality for a variety of reasons, not the least of which is that none of these approaches works. On the contrary, the probing, questioning and desire to attack a problem from all angles unite the disciplines of engineering, law and communications in a unique synergism.

Before discussing methodologies, it is essential that the public relations person have at least a basic understanding of some of the key laws and regulations that cover the field of environmental affairs. Two such major U.S. federal laws are the Resource Conservation and Recovery Act (RCRA) and the Comprehensive Environmental Response, Compensation and Liability Act (CERCLA), better known as Superfund, the trust fund it established to pay for cleanups and then to sue polluters to recover the money.

Reader's Digest magazine called Superfund "one of the nation's biggest, costliest and most controversial environmental programs."[6] Even a superficial look at these two acts makes it clear that the emphasis in environmental control is shifting and the possibility of adverse publicity for your organization in spite of its innocent intent is rapidly increasing. A closer look can serve to make us aware of the public relations ramifications of environmental legislation and what we as media relations professionals can do to help manage such issues.

Any company or organization covered by the RCRA would do well to have people intimately familiar with the specifics of the law, including characterization of hazardous wastes, internal handling, transportation requirements, disposal facility requirements, and local and state regulations. The implications for public relations became clear when it was apparent that not all disposal firms would be able to comply with the RCRA regulations for proper disposal of their customers' wastes. Because of the variability of site operations and the vulnerability of the sites' customers to improper disposal, responsible and forward-looking companies have evaluated disposal firms and developed a list of approved sites for disposal of hazardous wastes.

Liability of the sites' customers for past disposal of materials is not yet totally known. Companies and organizations have been using and disposing of significant quantities of chemicals for many years, and their wastes have been placed in hundreds of landfills throughout the United States. The unprecedented buyout of the entire town of Times Beach, Missouri, by the federal government is but another manifestation of the power and the trauma of hazardous wastes. The town was literally dying of exposure to dioxin, a toxic chemical waste mixed with oil by a salvage dealer and spread on dirt roads and other areas to keep down the dust.[7]

Legal responsibilities for such cases no doubt will be established in the courtroom, but public opinion as to who is the culprit is likely to be determined by media coverage. Indeed, pollster Lou Harris says that environmental protection "happens to be one of the sacred cows of the American public."[8]

Basic Preparedness

From both a legal and public relations viewpoint, the most significant aspect of Superfund is that fault does not seem to matter. With the best of intentions your company or organization could have contracted decades ago with a trucker or a landfill owner to dispose of waste that was considered nothing more than unneeded garbage. Yet tomorrow your organization could be hearing from the Environmental Protection Agency about a long-forgotten landfill on which barrels with your logo and traces of hazardous substances have been found. A few hours later your phone could ring, with a reporter on the other end of the line on deadline and asking you for a statement.

The first thing you might want to do after reading this section is **find out if your organization is covered by RCRA, Superfund or other such environmental legislation.** If so, an immediate planning session with your legal and engineering colleagues is in order. As public relations people, you can do a much better job for your organization when you know about potential problems in advance. Talk about the *facts* of the situation. Also talk about how the public might *perceive* the situation. In a crisis involving a gut issue like environmental pollution, reality and perception often can be two different things.

Second, decide who will be the spokesperson about the issue if a reporter calls. As emphasized in chapter 6, whoever it is should know the facts very well and be able to tell the company's story confidently and positively. Each organization will have its own reasons for deciding who should be the spokesperson—and the designation may change depending on the topic. The key is to decide ahead of time, before the crisis hits.

Third, work together on a standby statement, expected reporter questions and proposed answers. With this effort, you have probably accomplished the most important goal of all: You are ready for a reporter's call. If and when a reporter does call, you should make a quick check with the appropriate person in the organization to be sure you have the latest information. Then you should promptly and confidently call the reporter back and answer the questions. In any case, you will have avoided a crisis—assuming you view a crisis, as most people do, as an emotion-charged event characterized by hand wringing, awkward silences and confusion about what to do next.

Preparedness is not self-sustaining, however. It takes ongoing contact between you and the appropriate people in your organization so that you can continue to anticipate future issues and do the advance work necessary to keep them from erupting into public problems. Public relations programs can be valuable operations tools, but you are not a miracle worker. Too often public relations programs are based on impossible dreams. You should not be expected to keep all the bad news out of the paper or off the Internet and television screen. The vast majority of all reporters are professionals who will do a complete job. They know there are at least two sides to every news story, they want to get the complete picture, and they are more than willing to include your position in their report. The full story on such potentially emotional issues as a poorly maintained landfill often results in your turning what could have been a negative article into a neutral or balanced one.

Public relations people ideally should be brought into the act well before all of the decisions are made on a sensitive environmental issue. The critical counselor role of the public relations professional is covered in depth in chapter 12, but we mention it here because it is so vital whenever decision makers gather to discuss actions that will affect one of their many publics. If PR people are but privates in an army of generals, some of their most valuable skills are lost to their organizations. As CNN Headline News Anchor Bobby Batiste put it: "The public relations person is more important than anyone else in the organization as far as we are concerned—and should be briefed accordingly."

Public relations people often can counsel their operations and staff colleagues on how the public might perceive a planned action. Working together, you can avoid many problems. Sometimes that may require modifying an action plan to demonstrate your organization's commitment to environmental protection. Good relations with the public are, after all, based on a solid record of good performance. Organizations achieve credibility primarily by what they do, not what they say. Many times addressing the problem successfully will require developing a communications program to explain your plans internally and externally.

The Brighter Side of Building Credibility

It would be a disservice to all public relations people to end a discussion of environmental affairs after reviewing only the negative aspects of the topic. On the contrary, we much prefer to work on positive news.

Reporters—particularly on the smaller newspapers and stations—often are looking for good feature material and information that affect their readers or viewers. Offering them story ideas helps them do their jobs better—and is an excellent vehicle by which you can get to know them. They will come to respect you as news sources and are much more likely to check in with you on any news affecting your organization if you have worked with them before. Also, there is a plus on a personal level for PR people. When you are responding, it is often to bad news. When you are initiating, it is often to "tell and sell" good news. Obviously, it is much more fun to be in the initiative mode. Energy and environmental issues are news these days. In spite of what we may think on occasion, reporters want to cover good news as well as bad.

AT&T has been successful at placing news of its energy conservation efforts with the trade and technical press that cover both the telecommunications and the environmental industries as well as the general media in towns where the company operates. For example, in the years after rising oil prices prompted a concerted conservation effort, the company issued an annual energy usage report giving overall corporate results and citing the best efforts of its hundreds of facilities—factories, office buildings, service centers and warehouses—around the United States. A national news release on this report resulted in coverage in the trade press. It also provided offices around the country with a pattern release they could adapt by featuring their facility's results and quoting their local manager. For locations which won awards in the conservation contest, the lead becomes obvious and can result in positive headlines like, "Western Conservation Drive Cuts Light Bill by $91,000."[9]

If your company or client has recycling efforts underway, they provide fine opportunities for news releases—and also excellent "before and after" photo opportunities—in these resource-conscious times. As an example, a feature on recycling the excess plastic left over from the molding process used in manufacturing telephones resulted in a lengthy feature in the trade publication *Design News* under the headline, "Recycling Plastic Trash into Treasure"[10] and in *Telephony*,[11] one of the leading magazines covering the communications industry. Because of the dramatic photo and catchy subhead, "Raking It In," the photograph ran in a wide variety of newspapers across the country ranging from the *Lexington* (Kentucky) *Leader*[12] to the *Phoenix* (Arizona) *Gazette*.[13] All included the fact that AT&T had the biggest and most efficient plastics in-plant reclamation system in the United States.

This positive—and almost priceless—media coverage resulted from company-initiated news releases. Often equally fine results come from responding promptly and factually to a reporter's request to you—as we did to a call from *Electronic Engineering Times* asking if we would like to participate in a series of columns featuring chief executive officers of leading U.S. companies. The resulting article, "Energy Conservation as Corporate Policy,"[14] was later reprinted in a special booklet that was a fine handout for subsequent media and community contacts. AT&T's active environmental program got another boost in a major *Fortune* article pointing out, "AT&T has embraced Total Quality Management (TQM) principles to solve the most universal office pollution problem: too much paper."[15]

These articles are not merely corporate puffery. To make the news pages, your story has to have a news angle. You must be the first, the biggest, the best or some other superlative. Your news must be unique enough to be of interest to others in the industry or important enough to be of interest to the general public.

Organizations and companies involved in disputes over landfills, oil spills, air and water pollution or other negative environmental issues will settle their criminal and civil liability in courtrooms. The monetary stakes admittedly are high. Even so, they are likely to be less damaging in the long run the public's belief that your organization is unconcerned about protecting the environment or managing its resources. It is for this reason that you need an ongoing effort to tell your positive environment stories to the public via the media. You have to build a base of credibility to stand on if negative news forces you to implement that crisis contingency plan you developed.

Although it is unwise to become preoccupied with counting press clippings, radio or TV mentions and Internet hits, they are one important measure for the simple reason that they indicate how often you are getting your message—in this case a positive environmental message—out to the public. It is an accepted fact from advertising research that you have to expose your message to your audience over and over again before it is remembered for any length of time and results in changes of attitude or behaviors.

Case Study—Long Memories

AT&T once found itself in a situation with its Nassau Recycle Corporation subsidiary which caused us to wonder if we would use up every drop of goodwill our previous media relations efforts had generated. When polychlorinated biphenyl (PCB) contaminants were found at the South Carolina facility, AT&T immediately shut down the offending operation for a brief period until it was cleaned up, took additional steps to ensure that the companies dealing with the facility knew PCBs had to be separated out before scrap was shipped to Nassau for recycling since it is not equipped to handle them, paid a fine, and answered reporters' questions honestly and factually. Those of us handling the media relations were satisfied that the resultant press coverage was balanced. Actually, it was very fair considering the emotions that news of PCBs tends to generate.

Then the unthinkable happened: A neighbor's cows died and he publicly blamed Nassau. The engineers assured us the company could not be at fault, but we had to wait for government-sponsored tests by outside experts to prove our innocence. As we waited, we read the headlines: "Cows' Deaths Have Residents Suspicious," and "Thirty-eight Cows Die; DHEC Alerted." It was a little like watching a horror show—the monster is so terrifying you find it hard to convince yourself life will return to normal as soon as the film is over and the lights come up. A month and a half later we got the clearance the engineers had promised. Headlines dutifully reported, "Nassau Contamination Not Causing Cows to Die, Test Results Indicate" and "Nassau Plant Cleared in Probe."[16]

It is impossible to know, of course, how many people read of the cows' deaths and then missed the later headlines telling of the company's innocence. It was, however, some consolation that the media consistently included our statements in their reports and that we previously had been given extensive coverage of Nassau's leading-edge recycling efforts in those same papers. In a situation like this you want to guard against overreacting to coverage of your bad news. Do not be like the parishioners who caused their preacher to chide: "We use our religion like a trolley car—we ride it only when it is going our way."

However, a lesson learned once does not always last. Some years later, when relationships between Nassau Recycling and its publics had been allowed to wane, neighbors again began complaining about problems with "smoke" seen at the facility and excessive copper in their water.

The "smoke" turned out to be steam and the amounts of copper in the water were safely within all government standards. Then, a neighbor's pig died and he publicly blamed Nassau. As Yogi Berra said, "It was déjà vu all over again." Tests proved the pig had died of numerous ailments, none of which related to Nassau, but the germ of a concern was now in the community.

Suddenly, neighbors began complaining of skin rashes, itchy throats, watery eyes and other ailments. Such charges are taken extremely seriously by the company, and Nassau immediately joined forces with local and state officials to find the cause of the growing "epidemic" even while the neighbors were recalling the stories of the PCB spill of almost a decade earlier.

No conclusive evidence ever was found to indicate the cause of the neighbors' various ailments. Also, Nassau went on a strong offensive program, pointing out that of its 600 employees, most of whom had been employed since the opening of the facility, none had ever exhibited any of the so-called symptoms. Additionally, the water that left the site after it was used at the facility was more pure than water that came onto the site.

Eventually the furor died down, only to be resurrected a couple of years later when AT&T decided to sell the operation and get out of the recycling business. Opponents to the sale argued that the company was deserting a contaminated and polluting site, dredging up—again—the dead cows, the dead pig and unexplained ailments.

The public—and the media—have long memories when it comes to environmental issues. You must be prepared to have a long memory as well—and handle today's incident in the context of yesterday's or yesteryear's.

Case History—Planning for Negative Environmental News

Hailed as one of the most potent pieces of environmental legislation in 20 years, the Emergency Planning and Community Right-to-Know Act's (EPCRA) primary purpose is to inform communities and citizens of chemical hazards in their areas. The goal is to reduce risk for communities by providing the public direct access to emission data. Through EPCRA, Congress mandated that a Toxics Release Inventory (TRI) be made public. TRI provides citizens with accurate information and potentially hazardous chemicals and their use so that communities can make informed decisions and have power to hold companies more accountable.

In May 1997, for the first time, Bayer Corporation appeared as a "top polluter" as presented to the public by the Environmental Protection Agency (EPA) via a national news conference and the launching of a revised and very extensive Internet Web site. The EPA also announced that they intended to make additional information available to the public about companies' environmental performance later in the fall. Bayer projected that it might be identified as number seven in the nation for releasing toxic chemicals to waterways in the United States and number three in releases to the water when focusing on the chemical industry alone.

Bayer's goal is to be the leading chemical and pharmaceutical manufacturer in the United States and the world, and a leader in terms of environmental performance. As such, the company knew it had to communicate its positive environmental story clearly and proactively to all its target audiences to protect and build its reputation—before that fall TRI release date. The Corporate Communications staff arranged meetings with key local community officials and public opinion shapers, established a rapid-response internal communications network for real-time responses to queries from journalists and others, and conducted management briefings in all the affected facilities so local managers would be prepared to act as spokespersons.

When the TRI results came out, virtually all the news coverage included Bayer's messages. As well, the extensive planning enabled the company to keep the coverage a one-day event because of its quick response. The training sessions for local spokespersons at affected Bayer facilities enabled the company to tell its local story for each facility individually and personally. And within Bayer, the leadership role PR played heightened the awareness about environmental challenges and public perception significantly within the organization.[17]

Case Study—Nuclear Energy as News

Nuclear energy is another controversial environmental issue that tends to generate dramatic headlines and lengthy news coverage. When Seattle-First National Bank (Seafirst) was named bond fund trustee for a new issue of state power system bonds, its officers had no idea that this action would result in the bank's becoming the center of a nuclear controversy. As events unfolded, the bank appeared to be in the position of defending massive cost overruns at a nuclear power plant construction site and supporting increased electrical costs for Washington State consumers. The controversy threatened to disrupt the bank's annual meeting and affect profits as customers withdrew deposits and closed their accounts. It was contained with a quickly conceived but well-thought-out public information program in which bank executives' face-to-face meetings with selected media representatives were an integral part of a successful strategy.

Like any full-service bank, Seafirst routinely assists corporations and public agencies when they issue bonds. In 1975 the bank was low bidder among several major banks for trusteeship of Washington Public Power Supply System's (WPPSS) Project 3 bonds, to be used to build a new nuclear plant. (These bonds are different from the issue that made headlines when it became by far the largest municipal bond default in U.S. history.) The bond resolution defining the trustee's responsibilities for this project was not unusual: It was to monitor the issue's compliance with the terms of the bond resolution and to take whatever actions appropriate on behalf of the bondholders as well as to administer debt service, including payments of principal and interest, to bondholders. The phrase "whatever action appropriate on behalf of the bondholders" is standard to such agreements, so it aroused no undue anxiety in the minds of the bank's officers signing the contract. No one noticed or had any reason to point out that the letters WPPSS sound suspiciously like "whoops" when turned into an acronym and said aloud.

The first signs of trouble occurred when Initiative 394 generated enough support to appear on a ballot in Washington State. The measure required elections before additional bonds could be issued on such big energy projects as WPPSS nuclear plants, which were experiencing huge cost overruns. In effect, its supporters pointed out, it gave consumers the right to vote before they would be required to finance expensive nuclear power plants. Thus they would have some control over rising electric bills that carry the financing costs. It was a powerful argument, and the initiative passed. Seafirst officers and lawyers conferred among themselves and with two other banks which served as trustees for bondholders at other WPPSS sites. The result was a public relations problem of the highest order: The three banks took legal action to overturn Initiative 394. Bank officials said they had no choice. Indeed, they argued, they had a moral and legal obligation to file suit against the initiative, and Seafirst would have left itself open to a lawsuit by angry bondholders if it did not act. The bank pointed out that as a result of the initiative, two other nuclear projects had been terminated and their bond ratings suspended.

Public reaction was swift and pointed, led by a new activist movement called Irate Ratepayers which recruited members throughout the state. Thousands of consumers gathered at Public Utility District meetings to demand explanations from their commissioners. Citizens and politicians called for a boycott of Seafirst, and some branches experienced pickets and account withdrawals.

The Irate Ratepayers group set April 1 as "draw day" and generated wide publicity to encourage Seafirst customers to join together and close their accounts that day.

When the bank filed its lawsuit, its top two public relations positions were vacant, and the PR department was given no advance warning. It was thus behind from the start. The PR people's greatest efforts initially were focused internally—to explain the bank's complicated position to staff via normal media while at the same time educating top management to the severity of the situation. Many executives thought the problem would go away, but it got bigger and bigger. The Irate Ratepayers were front-page news around the state as they brought their demands to various Seafirst branches, held impromptu news conferences at the bank's facilities and hosted statewide meetings with news conferences afterwards. Seafirst's media relations people were busy "fighting fires"—responding to questions from scores of reporters around Washington State.

Taking the Initiative

Clearly, the bank needed a broad plan to tell its side of the story aggressively. It developed a multifaceted information program to reach its customers, employees and the general public via a variety of means, ranging from internal bulletins and special teller briefings to newspaper advertisements and information sheets prominently displayed in branches. Integral to the plan was a media visitation program. "It was obvious that there was wide confusion and misinterpretation about the bank's involvement in the lawsuit," said Arthur P. Merrick, then Seafirst's vice president and manager of corporate communications. "The Irate Ratepayers had a consumer-oriented message that was getting a great deal of media coverage. We needed to use our top people to tell our side to the media—and get our position out to a wider external audience, particularly our customers, who were being told to withdraw their money from the bank."

The strategy was to send a small group of senior executives from the bank to major television stations and newspapers to explain the bank's position. Primary focus was on reaching news directors and assignment editors, editorial writers and commentators, business editors and reporters, labor writers, energy writers and city editors. Influential journalists were identified by name as key contacts. Individual meetings were arranged by the corporate communications department but held at the papers' and stations' offices, not at the bank, to make it easier for as many editors and reporters as possible to attend. They were scheduled to occur before April 1, "draw day." Their message was threefold: That claims were being made about Seafirst and its policies that were generating unusually high media attention; that the bank executives wanted to lay their facts and positions on the table to ensure accurate treatment of the bank in ensuing stories; and that although the bank was not seeking coverage of this meeting in particular, it would welcome contact from reporters whenever they were writing stories on these issues. In addition, the spokespersons were prepared to answer questions on other subjects that Merrick's media relations staff thought might come up during the meetings. The sessions were informal, moderated by a public relations senior executive and usually lasted about an hour. Questioning was tough and probing.

Strategy Gets Results

Almost immediately there was a noticeable change in the thrust of media coverage on the issue. Headlines like "Energy Rebels Taking Aim at Seafirst"[18] and "Irate Ratepayers Urge Boycott of Seafirst Over Nuclear Bond Issue"[19] changed to "Seafirst Says It's Getting a Raw Deal"[20] and "Seafirst Caught in the Middle."[21] Opined the *Seattle Post-Intelligencer* in an editorial appearing the morning before "draw day": "Seattle-First National Bank, through no fault of its own, is caught between the proverbial rock and a hard place. . . . If Seafirst failed to challenge the initiative, the bank convincingly observes, bondholders could make a legal case against Seafirst for neglecting its responsibility as trustee to seek protection of their interests. . . . The net result of Seafirst's uncomfortable trustee position is that it has incurred the wrath of the state's rapidly mobilizing irate electrical ratepayers and the bank has become a convenient target for their anger at the documented financial profligacy of WPPSS. . . . Such action in the *P-I's* view, while understandable, is unfair to Seafirst, which in the final analysis is as much a victim of WPPSS mismanagement as the state's ratepayers. . . ."[22]

This turnaround in media coverage demonstrates once again the fact that most journalists want to include both sides of an issue in their stories. They will support your organization editorially if you have convincing arguments. Where corporate America's leaders in particular often go wrong is in not going to the media with their views and then criticizing the resultant media coverage as being unfair or inaccurate. The power of the press and bottom-line benefits to the organization of supportive external news coverage are also demonstrated by this Seafirst case. Only 341 people responded to the calls to pull money out of the bank on "draw day" and only $640,000 was withdrawn—about a penny and a half for every $1,000 on deposit at the bank.

Merrick offered several tips to others involved in similar situations. "First of all, get management and staff on your side and get them involved in telling your story," he said. "We did that in the branches—we even had branch managers writing articles for the op-ed pages of their local newspapers. And we used our executives in talking to the media. It humanized us as an institution in a tough spot. It also is critical to plan—jointly with the operating departments—on a worst-case basis. We worked together on security precautions, cash reserves for any large runs on branches, reporting processes so we could provide accurate data to the media on a same-day basis, plus internal and external communications."

And from a media relations perspective? "Be aggressive with the media when it serves your cause," he advised. "We fought the battle for the headlines on 'draw day' and we won. We knew we had to frame the stories on our terms, so we called it 'a fizzle and flop.' The other side said it was 'just a beginning.' But our words prevailed—or at worst, got equal treatment. Clearly you don't have to say 'no comment' about a case that's in litigation. In no way did we do or say anything that jeopardized our legal position."

Not only did Seafirst's active information effort turn around public opinion, it also made a direct contribution to the bank's business results. "We actually had many people come in to our branches to open accounts as a result of our strong stand on behalf of our bondholder customers," Merrick said.

Equal Employment and Sexual Harassment Issues

Other emotional issues that can escalate quickly to the crisis level are equal employment opportunity and sexual harassment. Many organizations find out the hard way—through expensive litigation and well-publicized court cases—that it is almost as important to spend time ensuring that the local community is *aware* of your affirmative efforts in the field of EEO as it is to actually *implement* your programs.

For the community to believe you are truly an equal opportunity employer, it is essential that local media reflect that position in their ongoing coverage of your organization—or at a minimum, not negate it.

The concept of equal opportunity is not a new one, but its emphasis has changed over the years. During the 1960s, recruiting efforts and special training programs were principally concerned with fulfilling the most urgent need of the times—providing more entry-level jobs for African Americans and other minorities. With success, social and business customs changed—and people's expectations and aspirations expanded. The focus today is on providing greater opportunities for qualified women and minority group members to break through the so-called "glass ceiling," to progress in their organizations to positions of greater responsibility and influence, and to establish programs for the disabled.

Equally sensitive, and more subtle, aspects of the EEO issue are surfacing and demanding resolution. The equal-pay-for-comparable-work issue has developed because women continue to earn significantly less than men. Its proponents cite as evidence of systematic discrimination the fact that jobs traditionally held by women—for example, nurses—are routinely paid less than those dominated by men—such as electricians. This so-called "comparable worth" issue is attracting Congressional attention and judicial rulings—and thus, media attention as well. There also is a greater emphasis on age discrimination as companies trim their payrolls to become more competitive and profitable.

Sexual harassment is another current EEO issue. Defined under Title VII of the U.S. Civil Rights Act of 1964, guidelines issued in November 1980 and administered by the Equal Employment Opportunity Commission make an employer liable for employees who are guilty of sexual harassment, since they say employers have an affirmative duty to prevent it from occurring. These regulations make clear that harassment is illegal not only when a woman loses her job or is denied a promotion but also when sexual harassment creates an "intimidating, hostile, or offensive working environment." Similar laws exist in Canada, where the subject is also getting publicity. Indeed, about 1.2 million Canadian women and 300,000 men believe they have been sexually harassed, according to projections in a Canadian Human Rights Commission survey. The figures mean 15 percent of Canadian women and 4 percent of Canadian men have at some time had an experience they felt was sexual harassment.[23]

Another recent entry into the world of equal opportunity is an organization's maternity benefits policy—and, once the baby is born, its child-care practice for both mothers and fathers (the latter dubbed "paternity leaves" by the ever label-hungry media). These types of cases make good copy from a journalist's perspective because they have a strong human interest factor. They can be particularly troubling from the organization's viewpoint, not just because they are intrinsic "no win" situations but also because they tend to take years to resolve and each stage in the litigation offers the possibility of another news story.

How your organization is portrayed by the media if such cases become local public issues will depend to a great extent on three factors:

1. Whether the reporter knows who you are and how to reach you so that your organization's position is carried in the story (proof that establishing ongoing relationships with local reporters is a must);

2. What type of previous coverage the journalist's files and Internet search reveal your organization received on equal opportunity issues (reporters are usually in a hurry, so when they check the Internet, morgue or library, you want to be sure they get accurate facts—the key reason for asking for a correction on the file copy if there is a significant error in any news coverage);

3. The general feeling that reporter has about your organization (a highly subjective reaction that could be based on such a substantive rationale as several interviews with your CEO and detailed knowledge of your product line, or formed merely from casual conversations with employees who are neighbors or being held up by traffic each morning as your workers turn left at a busy intersection).

Handling the Media in an EEO Case

When an equal opportunity case is filed against your organization, the same type of advance alerts and close communication discussed for environmental issues are essential for you to do your job—only this time your teammates are legal and human resources experts. You need to be informed of the existence of any such cases, be they informal complaints to the local Equal Employment Opportunity Commission or formal suits in a court of law. You need a copy of the plaintiff's complaint and your organization's reply when it is filed, since these are matters of public record. It buys you a great deal in relations with the news media to cooperate by providing such public information materials to key reporters, and the payback is usually more accurate coverage and inclusion in the story of your organization's position.

Almost inevitably, the first time you check with your organization's lawyer before responding to a journalist's query on a case such as an EEO complaint, the immediate response will be to have no comment at all while the case is in litigation. "We will try this suit in the courtroom, not on the front page of the newspaper" is often the pompous response. This position is dangerous, for it ignores the fact that the court of public opinion will indeed rule on your case whether or not you approve—and whether or not your organization's position is included in the evidence before it. It is much more satisfactory to your employer or client, to the reporter and to the public to have a plan in advance that meets each of these constituencies' needs.

One complicating factor is that often a reporter hears word of a suit before you do and is clamoring for a response on a very short deadline. Do not be content to issue a standard "We have not seen a copy of the complaint and thus cannot comment" reply. Many readers or viewers will take that to be an expression of guilt because your organization did not take the opportunity to defend itself. You may never get another chance to tell your side of the story to the public. Rather, answer such a request for comment by first positively stating your commitment to equal opportunity and citing some concrete results—and only later responding to the specific suit.

For example, if a female employee charges your organization with discrimination based on her sex, and your lawyer either has not yet received a copy of the complaint or filed your response, a standby statement previously cleared by you and ready to give reporters might read: "The Jones Textile Company is committed to equal opportunity for women—and our record of hiring and promoting women proves that. Last year almost half of the promotions in our company were earned by women. Women are actively involved in training programs that we sponsor to help them expand their technical and management skills. We have not yet received a copy of the suit to which you refer [or, We are currently investigating this specific complaint], but we are confident our equal opportunity record will hold up well under any objective review." Put this statement on your Web site as well.

Be sure your lawyer gives you a copy of the legal reply once it is filed in court. It is a valuable document in that it affirmatively enunciates your organization's defense to each of the specific charges. It is a public document once filed, so there should be no objection to your using information from it if a reporter calls.

If an EEO case goes to trial, you will want to be prepared with a statement previously cleared by your legal and human resources people that briefly states your position—again taken from the official papers your lawyer has filed with the court. Be sure it includes a positive "quotable quote" in the opening paragraph—and saves legal and other background information for later in the story—so that even the tightest editing by the broadcast media does not eliminate your main point. Whether you choose to be in the courtroom to personally hand out the statement, issue a news release including it or merely have it handy to reply if reporters call in with questions will depend on the severity of the case and your judgment as to whether or not the media will cover the trial in person. Often your being in court adds a significance you do not wish to give the suit. As long as you are comfortable that reporters know how to reach you, you often are better off operating in a "business as usual" mode from your office—with the standby statement handy in case it is needed and posted on your Web site.

If your organization decides to settle an equal opportunity suit rather than let it go to trial, you also will want to weigh the pros and cons of initiative versus responsive courses of action to let the news out. If the case has had pretrial publicity, or the plaintiff or other lawyer has a practice of going to the press with their version, you may want to issue a news release—or at least call a few key reporters and the local wire service bureaus if the case has drawn statewide or nationwide attention—to ensure your organization's statement is carried in any story. If the case is not widely known, you may be better off merely being prepared to answer media queries. In any event, your statement in a settlement should enunciate your organization's commitment to equal opportunity and perhaps include something like "We settled this case so we could devote our energies to continuing to work on equal opportunity programs at the Smith Association, rather than waste our resources in a nonproductive effort like a trial. Much has been accomplished—but much more needs to be done." Thus you have not admitted guilt and you have neutralized a negative story and used it as a platform for a positive message.

Telling the Positive EEO Story

Responding to difficult queries and combating negative press is like assuming command of the troops when the battle is nearly lost. Fortunately, however, there are times when you can mount a major offensive and move positively into newsrooms armed with an arsenal that will put out the fire—at least temporarily. On an ongoing basis, there are many practices you can integrate into your media relations programs to specifically and positively influence journalists'—and through them, the public's—views of your organization's equal opportunity track record.

1. Look for ways to publicize the upward movement of women and minorities in your organization by issuing news releases on their promotions or significant achievements to their community papers, professional or technical publications, alumni association newsletters or minority publications in your area. They make good feature stories for editors who usually welcome "hometown person makes good" material, they provide role models for younger readers or viewers who have not yet chosen career paths (or need positive reinforcement if they have), and they demonstrate that your organization has more than a "paper" commitment to equal opportunity.

2. Review your news release distribution lists to be sure they include media geared to minorities, women and the disabled. Translate releases and radio tapes into Spanish or another language if you have significant foreign language media in your area.

3. Look for opportunities to use women, minorities and the disabled as spokespersons for your organization. Issue news releases when they give public talks to local clubs or associations.

4. Try to interest feature writers in stories on your employees taking leadership roles in minority organizations like the Urban League or United Negro College Fund, professional or technical conferences such as "women in engineering" days or unique working mothers' child-care activities and "Bring Your Child to Work" days.

5. Issue news releases and invite reporters to attend if your organization participates in minority supplier fairs or career days. Write feature stories on minority businesses with whom you have signed supplier or distributor contracts.

6. Take a look at the brochures you distribute and videos or films you show to external and internal audiences to see if they demonstrate—or conflict with—your organization's claim to support equal opportunity. All of these materials should be visual ambassadors for your organization and its employment practices. If your employment advertisements carry the tagline "An equal opportunity employer" but the brochure you give a reporter carries photographs of women only in traditionally female jobs and white males only in management roles or historically male disciplines like engineering, the journalist is likely to question your company's or client's sincerity. From a jaundiced reporter on a slow news day, this disparity could even result in a feature story along the lines of, "Jones Shoe Company Claimed EEO Policy but Internal Documents Show Actual Practice Different."

7. Conversely, **do not use set-up pictures** for news photos or your organization's other materials that could be misleading. To imply that you have the "perfect" employment mix in all levels of your organization by taking a photograph of several women and minorities in a boardroom situation, for example, might result in even more negative reaction. It is equally important not to leave the impression by showing only women or minorities that reverse discrimination is inevitable.

8. Be careful of letting your publicity get ahead of your progress. Even though effective crisis management usually requires speedy action, remember that sustained, good performance is the foundation of credibility.

9. Review your material as a sensitized person might interpret it, to guard against inferred discrimination. If an attractive woman is posing with a new product, be sure there is a concrete purpose to having her in the picture—a much stronger reason than just to attract attention in a "cheesecake" manner. If your CEO is giving a recruiting speech to a university class, be sure it does not call for "young, innovative managers" to join the business. Make it simply "innovative managers." If you are writing a news release, avoid characterizing executives, decision makers or even customers as "he" while speaking of secretaries and clerical workers as "she." Few businesses can afford to alienate women who might be offended by such stereotyping, albeit inadvertent. Better to avoid the individual pronoun altogether by using the plural—or use the affirmative "he or she," which has become so common it is no longer awkward in most situations.

Reporters also are making special attempts to avoid biased communications that might unintentionally offend readers or viewers. Indeed, the media's own stylebooks have been updated to carry antistereotyping advice down to details such as eliminating descriptions of the hobbies, number of children and shoe color of women presidents unless such homey touches also would be included in stories of male leaders. An editor in New England once apologized in print for the use of the phrase "deaf and dumb" in a news story: "We realize now the terminology did a great deal of damage and we will live uncomfortably with that fact . . . though the mistake was inadvertent and without malice," editor William Ketter wrote in the *Patriot Ledger* in a message to his readers. "We regret it and promise to learn from the experience. We do not take lightly our obligation to print the news with good taste, common sense, and with proper attention to human dignity."[24]

A strong desire to avoid offending current and potential employees, customers, shareowners, clients or suppliers is reason enough for most organizations to pay careful attention to the words and tone of their communications. In addition, there is a federal law in the United States relating to such efforts. In December 1971, a new regulation was issued to apply to all companies that work for the U.S. federal government either directly as suppliers or indirectly as subcontractors. Called Revised Order No. 4, the law's best-known provisions set numerical goals and timetables for companies to meet in employment matters. Its communications section included two rules of specific interest to public relations people: "When employees are featured in advertising, employee handbooks or similar publications, both minority and nonminority men and women should be pictured"; and, "When recruiting brochures pictorially present work situations, the minority and female members of the work force should be included."

At least one company recognized the far-reaching implications of this new law. Pacific Northwest Bell gave one of its managers the special assignment for six months of reviewing all its corporate information pieces and training its managers on how to bring communications materials into compliance with the forward-looking provisions of Revised Order No. 4. This unusual effort made it clear the company was dedicated to carrying out the letter and the spirit of the equal opportunity laws and regulations. It also helped ensure the many printed and audiovisual materials Pacific Northwest Bell produced for internal and external audiences, including the news media, avoided even a hint of inadvertent typecasting of particular kinds of people into particular jobs.

Guidelines for Employee Layoffs

Employee layoffs represent another sensitive issue that can result in either negative news coverage or straight, matter-of-fact reporting depending upon how well you are prepared to explain your actions to reporters. Once again, careful planning and good relationships with the media are the keys to your success. Because people's lives and self-esteem are so directly involved, this subject calls for keen sensitivity on the part of corporate spokespersons.

You will need to decide whether you should issue a news release or merely respond to reporters' questions. If there are only a few people involved, relatively speaking—say, 40 or 50 out of a workforce of several thousand—no release may be necessary. But if reporters have been calling to ask the status of your employment situation, or if this layoff is the second or third in a series that the media and the community might perceive as a pattern requiring further explanation, you will probably feel you should distribute a news release, post the information on your Web site and at least phone major reporters with the facts. Often initiating contacts with the media in an essentially negative situation can result in the reporter's making a special point to carry your position—and even turn a negative story into a positive one.

In either case, a written piece—be it a news release or a standby statement—is a must. Questions and answers are advisable also—not only for your use but also for local managers who could get queries from reporters calling for an on-the-scene reaction and almost certainly will be questioned by their employees and neighbors. It is essential in handling any critical issue that all spokespersons for your organization "sing from the same song sheet"—that is, enunciate the same facts, rationale and tone whether they are talking to workers, union representatives, civic leaders or reporters.

To facilitate such consistency, if you work for a national or global organization, it is wise to keep track of all locations' layoffs at headquarters and share that information with local spokespersons who are putting together information materials before a layoff announcement. Reporters often want to know if the problems are isolated to your immediate area or part of a bigger picture. You also may want to prepare a general statement that can be used as a pattern piece by all your locations. You should advise other facilities whenever one is going to release news of a significant layoff in case that announcement generates queries from their local media.

When you are putting together Qs and As in a layoff situation, think of the kinds of questions your spouse or friends would ask if you went home and told them the news. How many people are affected? How long have they worked for the company? What types of jobs are involved? Why did you lay them off? What did you do to try to avoid this layoff? What chances do they have of getting hired back? And the inevitable, do you think there will be more layoffs in the future? Reporters ask the same types of questions any interested person would. Your ability to answer them promptly, candidly, in human terms and in simple English (rather than corporate bafflegab) will do much to contribute to objective media coverage.

An example of a down-to-earth answer to the difficult question of what the future holds was given by AT&T spokesman Dick Birkmeyer, who was quoted in the Baltimore *News American* at the time of a layoff: "I hate to give people false hopes, and yet I don't want to paint a 'gloom and doom' picture. It's just that we don't know what's going to happen. We're the last ones who would be sitting here with a crystal ball. We hope the national economy won't deteriorate further and impact on us. . . ."[25]

Look for ways to stress your organization's concern for the laid-off workers and their families. For example, are you offering extended medical insurance coverage, generous severance packages, career counseling, education and training assistance, or relocation aid?

It also is critical that you be intimately familiar with the provisions of the contract if your employees are represented by a union. Labor negotiations are much like international diplomacy—

words and phrases that sound innocuous can have special meanings to those involved. For example, citing advances in technology or the introduction of robots on the factory floor as one of the reasons for a layoff could result in your organization's having to make a special severance payment to affected workers, depending on the provisions of their contract.

Gain the confidence of those responsible for labor relations for your company or client before a layoff is imminent. Have them review your proposed news release, standby statement and answers well before you need to use them. Ask them to alert you in advance to any sensitive or negative issue a disgruntled worker could plant with a reporter or post on the Internet so that you can work together on an appropriate response.

It also is important to get everyone's agreement in advance to a detailed announcement timetable. To avoid leaks, your labor relations people should not inform national and local union leaders in advance unless your contract or local laws have a specific provision that you must.

Employees are the most important audience in a layoff announcement, and their feelings should be paramount in your planning. Not only do they have a personal stake in the news, but they also become unofficial messengers who relate and translate the information to the community. Fax or electronically send the news release to the media at the same time as the internal announcement—never before.

If the layoff is a major one, your CEO also may want to alert the mayor, legislators or other key community leaders after employees are told and the news release is on its way.

Television assignment editors often call in a layoff situation to ask permission to go inside your plant or office to interview your employees on camera and get their reactions to the news, or radio stations ask to tape interviews with your workers. Their intent is to go after the human side of the story. You may feel this type of request not only will disrupt operations within your facility but also will intrude unnecessarily on your employees' privacy. Indeed, many feel such "bad news" stories bring out the worst in electronic journalism. Commentator James Wolcott summarized many people's views of television news when he criticized one program because it "does not really believe in covering stories—it simply takes a swipe at them, like a bear pawing the water for fish.[26]

If you do not wish to grant requests to film within your facility, your best course of action is, as always, simply to tell the truth: "We feel that arranging interviews with people who have just been told they are going to be laid off is not a very considerate thing to do. However, I [or another spokesperson] will be happy to give you an on-camera interview and provide background footage [or slides] showing our operations." That kind of explanation and cooperation sometimes will satisfy TV stations—especially when you offer footage, since theirs is a moving and visual medium. Similarly, taping an interview with your CEO and offering it to a radio station as an actuality can result in good pick-up of your statement.

However, broadcast journalists often will insist on on-site coverage outside your building, and you would do well to cooperate with this request. As well, with or without your permission, some will assign their reporters to interview employees as they pour out of the gates or drive out of the parking lot. As long as the interviews are not taking place on the job and the reporter has no way of talking only with people actually laid off, you would do well to avoid narrow arguments over the location of the public property line. Better to stay in your office and let your employees decide for themselves if they want to be interviewed, because they now are on their own time. It is on occasions like this that companies and organizations discover how their workers really feel about them and how successful their ongoing internal communications programs have been. Some have been pleasantly surprised to hear their employees look right into the TV camera and say the company did everything it could, including offering voluntary time off and early retirement incentives, to avoid a layoff but sagging sales left them no choice. Such unsolicited testimonials are priceless in positively influencing the local community's reaction to your news.

Case History—Avoiding a Strike

We all know that CEOs and other senior executives care much less about media coverage and Internet hits than they do about the answers to vital questions such as whether this communications program will make people more likely to do business with the organization, buy the stock, apply for a job and become a supplier. This Federal Express case demonstrates the long-lasting impact a PR team can have when communications are professionally planned and implemented to meet business demands in a crisis.

During the hectic pre-holiday business season, the threats of a pilots' strike at Federal Express Corporation jeopardized the very foundation of FedEx—its reliable service—and loomed over the company's relationships with four key audiences: Customers might be forced to divert business from FedEx to protect their 1998 holiday business. Employees feared massive layoffs if the company were forced to restructure to survive a strike. Shareholders saw the potential earnings drain of a prolonged job action, and pilots were influenced by a formidable negative campaign by their union.

The stakes were high—and global. Working hand-in-hand with senior management and the negotiating team, FedEx's Corporate Communications Department faced a daunting task: To create an integrated communications plan that would reassure all key audiences and turn crisis into opportunity. By leveraging all resources—the external counsel of Ketchum Public Relations plus internal resources from media relations and other divisions—the team made critical contributions to the timely resolution of this potentially damaging crisis.

National and local research was conducted intensively from mid-October to mid-December. Customer focus groups were held in Chicago, New York and Phoenix to gauge awareness of contract negotiations between FedEx and its pilots union. In mid-October few customers had heard of a possible service disruption. But those who had been hurt by the previous summer's UPS strike stressed the importance of advance, honest communication about any service problems. During November, telephone polls of express shippers continued to show low awareness of a potential strike.

FedEx researchers also conducted weekly polls of residents of Memphis, the company's headquarters city and home to one-third of the pilot force. While early polls revealed a neutral stance toward FedEx and the union, later polls reflected a dramatic shift in favor of the company—the city's largest employer—against a strike. As well, the communications team analyzed case studies of companies such as UPS, Northwest Airlines and Caterpillar, Inc. that had faced similar labor situations. Meanwhile, several times a day the team monitored media outlets, Web sites, chat rooms and on-line news groups to track relevant commentary. This ongoing "litmus test" of public opinion helped them continually fine-tune strategies and messages.

Anticipating the negative tactics of the pilots union, the team took a true campaign approach with a positive and disciplined communications plan that focused on the strengths of the FedEx organization. The campaign had to build a compelling case that FedEx had the resolve, financial muscle and additional resources to restructure, if necessary, in order to survive a pilots' strike—unlike UPS, which had been shut down by a Teamsters' strike. Early in the planning process the team set up a central "war room," clearly defined all communications responsibilities, and met daily to map out key messages and strategy. Full-scale scenario planning provided flexibility to adapt to constantly changing conditions, and risk management was an overarching goal.

There were four key objectives to the communications effort:

- Retain customers and maintain package volume during this peak shipping season.
- Keep morale and service levels high among more than 143,000 non-pilot employees.
- Maintain stock price and shareholder confidence.
- Persuade pilots to return to the bargaining table and reach an equitable settlement.

There were four related strategies:

- Reassure customers that FedEx would remain operational, no matter what.
- Keep non-pilot employees informed and assured of their importance.
- Reinforce the strength of the company to shareholders via national financial media and analysts.
- Correct pilots' misperceptions by relaying details of the company's proposals to them.

The team used press releases, video news releases and B-roll to drive national media coverage of FedEx's "business as usual" commitment. They used their Web site for customer communications and coordinated one-on-one messaging with Customer Service and the global sales staff. Non-pilot employees were reached by a massive internal communications campaign involving face-to-face meetings with management, posters, buttons, banners, bumper stickers, T-shirts and sweatshirts, and special programming on the internal video network and Intranet—as well as via the external national and local media. To maintain shareholder confidence, there were financial media interviews with the CFO to detail specifics of the company's contingency plans in the event of a strike.

After a neutral third-party analysis characterized FedEx's proposal as favorable, fair and industry leading, the company sent the proposal and the analysis directly to pilots' homes. To fight union officials' pleas that pilots not read the information, FedEx appealed to the pilots through frequent local media interviews. This local media strategy reached pilots and the 30,000 other Memphis-based employees as well.

During the volatile negotiation process, the communications team took its "seat at the table" to shape the strategy and help protect the company's relationships with key audiences. Few if any valued customers switched their shipping business. Nightly package volumes remained steady throughout the strike threat and eventually reached more than 4.5 million packages, up 12 percent over the prior year.

Media interviews resulted in broad discussions of the FedEx business in key national outlets, with major customer testimonials getting prominent play. The company's stock price actually soared, instead of plummeting. Employees turned their "Absolutely, Positively Whatever It Takes" spirit into a customer focus. In fact, during the negotiations internal service measurements were the highest in the company's history. Just weeks after the integrated communications program was launched, the union postponed any job action, went back to the negotiating table, and overwhelmingly approved an industry leading contract.[27]

Case Studies—Major Accidents and Other Catastrophes

Handling media relations after an accident or during a crisis such as a product recall that runs on for several days or weeks will tax the talents of the most seasoned professional. Your ability to function well—to meet the needs of the media and the community for public information while not jeopardizing the personal and legal rights of employees and your organization—will depend on split-second decisions and uncommon judgment.

Some organizations put their heads in the sand and pray an emergency will never develop. Savvy ones, on the other hand, devise strategies to deal with the worst eventuality. For the sake of both you and your employer, it is wise to develop a detailed written plan for dealing with catastrophes—and get it reviewed and blessed by upper management long before it is needed. Circulate the plan widely throughout your organization with a cover memo from your CEO summarizing its purpose and stressing its importance. Then review it annually to see if it needs updating.

Here are several case studies that provide lessons about how—and how *not*—to handle media relations during a major crisis like an accident or product recall. Some, like the *Exxon Valdez*, Perrier and Coke examples, are classic "how to *not* do it" case studies. Others, like the Pepsi tampering hoax case, demonstrate open communications practices in an aggressive and timely way, with a clear concern for consumer safety. Still others generated less worldwide or nationwide attention but nonetheless provide valuable tips to media professionals who might face similar problems. Interestingly, major corporations with seemingly impeccable credentials and giant staffs sometimes do not handle crises well at all.

The *Exxon Valdez* Case

The Exxon Corporation's reputation was bound to suffer after the *Exxon Valdez* ran aground off Alaska and dumped 11 million gallons of crude oil into Prince William Sound. Exxon's problems were dramatically multiplied and the residual harm much more severe because of the way the company handled the accident.

How the spill happened, why an unlicensed third mate was at the helm at the time, why more equipment needed for the cleanup was not available and how the country could ensure such a horrendous disaster would never happen again—these are critical strategic and operations issues that need to be analyzed and answered. As Stephen McAlpine, Alaska's lieutenant governor, later said at the Second International Conference on Industrial and Organizational Crisis Management at New York University, "We have heard since that time that no one has the capability to clean up a spill of the magnitude of the *Exxon Valdez* incident."[28]

From a public and media relations perspective, in any case, crisis management experts point out that Exxon failed to follow proven public relations wisdom and well-established procedures:[29]

- The biggest mistake was that Exxon's chairman, Lawrence G. Rawl, sent a succession of lower-ranking executives to Alaska to deal with the spill instead of going there himself and taking control of the situation in a forceful, highly visible way. This gave the impression that the company regarded the pollution problem as not important enough to involve top management.

- Exxon decided to concentrate its news briefings in Valdez, a remote Alaskan town with limited communications operations, complicating the problem of disseminating information. Further, the company did not update its media relations people elsewhere in the world so they could answer questions from reporters unable or unwilling to travel to Alaska.

- Top Exxon executives declined to comment for almost a week after the spill, increasing the impression of a company that was not responding vigorously to a major environmental disaster.

- Public statements by the company sometimes contradicted information from other sources in the industry. At one point, an Exxon spokesman said that damage from the spill would be minimal, while other industry watchers were saying that the damage was likely to be substantial.

- An advertisement that Exxon ran in newspapers around the country 10 days after the spill appeared too late, and although the company apologized for the spill, it did not accept responsibility. To some readers that ad seemed platitudinous and failed to address the many pointed questions already being raised about Exxon's conduct.

Exxon officials defended their handling of the incident, saying the first priority was getting the remaining million barrels of oil off the tanker. Asked why he did not go to Alaska, Rawl said: "I'm technologically obsolete. Getting me up there would have diverted our own people's attention. I couldn't help with the spill; I couldn't do anything about getting the ship off the rocks."

This emphasis on operations overlooked public reaction to the largest discharge of crude oil in the nation's history, crisis experts say. Even if Exxon had been right from an engineering point of view, it lost the support of consumers, journalists and opinion leaders by the way it appeared to ignore public opinion. Further, the Exxon case reminds us that all crises have a short "window of opportunity" when you have to make it clear you are in control and managing the issues involved. If you miss that chance, it can be difficult—or virtually impossible—to recover.

The Coca-Cola Case

Lack of prompt, visible management response also was key to what *Fortune* magazine called "a product-safety fiasco in Europe."[30] In the summer of 1999, hundreds of consumers of Coca-Cola products in Europe began getting sick, prompting four governments to pull Coke from shelves and European newspapers to speculate that Coke cans were contaminated with rat poison. Three weeks after the crisis began, the company's chief scientist acknowledged that Coca-Cola, which the *Wall Street Journal* called "a company famed for its attention to quality control, brand protection and public relations," had "blundered badly." The result, said the paper, was one of the most serious crises in Coca-Cola's 113-year history.

Cause of the problem was failure to follow crucial quality control procedures in plants in Belgium and France. This operations debacle resulted in 14 million cases of Coke products being recalled in five European countries, but no deaths ever were reported. In the end it was the PR failures and other miscalculations that worsened Coke's problems.

The company missed several early warning signals, including sick school children in Belgium and foul-smelling Coke cans from a vending machine in a nearby village. A school official who called a hot line set up by Coke was told there was no real problem and given an incomplete list of codes on the bottom of Coke cans that should be removed from the vending machine. "For such a big company, they have very bad communications," he said. He called the company back and told them, "There's more of a problem than you think." The situation was fast turning into a PR nightmare.

A week after the crisis began, at what the *Journal* called "a chaotic press conference in the Brussels Hilton," Coke finally provided an explanation for all the illnesses, blaming bad carbon dioxide and fungicide problems. But few were convinced, in part because different officials used different terms to describe the problems. "That a company so very expert in advertising and marketing should be so poor in communicating on this matter is astonishing," said France's health minister. The *Wall Street Journal* quoted Coke's vice president of global communications and chief spokesman as saying, "With hindsight, you can certainly do things differently and better, and that certainly applies in this case." He was not willing to elaborate.[31]

It turned out that the actual health risks were relatively minimal. But the *Journal* reminds us of the value of good crisis planning and rapid implementation: ". . . the company's inability to contain the growing alarm shows how quickly a global icon can be knocked off center." Said the paper: "Every hour of uncertainty . . . seemed to be making the public relations problem worse."[32]

Negative media coverage and consumer concern spread across Europe and around the world. Wall Street, which initially had shrugged off the crisis, became increasingly concerned and Coke's stock price started to drop.

Finally, in what the *Journal* called "an act of contrition following days of criticism," Coke's Chairman and CEO M. Douglas Ivester came to Brussels, and the company launched a major advertising campaign in 15 Belgian newspapers to apologize and explain. The ads addressed accusations that the company's initial response to reports of more than 200 people becoming nauseated and sick after drinking Coke was impersonal. They featured a picture of Ivester and a message beginning, "My apologies to the people of Belgium: I should have spoken with you earlier."[33]

Obviously, the huge product recall in Belgium, Luxembourg, the Netherlands and France hurt sales. The situation was exacerbated by a product recall a few days later in Poland that involved mold. Financial analysts reduced their estimates of the company's next quarter earnings "to reflect the company's debacle in Europe."[34] When the quarterly results came out, it was clear the crisis had been not only embarrassing but costly. Earnings were down two to three cents a share, or about $50- to $75 million, as a result of the European crisis.[35]

The Perrier Case

The success of mineral waters depends on the strength of the brand name and its reputation for purity and quality. So when scientists at the Mecklenburg County Environmental Protection Department in Charlotte, North Carolina noticed that the water in several Perrier bottles contained minute quantities of benzene, an industrial solvent and a carcinogen, the company should have moved swiftly and carefully. Instead as *The Economist* put it, Perrier "started breaking every rule in the book." Here's that publication's analysis of what went wrong.[36]

- After moving fast to recall Perrier bottles in North America, the company then broke the first rule of crisis management:

Don't play the problem down. Before it knew the size and scope of the problem, Perrier's American arm was confidently announcing that the contamination was limited to North America.

• In France, the company first reacted decisively and halted global bottling of the sparkling water. Then, two days after the crisis had broken, a spokesman announced that the source of the problem had been discovered and fixed—a cleaning fluid mistakenly used on the bottling line that served only the North American market.

• Less than three days later the company discovered the real cause. Employees had failed to replace charcoal filters used to screen out impurities in the natural gas that was present in the Perrier spring. Six months of production was affected, covering the firm's entire global market, so it had to change its story.

• In Paris a few days later, Perrier still did not seem to have grasped the enormity of its problem. A press conference was held in a room too small to hold the hoards of journalists covering the story. Remarks—including quips and weak attempts at humor—by Perrier executives indicated they were making light of the problem. As well, Gustave Leven, the firm's chairman, revealed that benzene as well as other gases are present in the Perrier spring. Yet the spring had not been the first place that the company had looked when the crisis began. Further, the chairman did not seem to understand the ramification of this damaging admission, especially in the United States where the company's advertising slogan was, "It's perfect. It's Perrier."

• Interestingly, in the U.K. the Perrier people did have a plan and a crisis management team in place. They talked to journalists one on one. Importantly, they candidly confessed they did not know the cause of contamination until they were sure—a key rule in crisis management. U.K. journalists were much more impressed with the company's performance there—and news coverage showed it.

The Perrier case provides a good example of the importance of international coordination when you have a global brand. Above all, perhaps, it reminds us of the necessity to apologize early if the problem was caused by a company error. Only later, when Perrier started running global relaunch ads, did it concede that "for a product known for purity, [the problem] was definitely a mistake."

The Sears Auto Service Center Case

The controversy erupted when California's Consumer Affairs Department announced publicly that it would seek to suspend or revoke Sears' license to perform auto repair work in the company's 72 service centers in that state. The action followed a year-long undercover investigation, which California state officials said resulted in recommendations of unnecessary auto repairs 90 percent of the time at 38 Sears service centers that were investigated.[37]

Before the controversy died down, it did untold damage to Sears' reputation—to a great extent because of the way the company handled the crisis. It was not until almost two weeks after the controversy that Sears' chairman accepted responsibility for the problem, telling a news conference, "The buck stops with me."[38] In the meantime, Sears made several mistakes that crisis management experts say could potentially alienate customers and make it more difficult for the company to regain its reputation for trustworthiness:[39]

- Sears' first response to the accusations was to call them politically motivated and to deny any fraud. The company accused the California department of trying to gain support at a time when it was threatened by severe budget cuts. Using lawyers as its primary spokespersons, it held to that position for several days as the crisis intensified and spread. Nationwide news reports, meanwhile, concentrated for days on the findings of the undercover California investigators, who said Sears routinely overcharged for work, made unnecessary repairs and charged for work that was never done.

- Later, Sears sought to contain any damage with newspaper advertisements, in the form of a letter from Edward A. Brennan, then the company's chairman. The ad had a more contrite tone and pledged that the retailer would satisfy all its customers.

Clearly Sears at last had decided to shift from a response based on legal issues to one addressing the concerns of customers. Many media relations and crisis management professionals point out, however, that advertising lacks the third-party credibility of a news story, noting that Sears missed many earlier opportunities to take control, state its case and explain its action plans in a concerned, timely way to consumers via the news media.

The Pepsi Tampering Hoax

When the Pepsi-Cola Company faced product tampering claims at the start of its crucial summer soft-drink sales period, its confident and forthright handling of the crisis prompted *Advertising Age* to call its effort "a textbook case of how to come through a PR crisis."[40] In the end, of course, Pepsi had the great advantage of having the charges proven false. Nonetheless, less sophisticated management of the situation would have resulted in many more credibility and reputation problems.

Pepsi executives believed it was clear in the early hours of the crisis that the claims were untrue because they were coming from so many parts of the country rather than from one area, which might have indicated a contaminated production line. So Pepsi decided not to recall any products—and to "fight the media crisis with media."[41]

- Pepsi set up a crisis command center in a conference room at its Somers, New York, headquarters. For the next week this room also served as the office of Craig Weatherup, then Pepsi's North American president.

- Weatherup made himself available for interviews. Journalists said that in his personal appearances on TV news shows *The MacNeil/Lehrer Newshour* and *Larry King Live* his earnestness and factual explanations came across well.[42] The Pepsi media relations team furnished journalists with an ongoing stream of visuals and facts. They produced video news releases demonstrating the canning process and showing that it is almost impossible to insert a syringe into the cans.

- Members of the core crisis team, including Weatherup, media relations and product safety experts worked around the clock. Lawyers and others were brought in as needed.

- Anxious bottlers received faxed updates twice a day, and two dozen employees took calls from various consumers and bottlers asking for more information.

- When the hoax finally was exposed and arrests were made, Pepsi took out a full-page ad in *U.S.A. Today, The New York Times* and a dozen other major U.S. papers that boldly headlined, "Pepsi is pleased to announce . . . nothing." The copy said, "As America now knows, those stories about Diet Pepsi were a hoax." It also mounted a massive coupon promotion whereby each of the 50,000 company and bottler employees were given up to $50 in coupons to distribute to friends and family. Coupons also ran in newspaper ads that said simply, "Thanks America."

The Hyatt Regency Skywalk Crash

Kansas City communicators learned firsthand the value of written crisis plans when two skywalks in the Hyatt Regency Hotel there crashed to the floor amid revelers at a weekly tea dance. The hotel disaster was the worst in the city's history, with 111 dead and 188 injured.

Judy Hasse, then public relations coordinator for St. Luke's Hospital, explained that a control center was quickly set up to handle the information needs of the public and the media. "We have a mass casualty plan, as do all hospitals," she said, "and specific guidelines for the communications staff are included. Our plan worked. It's terrible that it had to be used, but it worked."

Possibly the most complex communications task fell to Crown Center Redevelopment Corporation, a wholly owned subsidiary of Hallmark Cards and owner of the Hyatt building. Hyatt Hotels, a division of Hyatt Corporation, operates and manages the Hyatt Regency under a management agreement. "The situation was unusual because there were so many entities involved," said Steve Doyal, public relations director for Crown Center. "Our first activity was to provide the media with clearance for photos and facts about the hotel. The next move was to attempt to organize information about the disaster. Our efforts during the week following the tragedy were focused on the investigation. We tried to provide as much information as possible. None of the crisis communications sessions I've been to could have prepared me for something of this magnitude, but it certainly helped to have a detailed plan to work from."[43]

Keeping the plan current also is a necessity. E. Zoe McCathrin, director of public relations for BancOhio National Bank in Columbus, says: "When a crisis occurs you need to move. It's too late to worry about putting together a plan of action." McCathrin speaks with the voice of experience, after living through more than 50 robberies, attempted robberies and other crimes against various branches around Ohio. "In each case public relations professionals, armed with a step-by-step crisis plan, facilitated the flow of information from bank protection and law enforcement officials to the media, while protecting the identity of the victims," McCathrin said. The plan, developed in 1976 in response to increasing crimes of violence against the bank, is reviewed and updated regularly. "After each crisis situation the bank personnel involved meet to discuss what happened, and make suggestions for improving the procedure."[44]

Preparing Your Crisis Plan

Helping senior management understand the impact of poorly considered responses to a crisis is one of the most important strategic services a media relations professional can provide. Says James E. Lukaszewski, a White Plains, New York-based crisis communications management consultant: "To have a strategic discussion requires a tool that has value without insulting the executive's intelligence, has impact without belaboring the obvious, inspires action without oversimplifying, and illustrates options and choices without teaching unnecessary, ill-advised lessons in public relations."[45]

As you develop a written crisis communications plan, a key point you will want to make clear to the top decision makers of your company or client is that the definition of a crisis—and thus of a legitimate news story—is a relative thing. In a small town, one person hospitalized as a result of an accident on a production line can generate more coverage in the local newspaper than a major earthquake in China because the community editor knows readers care about their neighbors. A few people picketing in front of your office over a work dress code can be big news—and front-page photograph and television footage material—even when you feel the issue is trivial in light of broader labor relations matters.

Incidents like these do not require activation of a full-fledged crisis plan, but they do require attention to many of the same principles. Indeed, your prompt, matter-of-fact management of smaller incidents will go a long way toward containing them so they do not develop into major media events. You may even convince reporters the issue is so routine as not to be newsworthy.

The first step in a crisis communications plan is a detailed procedure for alerting whoever must know that a major accident or other critical event has taken place. As the person responsible for media relations, your name should be right near the top of the list—immediately after the CEO's and the police or fire department. There should be at least one back-up person for each of you. The guidelines should be written with a "when in doubt, call" tone. You want the night foreman or security guard to feel you would rather be informed about something that turns out to be minor—even if it involves a phone call in the middle of the night—than have an unexpected crisis explode in your face. There should be one or two people on this first-team call list who are experts in any field that might make crisis news—including legal, finance, human resources and technical expertise.

The second step is to establish who will be in charge of the disaster team and thus your source of information—and to get agreement on the fact that you or your staff will be the only source of information to the news media. This is the single most critical element of the plan. Only if you have a direct line to the place where all policy and corrective action decisions are being made can you function properly. Only if the media know who to contact can you expect accurate presentation of the facts and your organization's position. Immediate response to journalists' queries—often measured in minutes rather than hours—is critical in a crisis situation. You do not want to shoot from the hip. Nor do you want to be so deliberate that you approach paralysis and miss a reporter's deadline. As a corollary, you need to designate backups for yourself and the head of the operations team in case the crisis demands 24-hour-a-day staffing. You should arrange for contact people at any remote location who would handle reporters on the scene under your direction or until you could get there.

After the initial contact list and the designations of who is charge, other components of the crisis plan should include the following:

1. Determine an appropriate location in your headquarters or main office where you could set up an operations and news center if it were necessary. Make sure it has adequate telephone and data facilities, cellular phones, small portable radios and TV sets, computers, fax and copying machines, news release paper and other office supplies. Locate the nearest food sources and hotels or motels and arrange contingency credit and billing procedures—they may be necessary not only for your organization but also for the media.

2. List appropriate public officials, including the mayor, legislators, senators, union leaders, heads of local consumer groups or other key opinion leaders whom you might want to keep informed on an ongoing basis depending on the nature and severity of the catastrophe. Include their office and home phone numbers. Initiating contact and opening up a communications channel in a crisis situation often can turn a potential protester into an ally.

3. Ensure the availability of a large supply of background information kits including photos and other basic materials about your organization. Put all this material on your Web site, translated into other languages as necessary. A crisis often is covered by spot news reporters who normally are not familiar with your business or industry.

4. Create a responsibilities list for your staff using a worst-case scenario. For example, if you decided to host an on-site news conference, who would arrange for transportation to the disaster site for the media? Write a news release? Get it duplicated? Update your Web site? Hire a photographer? Get pagers or cell phones? Brief your CEO or chief spokesperson? Arrange for technical experts who also can communicate in everyday language with reporters? Refresh their interview techniques skills? Control media access to the disaster site? Control statements issued by the hospital?

5. Find out where the nearest hospital, fire, police, poison control, ambulance and other emergency services are for each of your facilities. Make that list available to the management and security people at each location—and a part of your written crisis communications plan.

6. Major catastrophes can affect the price of your company stock. Make sure your plan includes an investor relations or financial analyst contact person you can alert if necessary. Make sure your CEO contacts your board of directors or trustees so they hear the news from your company rather than the news media.

7. Similarly, there may be a need for someone in your organization to contact regulatory agencies like the Food and Drug Administration, Occupational Safety and Health Administration, Securities and Exchange Commission, or a state or local commission. Many "bad news" situations have government implications. Also, be prepared in case any information given to a government agency finds its way to the media.

8. Legal and insurance ramifications must be foremost in your mind during any significant crisis. Establish a legal liaison with whom you can have instantaneous access or minute-by-minute contact if you need it. Statements to the media should describe the nature of the crisis—but not speculate on its cause or give a dollar estimate of damage.

9. Employees are a key constituency during any crisis. So are distributors, wholesalers, retailers and suppliers. Establish separate communications channels for them, or they will tie up phone lines into your news center that were intended for reporters' use. Tell them how to access your Web site. If they know the facts, they are less likely to speculate or spread rumors. Make sure your labor relations people are involved in any decisions affecting union-represented employees.

10. If the crisis continues for several days, establish and stick to a briefing schedule. Your spokesperson, advisers and the media all will be grateful for a respite from their vigil. Tired participants can result in indiscreet revelations, inaccurate quotes and safety problems. Even when you do not know all the facts and answers, let the media know what you know on a continuing basis—before they find out from other sources.

11. Continually remind yourself and your spokesperson to be sensitive to the needs of audiences as they discuss an accident or other disaster. Business people tend to be concerned with money, facts, figures and the reality of a situation; reporters and their readers or viewers are normally more interested in the emotional, dramatic, human aspects of the case. Remember the adage "Soldiers fight for their country but die for their buddies." Both your attitude and your actions should show serious concern for your employees and the public—particularly if anyone has been injured or killed. It is not necessary to accept blame; in fact, for legal reasons you will want to avoid that. But your answer to the question, "What are you going to do about it?" should clearly explain your corrective action in terms people will understand. Be succinct—especially if you are on radio or television. To those who say their story is too complicated to be told in 30 seconds, ABC-TV News economic correspondent Dan Cordtz has responded that corporations spend billions of dollars every year on commercials which are 30 seconds long—and presumably informative enough to be worth the expense.[46] It is not easy to boil your position down to a paragraph, but it can be done. It must be, if you want your point made on broadcast media.

12. If you are launching an investigation, it can be valuable to name outside experts who will be asked to give an independent evaluation. Your objective should be not merely to give information but also to generate support for the way your organization is handling the incident.

13. A decision to withhold negative news should be made only after you have considered the implications of the fact that subsequent revelations of your containment activities may generate more publicity than the news would have. Remember that the ubiquitous presence of the Internet and copying machines, plus the wide-ranging powers of legal subpoenas, have made the private memo or report almost obsolete.

14. Conversely, do not overreact to a problem in one branch or area and assume it automatically is an issue elsewhere. Gather the facts and scope the problem before you act. If you alert offices all over the country without determining you have only an isolated incident, you could create news problems that never need arise.

Advantages of Approved Plans

There are many advantages to having an approved crisis communications plan in place for your organization long before an accident, fire, strike, product recall or other disaster occurs. Obviously, such a plan limits the number of decisions that must be made in an emergency mode. It also legitimizes your role as a valued member of any crisis team, and it serves to remind others of the importance of long-term relations with the news media. On the tactical front it can also encourage participation in interview techniques training as a matter of course for anyone who might be involved in crisis communications.

Businessmen and women know their subjects far better than any reporter who will ever interview them—but their performances during an accident or other catastrophe can make it appear they are ignorant or—worse—covering up something. When the emergency hits, it is far too late to learn spokesperson skills and cultivate relationships with the media.

Further, when you have set procedures in place you are prepared if you want to be the first to reveal negative news. There are many advantages to this course of action. You are more likely to get your story accurately reported by the media. You are less likely to be on the defensive. You may get credit for honestly admitting a mistake—and caring enough about your customers and the public to speak up and let them know about it. You will establish yourself as the source of information, a partnership position most reporters will think twice about before exploiting. Taking the initiative may avoid making a hero out of your attacker, be it an unhappy employee or a self-styled consumer advocate. You also are more likely to have the story covered for only one day and then forgotten.

Your objective in handling bad news is to get it out of the way and prevent it from becoming a continuing news story. Forthrightly explaining the situation and emphasizing remedial action will usually accomplish this objective, since there will be little of the charges and countercharges between two sides that characterize ongoing news stories. Further, and of major importance to public companies, the Securities and Exchange Commission and major stock exchange regulations require publicly held firms to disclose negative news in a prescribed, timely way if it could have a material effect on the financial status of your company or client and affect shareowners' investment decisions.

Case Studies—Atlanta and Salt Lake City Olympics

Two crises relating to the Olympics dramatically demonstrate the value of having a well-thought-out crisis plan in place and an experienced PR person on the team—and the disastrous consequences when you have neither.

In Atlanta in July 1996, C. Richard Yarbrough was managing director-communications for the Atlanta Committee for the Olympic Games when a pipe bomb exploded in the middle of the night at Centennial Park in downtown Atlanta, killing one woman and injuring hundreds more. Yarbrough is a veteran PR executive who had occupied a key place on the Atlanta Olympics management team from the beginning. He had a crisis plan ready to go and years of experience to fall back on. Despite only two hours of sleep, he went to work, short on facts and details, knowing that the world was watching and that the future of the Atlanta Olympic Games lay in the balance.

"We had been told by law enforcement authorities from the beginning that international terrorism and terrorism of the type that occurred in Oklahoma City are always concerns. But the most unpredictable scenario, they warned, was that of some individual acting alone. That was my nightmare and it happened," Yarbrough recalled.

The executive management team, of which Yarbrough was a member, met with members of law enforcement about 3 A.M. and began planning for a 6 A.M. media briefing with the FBI serving as the lead agency. Atlanta Olympics CEO Billy Payne conferred with Juan Antonio Samaranch, head of the International Olympic Committee (IOC), and quick agreement was reached that the games would go on. At the 6 A.M. briefing, law enforcement agencies discussed with the media what information was known and how the investigation was to be conducted. The Atlanta Olympics' chief operating officer (COO) assured the press and people around the world that the games would continue in as normal a fashion as possible.

By 9 A.M. a total external communications strategy was established. Law enforcement agencies would conduct their own briefings to keep the Atlanta Olympics spokespersons from having to answer questions speculating on the investigation. Meanwhile, Payne would make the rounds of the TV networks—ABC, CBS, CNN and NBC—with a tight message that expressed sympathy for the families of the victims, assured TV viewers and the media that the games would go on, and stressed that the incident vividly demonstrated the need for what the Olympics movement stood for. NBC's *Today Show* was Payne's first appearance because NBC was the rights holder and Olympic Games broadcaster. Payne also did one-on-one interviews with major print publications, including local media. As well, the COO provided reporters with a host of factoids designed to show the games were on schedule and running smoothly.

"Our first goal that day was to keep the games going and show a 'business as usual' attitude," Yarbrough explained. Twenty-one competitions were held and stadiums operated at 95 percent capacity that first day after the bomb. Eight-five percent of the volunteers showed up and 27,000 additional tickets were sold that day to future events. Buses ran on time and competition results were delivered to the media efficiently and accurately. "Our second goal was to avoid linking the park bombing to the Munich massacres in 1972," Yarbrough said. Did it work? Two days after the incident they held a press conference, and in a 30-minute Q and A session not one question was raised about Munich. Throughout the crisis, coverage was positive and sympathetic, and journalists gave high marks for accessibility.

"Much of what we did the day of the explosion worked because it had a logic about it," Yarbrough said. "One key to the plan was that we quickly separated out the law enforcement investigation piece so that we could focus the media on the games and not have to answer questions about the investigation. All of that was planned and worked well. What was not planned was that there was a sense of defiance, as *USA Today* put it, from the public that they were not going to be intimidated by an act of terrorism. If there was anything easy about the day, it was that kind of environment in which to execute the plan."[47]

Compare that professional execution and those excellent results with another Olympics disaster, this one in 1999 when the biggest corruption scandal in the history of the Olympics erupted in Salt Lake City. Organizers there were accused of bribing IOC officials with expensive gifts, travel, no-show jobs and other perks to help win the 2002 Winter Games. When bribery allegations broke in mid-December, letters were quickly sent by the IOC to sponsors assuring them of fast, decisive action by the end of January. But the so-called internal investigation dragged on, spawning public cynicism and three other investigations—by the U.S. Justice Department, the U.S. Olympic Committee and a local ethics committee.

Eventually some expulsions, resignations, sanctions and guilty pleas resulted, and the IOC pledged reforms. But Juan Antonio Samaranch refused to accept blame or step down as president because of the scandal, as some current and former Olympics officials had called on him to do. Many journalists, members of the sports world and general public sensed a coverup. At stake, opined the *Salt Lake Tribune*, was "the IOC's ability to regain the confidence of the public and corporate sponsors, and the integrity of the [Olympics] movement itself."[48]

Samaranch and the IOC mishandled this crisis in almost every way. They demonstrated the truth of an old warrior maxim that says you can do more damage to an organism by inflicting a series of little cuts over a long period of time than by attempting one giant kill. In this case, of course, the cuts were self-inflicted. In an analysis in the *American Journalism Review*, Alicia C. Shepard said that "the culture of the IOC also played a role in what happened. It has long been shrouded in secrecy and comes across as disdainful toward the press and resistant to public scrutiny."[49]

Shorter Case Studies

Recalling a defective product may be embarrassing and costly for a company. It also can make good business sense and protect both consumers and the corporate image from irreparable harm. For example, John J. Nevin, then head of the **Firestone Tire & Rubber Company,** said in retrospect that his company should voluntarily have recalled its infamous Firestone 500 tires long before the government insisted on the recall. Although it was concerned about the number of free replacements it was making, Nevin said Firestone should have initiated action before lengthy government hearings into the tire's safety tarnished the company's image.[50]

The candid approach worked well for **Bank of America** when a customer complaint revealed that the bank's service charges on consumer loans were exceeding state limits. Bob Feinberg, the vice president who directed news relations for the bank, said: "We recommended to management that the bank take the initiative, announce the mistake along with the remedy of paying everybody back in full, and station spokespeople around our branch system to answer press questions. Some executives felt uncomfortable about this and thought the bank would look silly. We said we'd look sillier if we refunded $1,000 to a reporter who would run the story and start an incident that would drag on for months. We announced the mistake and it was in and out of the papers in 48 hours."[51]

Johnson & Johnson adopted a similar strategy of openness and became a model for how to handle a crisis when cyanide-laced Extra Strength Tylenol caused seven deaths in Chicago in 1982. Media cooperation was a departure from the company's previous media relations posture, although in fairness such a decision must have been easier to make because company officials knew the tragedy was not their fault. Media interest was immediate and intense. "We decided right away to answer every single press inquiry," said Lawrence C. Foster, then vice president for communications. Over the weekend following the tragic poisonings, the company, which gets three or four calls from reporters on a normal day, answered nearly 300 media calls.[52] Chairman James Burke appeared on TV programs like *Donahue* and *60 Minutes*. When the company decided to keep the Tylenol brand alive in a repackaged container, it hosted a massive news conference via a 30-city teleconferencing hookup. Ironically, then, the media—which had unwittingly created a potential marketing disaster for Tylenol—became the vehicle for its comeback.

Johnson & Johnson said it received more than 125,000 press clippings on the tragedy, nearly all of them favorable. Tylenol regained more than 80 percent of the market share it held before the poisonings, a feat one market analyst called "a miracle, pure and simple."[53] "Johnson & Johnson has effectively demonstrated how a major business ought to handle a disaster," wrote Jerry Knight in *The Washington Post*. "From the day the deaths were linked to the poisoned Tylenol until the recall . . . J&J has succeeded in portraying itself to the public as a company willing to do what's right regardless of cost. Serving the public interest has simultaneously saved the company's reputation. That lesson in public responsibilities—and public relations—will survive at J&J regardless of what happens to Tylenol."[54]

Power of the Wire Services

Johnson & Johnson's Tylenol ordeal demonstrated the value of openness and consistency with the media when an organization finds itself involved in a major disaster. Such responsiveness does not always mean the end of the story, however. Sometimes publicity begets publicity.

If a wire service picks up your news and transmits it to their member newspapers or stations, you could get calls from reporters across the country or on the other side of the world. Or the news could be carried by smaller papers and stations with limited staff exactly as received—the so-called rip and read style of journalism.

This practice makes it critical in bad news situations that you maintain a close working relationship with local bureau chiefs of wire services so that they are more likely to call you for comment and to verify stories before they are sent out over the wires. It also argues for you to make a practice of delivering your releases to wire services first.

You may want to consider subscribing to Associated Press, Dow-Jones or other wire services, or hiring an agency to do so, depending on the nature of your business, so you can monitor and immediately correct any erroneous or misleading information that goes out on your organization over the wires. What wire services transmit in the first few minutes after news breaks has a significant impact on the way a story is covered in your area, throughout the nation and sometimes even internationally. Thousands of publications or stations reaching millions of people get much of their news from wire services, so their influence should not be underestimated.

Internet—Both a Curse and a Blessing in Crises

Ongoing monitoring of Internet coverage is equally important. The Internet has put a great deal of power and reach into the hands of individuals. Anyone with a grudge and a computer can spew out hostile messages. On cyber-radio, would-be disk jockeys and talk show hosts broadcast commentary around the world. Rogue Web sites spring up overnight and die in a matter of days or weeks, leaving serious damage behind.

Do key word searches regularly so you are not sabotaged by negative or erroneous information on your organization that could have been corrected or explained. The vast reach of the Web increases the visibility of any bad publicity, true or not. But if you track and promptly correct rumors on the Internet, they are less likely to make it into print or television. Burrelle's offers a tool that monitors Web dialogue: CyberTalk tracks what's being said in newsgroups, chat rooms, user groups and forums daily, matching new messages against key words defined by the client.

Terri Holbrooke, president of Ziff-Davis brand and market services, says that the Internet "is a Petri dish for gossip and rumor. I don't think we've ever seen a medium where there is so much ability for people to get completely unfiltered information about your company and for that to fester so quickly. It's like watching a film of a Petri dish where mold is growing, but it's in quick time. It can happen overnight."

She points out that the Internet makes communications more inclusive and less exclusive. "There are hundreds of messages going out every day. Figure out where they are going. Figure out who's talking about you in what chat room in which Web site. And make sure you know that stuff the way you used to in your early career when you read the press clips every Monday morning."[55]

As Harold Weinstein, CEO of Princeton, NJ consulting firm Caliper told *Fortune*: "The way the world does business—not just your office but the whole world—has changed irrevocably."[56]

HealthSouth Corporation learned the hard way the negative power of untrue information from anonymous critics on the Internet. CEO Richard Scrushy was making the rounds of investor conferences when analysts told him of a bulletin board devoted to his company that was carrying messages relating to billing fraud, executive wife swapping and love affairs. One posting called the company a house of cards starting to tumble. All the information was false. Using what the *Wall Street Journal* called "cybersleuths and shoe-leather detectives," HealthSouth began unmasking the message writers and sued to put a stop to their postings. One was the husband of a disgruntled employee. Another was an ex-employee.

Said the *Wall Street Journal*: "Until the Internet came along, the traffic in opinion about stocks and bonds was largely—and for the most part calmly—controlled by Wall Street analysts. The message boards, however, let all comers vent their feelings, and that's the root of a growing problem for corporate executives: To ignore the postings is to risk seeing them grow even more outrageous and spread."[57]

On the other hand, the Internet can be your first line of defense when your organization is under attack. It provides a wonderful capacity to speak directly to your target audiences, without having your messages filtered through the media. Go around them by directing your target audiences to your Web site and establishing a crisis update center on line. Put spokespersons in chat rooms—clearly identified as your organization's staff or you soon will be outed by astute chat room visitors. Establish multi-lingual sites if the crisis involves countries speaking languages other than English.

Especially during an emergency, monitor your site to determine not only the number of hits but, more important, how long your visitors stay there as a measure of its usefulness to journalists and others. Learn what makes reporters come to your site—what they need, not just what you want to tell them. Research has shown that when reporting breaking stories after normal business hours, reporters try for their regular source first and then turn to the organization's Web site.[58] And remember that the Internet is not a broadcast medium but an interactive one.

The Internet also can be a valuable early warning device to alert you to customer concerns. Consider how differently the Intel Pentium chip fiasco would have played out if they had paid attention from the beginning to the cascading customer complaints on the Internet.

Lessons Learned

George Stephanopoulos, long-time adviser to President Bill Clinton, offered advice to political candidates running in the 2000 elections that applies equally well to organizations preparing crisis plans: "Know your weaknesses," he says. "Research all your own vulnerabilities before your enemies do."[59]

Most misconceptions begin with a certain element of truth. Look at how your policies and practices could be perceived by others, especially those who are not admirers of your organization or industry. If there is even a hint of scandal, heed the advice of veteran *Washington Post* reporter Bob Woodward. In his 1999 book, *Shadow: Five Presidents and the Legacy of Watergate*, Woodward said it is imperative to release the facts as soon as possible lest questions harden into "a permanent state of suspicion and warfare."[60]

Ronald L. Levy, media expert and president of North American Precis Syndicate, Inc., advises: "Be pre-emptive. The best time to avoid a media disaster is the same as the best time to avoid a fire or explosion in the plant—before it starts." He points out that almost always when an industry is attacked, it is on the basis of the same two allegations—that the industry is making too much money or that it is endangering the public in its manufacturing process, product safety or waste disposal. Levy says the answer is to prepare for the "making too much" charge by showing "what you are doing with the money to protect the public." Examples might include additional safety measures to protect the environment, packaging the product in top quality and sterile materials, and supplying free products to those who serve the poor.

"Focus on the ultimate weapon of modern PR—the truth," says Levy.[61] Turnaround PR experts have shown that with good planning, communications skills and the facts, much of the potential damage of negative publicity can be mitigated.

Nonetheless, it is important that you and your management recognize that incomplete and sometimes inaccurate media coverage is inevitable in crisis situations. Perhaps all you can realistically hope for when you are involved in negative news is that the media get most of the facts right and portray your organization as being concerned and actively involved in fixing what went wrong. Including a positive and personable quote from your CEO high up in the news release or response statement, faxing or electronically transmitting the story to the media, beating your opposition to the wire services so your statement is carried first, initiating phone contacts and offering to set up interviews for key reporters, answering media questions late into the night—all these tactics will go a long way toward ensuring fair coverage for your company or client.

Clearly, honesty is always the best policy because reporters and the public will eventually learn that they have been fed half-truths or had information withheld. In the final analysis it will be the professional relationships you have established over the years with the news media—combined with the essential rightness of your organization's position—that will determine how reporters and editors handle your news.

Effective news media relations is much like effective selling—it takes time to position yourself in journalists' minds as a necessary and credible resource over the long term and to build relationships with new reporters who have come on the scene. Because they control the main channels for the rapid dissemination of information in a bad news situation, reporters' attitudes are of paramount importance to you. Their misunderstanding or hostility could garble—or perhaps completely change—your message before it reaches their readers or viewers, who are your customers, employees, volunteers, suppliers and shareowners. Whether or not they have a legal right to such information, these stakeholders are demanding to know how organizations that affect their lives socially and economically conduct their affairs—particularly when something goes wrong.

The true test of your media relations skills, top management's confidence in you and, ultimately, your organization's standing in the community will come in a negative situation. Indeed, it will be your record of accuracy, honesty and plain speaking that will give you credibility and carry your company or client successfully through the emergency.

Helpful Hints from Journalists

At the 14th annual spring seminar of the Arthur Page Society in New York in April 1999, two panels of journalists offered tips on how reporters and media relations professionals can best work together. Here are some hints relating to crisis planning and communications:

We haven't been 9 to 5 for ages. Increasingly, it's around the clock. It would make our life great if any time there is a story that breaks, there are PR people that we can find at 3 in the morning, 4 in the morning. . . . For us to go on the air and say, "This is what's happening but the company is not available for comment," I could be doing 10 reports before the company makes a comment. And each time we have to say, "They're not available," people are sort of sitting at home thinking about what it means. The other thing that's very helpful is when you call somebody early in the morning and they say, "I don't know. I just got in. We have no idea what's going on." Then they'll tell me, "Please call back in an hour. We'll have a statement." That's hugely helpful. I can say, "The company will have something available for us later."

—Rhonda Schaffler
CNN Financial News

There have been a number of companies where there were major scandals going on. And when something like that comes out, we want to report on it. And yet when we go to the particular company, the door is slammed in our face. That means we have to go to all these outside people, whether it's analysts or competitors or a board member who has left, to put together the story. So my question to you is, how can you help us get the information we need to do a balanced story? I have a suggestion, though. I think one of the best investments that any company can make right now, going into the new century, is to have a broadcast facility in your company. A number of companies have already done this so that we can interview your top management, whether it's the CEO or the CFO or whoever [without their having to leave their office]. And go digital, too, because that's where all of us are going.

—Susie Gharib
"Nightly Business Report"

The world today is non-stop. Markets trade 24 hours a day, and information is dispensed from so many outlets that never used to exist. And it is a lot more out of your control than it ever was before. I think an interesting reaction to the lack of control, or less control, that you have nowadays is a sense that I'm getting from many corporate communications people, that there is a tendency to pull back on information. You've got rumors, you've got dis-information, you've got the Internet, you've got newsletters, you've got all different kinds of places that are spewing out what may or may not be real facts. And there's almost a reaction of retrenchment on the part of some corporate executives. I think that's making your jobs more difficult because the fact of the matter is a journalist needs real information

and good data now more than ever before. And I think that companies need to get that information out now more than ever before.

—Gretchen Morgenson
The New York Times

We rely on a lot of B-roll and video that are sent to us. Although I
spend some time in the field, it's not as much as I'd like to, to be honest. We're expanding our staff and the number of producers because
we'd like to do more field work.

—Martha McCallum
CNBC Business News

From the perspective of a journalist, I think we all know that Wall
Street, even though it's harsh, can be pretty forgiving if someone is
straightforward on the news front. And extremely unforgiving if
something happens a couple of times in a row where promises are
not kept.

—Markus Koch
Germany's CNN affiliate

Test Yourself: Handling a Crisis

Here is an exercise that the public relations directors of The Reader's Digest Association discussed at the Global Public Relations Conference in New York City in 1992. Test yourself to see how you would handle this "crisis."

It is now 3:20 P.M. You are called to your CEO's office where he tells you that the Customer Service Department in your company is being restructured. Some of the work is being given to an outside contractor. As a result, plans call for 40 people in the department to lose their jobs.

- The department is a very important and visible one within the company, and the employees' absence will surely be noticed.
- The department has previously received mentions in the news media because of its important contributions to the company's results and your company's reputation for excellent customer service.
- Construction is underway in your offices and some members of the department have been moved to temporary quarters. The move makes them very unhappy, and they wonder if the company feels customer service is not important any more.
- Twelve of the employees are within two years of retiring.
- Eight have been with the company for more than 20 years.

You return to your office at 4:00 P.M. You have plans to go to the theatre that night, but a reporter calls from the morning newspaper. She says:

> I've heard from sources that your company is eliminating its Customer Service Department and sending all of the work to an outside contractor. I understand two hundred people will lose their jobs. Some employees in other departments say they believe the same thing will happen to them within the next three months. What can you tell me? I need to hear from you no later than 6:30 P.M. for a story that I'm writing for tomorrow's paper.

You call your CEO and he asks you to develop—in the next 50 minutes—a plan to handle the situation and report to the company's Management Committee before you return the reporter's call.

Short Term:
- What is your plan?
- What is your timetable for that evening and the next day?
- How do you address each of your company's target audiences?

Long Term:
- What do you need to do to avoid such a "crisis" in the future?

Chapter 11

MEASUREMENT/EVALUATION
How to Know if
Your Program Is Working

Globally, the number of Web sites used as part of organizational communication increases exponentially each day. In addition, there are hundreds of thousands of daily newspapers, Sunday papers, weekly papers and trade and consumer magazines worldwide. Add to this thousands of television and radio stations, and you can begin to see the scope of a media relations program for your company or organization. While it probably is not the intent of your particular media relations program to reach all of these media outlets, it should be your intent to know, insofar as possible, how many of your targeted media responded to your efforts to communicate about your organization and in what way, and—more important—what action the targeted audience took in response to your message.

Measurement of the various media relations activities is generally the forgotten element of the program. In fact, some handbooks on publicity do not even include a section on measurement. When measurement is mentioned, it is often as a knee-jerk reaction to the question "How did we do on that notice about the new widget?" Measurement should be as well thought-out, as well planned and as well executed as the rest of your media relations program.

You should know if you want to measure:

1. The relationship you have with media representatives;
2. The impact your messages have on the publics you wish to reach (Do they react to your messages the way you want them to? Do they understand your messages? Do they buy your product?);
3. The numbers of people you reach via the media;
4. The way your message is perceived by the public (Do they feel about your organization or product the way you want them to?);
5. How many media use your message;
6. Which media use your message;
7. An estimated value to the organization of your efforts (Was a boycott prevented? Did you receive favorable editorials?).

Organizations that have had a disaster also need to consider evaluating the spillover effect of that disaster onto subsequent public relations and media relations activities. Bad news stays in the public mind for many years and can heavily influence how the public feels about your company, organization, management or campaign.

Innocent attempts at new, positive media campaigns can revive old, bad memories. For example, a story of a new method of cleaning up oil spills can trigger an editor's memory of the Alaskan spill—inevitably linking a good story to a bad one. A long-term, professionally administered measurement of current levels of this "guilt by association" attitude can help you determine when, how and where to launch new media campaigns.

How to Measure

No matter how large or small your operation may be, every well-run media shop should have some method for monitoring and evaluating the results of its output and outcome. For too many years, the rule of thumb on media measurement was counting clips and column inches. That was sufficient unto the day—the day before fragmentation of audiences, electronic media and satellite transmissions. Then, "air time" was added to the mix. Along came "impressions," which is another way to describe circulation and viewing-audience numbers. Then, "advertising equivalents" were touted as a great measurement tool.[1] All of these efforts produce only abstract numbers. They measure output, not outcome.

Dan Burgess of Doe-Anderson PR says, "I would argue that media placement is not necessarily a result; it's just on the way to a result."[2] Dr. Lloyd Corder adds, "There is still greater focus on doing the marketing than on proving it works."[3]

Changes in the media field itself, combined with increased sophistication in measurement techniques, have brought about changes in the way we measure our work. True measurement will show how a designated audience responded or how an activity changed as a result of the media relations effort. Measurement begins with setting measurable objectives that are based on the organization's business goals and not on the process of media relations. If your media relations objective is "to get 1.5 million impressions," then you are measuring your process, not the company's goal of "increasing sales" (see chapter 2).

Do-It-Yourself

Perhaps the simplest way to begin measuring is to create a log of activity. This isn't anything elaborate: make a list of the media you deal with; each time you give them a story, check off if they use it. Over a period of time, you'll get a picture of who uses your material and who doesn't. You'll know which editors you need to see more frequently and which ones need less attention.

If your media relations activities are centered in a small geographic area—a city, county, state, region or province—consider creating your own monitoring/clipping arrangement for both print and electronic media. Begin by subscribing to all the print publications that receive your news releases or are likely to cover your industry or organization. These publications could run the gamut from business and financial publications to detailed engineering journals, trade newsletters and industry-specific magazines.

Assign one person responsibility for reading the publications. This reader will become familiar with the style and arrangement of each of the publications and will not have to waste valuable time wading through sections that would not carry your type of news. The reader also will be in a position to notice if certain publications are changing their style of coverage, if they increase (or decrease) coverage of your company and other trends. Reading should not be given as an extra assignment to a staff person who already has a full workload. Reading should be a primary responsibility, if at all possible. This assures that the reading is done in a timely manner so that results—and any ramifications—are on your desk as soon as possible.

You can create your own form sheet for clips. At the top of the sheet put lines for the name of the publication, the date of publication, and the page number. The reader can then cut or copy each article that pertains to your organization or subject matter and attach the article to the form sheet. Having a form sheet makes distribution, filing and retrieval much easier.

Television and radio monitoring can be as simple or as complex as you desire. The easiest do-it-yourself method is to assign people within your organization to watch specific television stations in your area and/or listen to radio newscasts. With the exception of an all-news network, television has few lengthy news programs and they generally fall into three primary time slots: morning, evening and late evening. Although there are numerous news breaks and news updates throughout the day, your interest probably will be in whether your organization appears during one of the lengthier, prime-time shows.

Radio, on the other hand, has newscasts quite often. They can be every half-hour, every hour or even constant. There are, however, two prime times that may be of interest to you: morning and afternoon commuting times when decision makers, thought leaders and overall business audiences are commuting to and from work.

For both television and radio, the viewer/listener has a relatively simple task of noting the name of the station (call letters as well as popular name), the name of the program and the time of day the item was mentioned. A one-line summary of the content also is useful, such as: "Repeated announcement of new company president," or "Used announcement, mispronounced president's name," or "Information was correct, used film footage of manufacturing facility."

Another way to check on coverage is to daily monitor on-line news sites and electronic newsletters, as well as retrieval services such as Nexis. Bookmark the sites and search for the key words from your release; then, download resulting clips.

Clipping/Monitoring Services

If your activities are far-reaching or complex (for example, a nationwide or international campaign), you may find it advantageous to use clipping and/or monitoring services. What you gain in convenience and peace of mind, however, you might lose in money, as such tracking services can become expensive.

The best way to make sure you are getting full value is to define clearly, both within your organization and with the service, what it is you want monitored or retrieved. By starting out with a well-thought-out program, you stand less chance of being disappointed later. For example, you may want only those clips that carry the name of your organization, such as the American Heart Association, or you may want to have clips that also talk generically of your product or service offering, such as heart disease information or heart transplants. There also might be variations of your organization's name which should be noted by the clipping agency. Be clear about which publications should be scanned.

If your organization is considering launching a media relations or public relations campaign, you may wish to monitor other organizations' activities to help give you an idea of how your campaign might be received. For instance, if your company is going to introduce a new method of installing solar heating units, you might want to see what the media is currently saying about solar heat generally and installation of heating units specifically. You might want to-determine the media's understanding of solar heating or the types of artwork or photography used most often. As another example, you might want to be aware of the public's attitude about care of the elderly before introducing a new senior citizen program.

As you can see, a tracking service can be as finite or as general as you direct. Certainly, such a service can be more thorough than you or your staff members because it has professionally trained people and the technology to scan and retrieve items. These tracking agencies vary in pricing methods. Some may charge a flat fee for a specified number of print clips; others may charge a monthly reading rate plus a cost per clip. The important thing here is to check costs ahead of time and try to anticipate which system will be better for your organization.

Many of the agencies offer electronic clips as well. They record both radio and television newscasts on a local, regional or even national level, sort through the newscasts on playback and listen for clients' names or subject areas. International tracking also is available, but because of costs and technology differences you should be sure you want to avail yourself of this service.

Electronic clips can be offered to the client in two ways: a copy of the audio- or videotape or a transcript of the segment of the program pertaining to the client. Either way can be quite expensive if you are in the media extensively. You should think out carefully the possible uses for such electronic clips before paying to search them. For instance, do you really need six variations of the same product announcement? Or ten radio spots naming your new president? What use do you have for the electronic clips? These tapes take up shelf space quickly and can devour a budget rapidly.

One advantage in using a tracking agency is that the service will provide up-to-date circulation or viewing/listening audience figures. A return of only one clip on your news release might not seem too successful until you are able to note that the item was used on network nightly news or in the morning paper with a circulation of one million.

What to Do with Results

In spite of claims of the "paperless office," many media relations offices look like the last vestiges of a pack rat convention. Clips, newspapers, magazines and tear sheets litter the confines. The problem is that few people know what to do with all the clips after they come in. There are several solutions to this dilemma, all of which clearly point to one thing: document your successes and failures, and let others in your organization know what is happening.

The simplest way to accomplish this is to organize your clips. Make copies of the articles found by your reader and/or your clipping service, and then present the copies to the key executives who should be informed on a daily basis of news about the organization or anything that might affect it. A variation of this procedure is to take the clipped articles and write a synopsis of each. The final piece, which should be no more than one or two pages, can be reproduced each day, again for immediate circulation to executives.

Either method performs a highly needed service for your key officers. They do not have the time to peruse all the publications that deal with your industry or service area. They look to you to perform that service. The clips or synopses do not have to be specifically about your organization, but they should be relevant to the business.

A more detailed presentation of clips should include an analysis. For example, if you have announced the closing of a manufacturing location that employed one thousand people, you probably are anxious to know how the media dealt with that story. Did they treat it objectively? Were the editorials damaging or supporting? Were the explanations of the closing repeated accurately? Was there additional pick-up on the wire services? What type of photo coverage accompanied the story?

Gathering all of the clips, both print and electronic, and answering these types of questions will help you identify certain traits about the media, reporters and newscasters. You might notice that one reporter seemed to consistently misunderstand, and thus misrepresent, the story behind the closing while all others got the story correct. You might also notice that all the headlines or television leads were straightforward and not misleading or of the tabloid variety.

This information tells you that you—and the executives who helped you—put together material that was easily understood. It tells you that the media have an understanding of the situation and that your story was handled fairly with only the one exception. You cannot ask for much more than that. The lone, differing reporter should be invited in for a briefing on the business; clearly, he or she misunderstood. The people who assisted you should be given a pat on the back for their efforts.

This type of analysis ideally should be done with each major news event. It also can be done over an extended period of time with an ongoing, low-key campaign. For example, a campaign might be created to increase public awareness of the many ramifications of drunk driving. Articles supporting this theme would be placed with general and trade media over a long period of time—a minimum of a year, although two to three years would be better. Remember: as with advertisements, the public begins to retain a message only after hearing or seeing it several times.

Clips of the articles would be gathered and kept. Periodic reports could be prepared showing: how many articles have appeared; how many people read those articles; which geographic regions used the articles the most; what type of headlines appeared; what types of audiences read the material; if the articles were completely rewritten or used almost in the original form; how many additional articles were created by the media based on information that was sent out.

The nice thing about a long-term project such as this one is that the program can be changed along the way to counter any negative items that might be appearing. For example, if the articles are being totally rewritten, then you need to look again at your releases to find out why. Are they not in the proper journalistic style? Are they full of typos? Did you fail to include your contact name and number?

If articles are not being run in certain publications, find out why. Do they not fit the style of the publication? Are they going to the wrong editor? Are they missing the deadlines?

The final report on a long-term project should talk about both the positives and negatives. It should tell what was accomplished by the campaign and explain both how the external audience benefited from it and what the internal media relations staff learned from it.

Clips also can be used to spot trends in your industry or service area. If coverage of your organization changes, perhaps it is because of new activities in Washington from environmentalists or labor lobbyists. Perhaps something else has occurred to make reporters and editors look anew at your company, industry or organization.

Where to keep clips—if you keep them at all—can sometimes be a problem. If you have announced the opening of a new office or the receipt of a major quality award, then all the clips of that announcement clearly should go with the archives. But what of the others?

A clever way to distribute clips is to look for people in the organization who might have an interest in the story. Attorneys, for example, often need clips that mention your company or association in regard to a particular activity, such as pending litigation, resolved litigation or just in reference to a general topic, such as safe manufacturing procedures, tariffs, labor regulations, environmental laws or international law. Attorneys also will be interested in clips that show possible trends that might affect them: increasing numbers of age discrimination suits, possible ramifications of transborder data flow or Good Samaritan laws.

Clips mentioning employees should be sent to those employees as a courtesy service from the media relations group. Even if an employee bowls a three hundred game in another league and it somehow shows up in your clips, send it to the employee with a congratulatory note. If one of your executives gives a speech to a local civic organization and it is written up, he or she would appreciate having the clips. When you send out a news release announcing a new executive, keep track of the resulting coverage for your own analysis, but also send copies of the clips to the executive. The subject-matter experts you use as spokespersons for interviews also would appreciate clips on their topics as well as copies of the articles in which they appeared. Clips on products can go to the appropriate product manager or market manager. Clips talking about what a good corporate citizen your company is should be shared with as many people as possible.

Technology to the Rescue?

Introduction of software tools can often help the beleaguered media relations person who is operating a one-person shop. Or not.

Some software, such as PRTrak, created by TRAKWare, Inc., easily calculates ad-equivalent data, which the company calls "media value," because they believe "a story has an objective value because it is sold daily in the market." This is still an abstract number measuring output, not outcome, and measuring the process rather than the result.

The software also has a qualitative side. Along with entering hard data (date of placement, outlet, air time, column inches, etc.), a user can enter self-selected subjective measurement fields such as number of messages delivered and story slant (positive, neutral or negative) on a 1–10 rating scale. The resulting information tells how the media used the story. It does not, however, tell how the audience acted on that information.[4]

Edelman Public Relations Worldwide uses its own Edelman Media Analysis and Planning tool which "doesn't just tell users where the story appeared—but also who exactly read it."[5]

Getting more detailed information about the audience is an additional help. However, the media plan should have clearly identified the audiences and the media needed to reach them. Determining who read or saw your news items after the process is completed seems a wasted effort.

While media relations software can be of great help in keeping qualitative data on your program and process, it probably isn't the way to try to measure outcome. Setting measurable objectives will result in outcome measurement.

Measuring Actions and Behaviors

Measuring how people react to a media relations campaign is something best left to public opinion experts and pollsters. There are times when this knowledge will be essential for strategic planning, so it will be worth the time and money invested.

Quite simply, all you are trying to find out is whether or not the public acted in a way you wanted them to because of your media program. It could be that one of the objectives of your campaign to increase public awareness of the ramifications of drunk driving was to get the public to write to their congressional representatives for new legislation. To get feedback as to whether or not your objective was met would require the assistance of professional public-opinion gatherers. On a more easily measurable level, you might just need to know how many people attended the open house of your new facility or the festival in the park as a result of your media efforts.

Determining Attitudes

Determining how people feel about your organization also is something that can be done professionally. There are ways to find out if your print and electronic clips are viewed as positive, neutral or negative. Although you might be able to guess at such responses based on key verbs and adjectives in the articles, it still is best to have an objective, outside firm perform this service for you. Such information can be vital during critical times in your organization's life—for example, during labor negotiations or a major catastrophe. The objective is to see if the message you are sending is received as a positive or neutral message. If the message is perceived as negative, you can at best hope to pull it up to neutral. The important item to note is that you can measure beyond the number of column inches and numbers of clips—*and determine impact as well as volume*.

Combining all these measurements for a long-term campaign can produce astonishing results. Returning to the drunk driving campaign as an example, we can find out:

1. how many people are reading/hearing the desired message;
2. in what geographic areas these people reside;
3. which media are using the message;
4. if the public is acting upon our message in the way we want them to;
5. if the public views our message in a positive, neutral or negative manner;
6. if we have done better in the last three months than in the previous three months.

Correlations then can be drawn between the number of drunk driving incidents in a certain geographic area before, during and after the media campaign. If the results are positive, you can share in the credit. If the results are negative, find out why and begin a new campaign.

Medialink Public Relations Research uses a software called InfoTrend to "inform its clients how they are being covered in newspapers, magazines and wire services, television and radio broadcasts and on the Internet. We tell them if they are receiving positive or negative coverage [and] whether their key messages are getting through to the public."[6]

Whatever the method used to determine results, you have evidence that your bottom-line approach to media relations is working.

Media Audits

Unless you are dealing with only a few media, you probably will want to consider a media relations audit every so often. For objectivity, the audit should be done for you, rather than by you.

The media relations audit works like this. An opinion research firm surveys editors, news directors and key reporters in the region you specify. The questionnaire can be structured to deal with any aspect of news media relations you want it to. Generally, the survey asks about several companies simultaneously to avoid the "halo syndrome" where the editor might say good things about your organization because you are asking and you are a friend. Having several companies participate also cuts down on the costs.

The surveyors ask such questions as how responsive an organization is to media inquiries, whether the editor knows whom to contact for information at an organization, the quality of the news releases received and the courtesy of the organization in dealing with the media.

This type of audit actually measures the relationship you have with the media representatives. So, when the audit comes back saying you have some journalists out there who do not think you are doing a very good job, you know you have to start from square one to build a better relationship.

An audit also will help you continue to meet the needs of the media, which should be one of your primary functions. An audit can be expensive, but it is well worth the effort if your media relations program is extensive and if you have several people in your shop and want to make sure they all have good relationships with the media on their beat. Unless you know your way around polling techniques and statistical analysis, you probably should not conduct such an audit yourself.

No matter what the extent of your media operations, you should have built-in measurement techniques. After all, you have put a lot of work into creating a program that will tell your organization's story to the public or offer your products to an audience. Surely you want to measure the impact of that story and relate how that helps your organization meet its goals and objectives. To do any less would be less than your best professional work.

Chapter 12

THE FUTURE
Expanding Your Counselor Role

There is an old saying among media relations counselors—and CEOs—that there is no such thing as a good surprise. The objective of effective PR counseling is to anticipate and identify developing issues early so your organization can help shape those issues instead of just react to them. This proactive posture guarantees a minimum of surprises, good and bad.

Important issues may surface in the community, the industry, or within the ranks of your own organization. They can have a nationwide or global impact. They might involve employee matters, politics, health care, privacy or the environment. The possibilities are endless. Many are fundamentally "wallet issues," affecting people's financial and emotional well-being.

If an issue has the potential to some day affect your organization, it is your job to understand that issue and share your knowledge with the decision makers of your organization. PR counseling, though, goes beyond sharing information. As a PR counselor, you also should help your organization develop a position on emerging issues, and manage the business to avoid negative situations and capitalize on opportunities. Think of yourself as an ombudsman. In addition to being the eyes and ears of your organization, you sometimes have to be the conscience as well. Being an effective counselor is one of the most important and demanding roles of the media relations professional.

As a counselor, you need to be part of the decision-making

process in your organization. You must:

- Have constant access to the CEO and other key executives.
- Be part of the strategic planning team for your organization's business activities.
- Have "a seat at the management table" when debate is underway and decisions are being made.
- Help management consider the long-term strategic and "image" implications of your company's response to an issue.
- Ensure that your company's policy-formation process gets the benefit of a broad perspective and variety of opinions, both inside and outside the organization.
- Have media relations and other communications functions included in your organization's business plans.

If you are being called in only after decisions are made, you are not practicing PR counseling.

Building Your Credibility

While media relations professionals generally are well informed, you can increase your chances of recognizing important issues early by paying careful attention to all media, traditional and new, not just those that cover your business and industry regularly:

- Read a wide variety of media—not just the business and trade press but also "alternative" press and publications devoted to subjects and ideologies outside the scope of your industry. Do key word searches on the Internet and visit opinion-leading Web sites.
- Read editorials consistently and be alert to new subjects and shifts in the opinions of thought-leaders.
- Monitor letters-to-the-editor sections in newspapers and magazines, especially in the more prestigious publications, as well as newsgroups, chat rooms, user groups and forums on the Internet. Important new issues or changes in viewpoints on old ones often get their first public exposure in these arenas.
- Pay attention to better-quality TV and radio talk shows and interview programs, which are good sources of perspectives on issues.

- Maintain informal contacts with key media people. Seek their opinions. Get them to share their experiences with you.
- Build internal alliances and a strong informal network of source people within your organization. They can alert you to developing trends within your industry and markets, and changes in courses of action that are needed.

To get the attention of your senior management, you have to earn their respect through your performance. Top executives and other decision makers within your organization will find it difficult to take advice on media relations and other communications issues from anyone who does not have a thorough understanding of the business. You must constantly update your knowledge of the organization, its strategy, its position in the marketplace, and its growth and expansion plans. Demonstrate this knowledge for the management team by connecting it to the advice you give.

When you make a presentation to management or the board on the importance of an issue, support your evaluation with facts—for example, opinion poll or research results, news media reports, speech excerpts from opinion leaders, and your operations colleagues' evaluation of its relevance to the business. Important issues—especially emerging issues—usually have many interpretations. Your own interpretation is part of the value you contribute as a PR counselor. To protect your credibility, though, you should make your management aware of other views on the same issue by different interest groups.

Expanding Your Role

The evolution from communicator to counselor is so natural and so subtle that you may not be aware of the metamorphosis until it has occurred. One day you are responding to a journalist's question on why your organization has a certain policy on drug abuse in the workplace. While your lips are providing the answer, your mind is asking, "Why indeed?" Or you might be briefing a spokesperson for your organization before a major media interview, when suddenly it becomes obvious to both of you that a particular personnel practice is woefully out of date. So together you work out a plan to change it. Perhaps you are writing remarks on your organization's global marketing strategy for your CEO to deliver at a news conference when you cross the line from simply articulating someone else's policy to actually participating in policy formation yourself.

Your role has changed. Your responsibilities expand. As a stained-glass window diffuses the light that passes through it, enhancing the light by the addition of myriad beautiful colors, you find yourself contributing to your organization's policies and helping to shape its future. You have become an entrepreneur in the broadest sense, whether or not you run your own company, because you are truly breaking new ground. You have become a public relations counselor.

You still will spend time answering questions from reporters and preparing media plans. But more and more you will find yourself focusing on communications strategy, being a champion and agent of constructive change, and giving advice—on issues as complex as your CEO's responsibilities, as broad as your organization's business, as fundamental as its culture and values.

Harold Burson, founder of Burson-Marsteller, describes the evolution brilliantly: When public relations was in its infancy, clients called on their PR people to ask, "How should I *say* it?" As the profession became more sophisticated, the question evolved to, "*What* should I say?" At the next level it became, "*How* should we *do* it?" And at the highest level it became, "*What* should we *do*?" As that question has changed over the last few decades, so our function has changed and grown as well.

Such breadth means that we must have a thorough understanding of our organization's business strategy and marketing plans, internal challenges and future opportunities, customers and competitors—and we must learn to think strategically. Indeed we must think—and regard ourselves—as general managers, not just as media relations professionals. We need to become, as management consultant Harry Levinson puts it, "organizational radar, taking soundings and helping to steer rather than expecting to be piloted."

Alumni of AT&T's public relations organization are very proud of Arthur Page, who first demonstrated the relevance of PR to corporate policy formation. He was recruited after the CEO, Walter Gifford, had read Page's articles about the responsibilities of business toward its customers and its publics. Gifford told Page that since he was so good at telling business how it should act responsibly, he should come to work at AT&T and try putting those edicts into practice. Page agreed—but not until he was assured he was being hired not as a publicist or a rewrite man but rather as a contributor to policy and a full-fledged member of the AT&T senior management team. He became an AT&T vice president from 1927 to 1946, the first person in a PR position to serve as an officer and member of the board of directors of a major public corporation.[1] Arthur Page's legacy has been passed on not only to AT&T PR people but to our entire profession.

Similarly, when President Kennedy asked Edward R. Murrow to become director of the U.S. Information Agency, Murrow reportedly responded that he would be happy to do so "provided it is understood that I shall be in on the takeoffs as well as the crash landings."[2] That is a position we all argue for—albeit perhaps not so cleverly. Too often the task of media relations people is to make the rough *appear* smooth, rather than to apply sandpaper carefully to make that objective a reality.

Influencing Actions and Behaviors

In chapter 10, for example, we discussed ways your expertise could offer temporary relief from the symptoms in crises. In this chapter we will address ways you can help cure the disease.

As Eli Lilly CEO Randall L. Tobias put it, too much emphasis on how and what we communicate

> is nothing more than a Band-Aid on some symptoms, not a cure for anything very important. Integrating what we speak and write is no substitute for integrated *behavior*—shared behavior that is single-mindedly focused on customers and their needs, as well as the needs of each of the other stakeholders of the corporation. . . . In my view, the activities of communications professionals are not simply the means to other ends, and not ends unto themselves.

> For me, communications must be defined to include all forms of a corporation's behaviors toward all of its stakeholders. For me, integrated communications is just another form of cross-functional teamwork. It's silo-busting—doing away with fiefdoms—doing away with turf. Another way, in other words, for an organization to do the right thing. . . . I believe the most effective public relations organizations are the ones who are embracing change and leading the transformation of communications integration within their own institutions. As I define it, communications is the sum of all the activities that demonstrate—through actions—what a business really stands for.[3]

Presidential speechwriter, political analyst and author Peggy
Noonan reinforces the importance of substantive policy rather than
merely pretty words:

> Style enhances substance; it gives substance voice, it makes a mes-
> sage memorable, it makes policy clear and understandable. But it is
> not itself the message. Style is not a replacement for substance, and
> cannot camouflage a lack of substance. And where there is no sub-
> stance, the style will perish. You cannot be eloquent about nothing.[4]

Involvement Brings Responsibility

The access that our media relations responsibilities gives us—
not only to top management but also to the decision-making processes of our company or client—brings with it a great obligation.
We can take apparently random sequences of events and help
translate them into an actionable agenda. We can ensure that our
organization's decision makers have access to public opinion and
attitudes so they can evaluate their actions against perception as
well as reality. After all, every misconception begins with a certain
element of truth. Much like products, public issues also have life
cycles. We can help identify emerging issues early enough so our
organizations can shape and manage them rather than merely
respond.

Counseling is much more than offering advice. It acts as a
strategic glue, bringing together input from all available external
and internal sources to ensure a "catholic" rather than a "parochial" view. It is selectively sorting information and focusing only
on events that are important and contribute to understanding. A
good counselor will relate and interpret the facts; a great one will
understand and enhance the meaning.

Harold W. Burlingame, an executive vice president at AT&T,
advises:

> You should try to get yourself positioned as one who has a special
> sensing system and thus can anticipate problems in time to solve
> them before they erupt publicly. Public relations people need to be
> an integral part of the planning process if you are to help your orga-
> nization anticipate and prepare for change. To be credible, however,
> you have to demonstrate a solid understanding of the business and
> appreciation for its operations problems. Without that knowledge
> you will have great difficulty being accepted as an equal member of
> the management team.[5]

Inevitably there will be those who continue to slot their line and staff people into different categories, tolerating discussion of emerging issues only in ivory-tower offices and insisting that concerns such as budgets, production timetables and inventory control dominate the time of operations managers. These executives must have forgotten the lessons learned by General Motors, which watched helplessly as the power of Ralph Nader and his consumer movement grew strong enough to kill the Corvair. Or they choose to ignore the experience of nonprofit associations and arts groups, which ceased to exist after government grants dried up because they had not previously developed community loyalty and deep financial ties with their constituents.

Business Problems Are PR Problems

Almost all the critical problems facing your organization today and in the future are public relations problems in the broadest sense of the term. Like Rubik's cube, the solutions can be deceptively simple in appearance. But the cosmetic touches of a publicity program cannot obscure deeper blemishes in organizational policy or practice for long. You can help your top management look at each problem strategically, searching for well-thought-out actions that contribute to permanent resolution. You can apply a touch of healthy skepticism since, as Carl Sagan put it: "Skeptical scrutiny is the means . . . by which deep insights can be winnowed from deep nonsense."[6] You can reflect shareowner sentiment, customer concerns and employee expectations, for you are their voice within your organization just as you are its ears and eyes in the community and the marketplace. Instead of expending energy criticizing the media for inaccurate reporting, you can help your top management address the policies and practices that prompt investigative journalism and negative news stories.

You have an opportunity to use the unique window you have to public opinion—those constant contacts with the news media—to act as an early warning system for the decision makers of your organizations, to perceive not only what is going on around you but also what is coming. You can become a catalyst for change. Like truffle hounds—dogs used in France to root out delicacies from under ground—you can search for signs of emerging concerns so your organization has a head start in addressing those that merit attention.

The length and breadth of the list may be awesome. Isolating and defining the underlying causes may be difficult, much like grappling with Jell-O. To be effective, solutions must reflect an objective analysis of the problem, rather than merely respond to the needs of your company or client. As Reader's Digest Association retired Chairman and CEO George V. Grune put it,

> The combination of knowledge, judgment, instinct and skills will result in a solid working relationship with your senior management. They will come to rely on you as one who provides added value when they are making major decisions affecting the business—decisions on a wide variety of topics from expanding into new markets and launching new products to downsizing a department and laying off employees.[7]

Some Current Issues to Watch

Throughout this book we have given specific examples of what you need to be aware of in your capacity as a media relations professional. Here we offer as examples a selection of some of the issues you may encounter as you move into the capacity of counselor. These are issues facing many organizations, depending on their type and on how they do business.

Corporate Governance

World-renowned, blue-chip American companies including AT&T, General Motors, American Express, IBM, Westinghouse, Sears, Kodak and Eli Lilly replaced their chief executive officers under pressure from their boards of directors or investors in the 1990s. "Shareholders were always the owners of public companies," explained Richard M. Clurman. "But in another era they quietly sold their stock and bought another if they were dissatisfied with their investment. . . . No longer. Today shareholder complaints are a noisy rock and roll amplified by the media around a bandstand labeled 'corporate governance.'"[8] John L. Grant, a director of Air Products & Chemicals in Allentown, Pennsylvania, agreed. In a *Wall Street Journal* article titled, "Shield Outside Directors from Inside Seduction," he wrote: "Corporate governance is a hot topic these days, inflamed by the lethargic response of boards to underperformance by corporate managements. The same questions always emerge: 'What are the directors doing? Are they asleep? Are they in management's pocket?'"[9]

Television commentator John Chancellor put it this way in the introduction to a PBS program titled, *Battles in the Boardroom*:

> As news about corporations and their executives moves from the business page to the front page, we're becoming aware of the changing dynamics of American business. Corporate chairmen and chief executives who once seemed unassailable are toppled from power. Powerful new forces are at work in today's corporations. Shareholders, management, employees, inside directors, outside directors and the community at large all have a vested interest in the successful operation of a company's business. But how does a board of directors resolve these conflicting responsibilities? How is that accomplished in the face of escalating executive compensation, global economic pressures and discontent in the ranks of shareholders who are becoming increasingly powerful?[10]

Corporate governance issues make front-page headlines, bringing dramatic media attention and widespread public interest to subjects that previously were buried in boardrooms or shareholder materials. They become important opportunities for counselors because the solutions cross disciplines from public relations and legal to investor relations and finance and affect virtually all the organization's target audiences.

Executive Pay

Few topics make management more uncomfortable and employees more concerned with fairness than the issue of executive pay. In the 1990s, the subject was splashed on magazine covers and the front pages of newspapers. It also became a hot issue on radio and TV talk shows, and in Internet chat rooms. In a cover story on executive pay, subtitled "Compensation at the top is out of control. Here's how to reform it," *Business Week* pointed out that American companies were losing competitive "ground to foreign rivals, whose chiefs are often paid pittances by U.S. standards." The magazine also quoted Stanley C. Gault, then chairman of Goodyear Tire and Rubber Co., as saying too often pay isn't linked to how well the company's owners do and "the only one who gets the short end of the stick is the shareholder."[11]

A year later *Business Week* again made executive pay a cover story topic. "Reform may be in the works . . . but so far, you wouldn't know it" the magazine headlined, acknowledging "the mounting controversy over the growing paychecks of America's CEOs—not to mention the finger-pointing at complacent directors—seems to be goading many boards into action. Directors are devoting more time to the issue of compensation, often challenging the assumptions that lie behind the pay packages. . . ."[12] *Business Week* also cited stock options as being a big part of the problem. *Financial World* zeroed in on stock options in a column by compensation guru Graef S. Crystal, calling them "stealth compensation."[13]

Shareowners are not the only interested observers following this issue. The topic is of concern to a broad cross-section of the country's population because huge compensation packages sometimes are being paid to management at the same time their organizations are laying off employees, closing facilities and announcing poor earnings.

Work and Family Balance

With record numbers of working women, single parents, two-career couples and an aging population that has made many employees also responsible for elder care, organizations have had to be much more flexible in their approach to employee relations and benefits. As *U.S. News & World Report* put it, "Beyond a doubt, companies today play a larger role in family life than they did a decade ago. Flextime, job sharing, telecommuting and elder care have moved off the pages of human resources journals onto boardroom agendas."[14] A study by the Conference Board, a business research group in New York, documents lower turnover and absenteeism and increased productivity at family-friendly companies.[15]

Today *Fortune, Business Week* and *Working Mother* all rank companies as to whether or not they are the best places to work. When *Working Mother* pioneered the "Best Places to Work" magazine list in 1985, it could barely find enough companies impressive enough to warrant a listing. Now organizations clearly recognize the value of being featured, and have modified their policies to gain recognition. *Fortune* magazine's list debuted in 1998 and immediately became an industry icon, according to *Chief Executive* magazine, since it measured such disparate aspects as a company's culture, work environment, financial security, and time and support for an outside life.

"Companies on that list were suddenly inundated with

resumes, enabling them to hire the cream of the crop," said Louise Rush, a work/life expert at Tandem Performance Institute in San Francisco. With the labor pool tightening and companies looking for ways to boost recruitment and retention, companies scrambled to add so many employee-friendly policies that scores of others fell off the list because they were eclipsed by the offerings of others. Getting on that list not only aids recruitment and retention of staff but also opens the door to new clients.[16] The broad work and family balance issues provide excellent opportunities for PR and human resources professionals to pool their expertise for the good of their organization.

Diversity

Another area where communications and human resources should work in close partnership is helping your organization deal with diversity. The issue first came to many people's attention in the late 1980s at the time of the publication of a landmark report called *Workforce 2000* from the Hudson Institute, a policy research organization in Indianapolis. The report showed that white males were already a minority in the American workplace, and it forecasted that 85 percent of the net growth in the U.S. labor force throughout the rest of the century would be workers who are minorities, white women or immigrants.[17]

By 1993, diversity in the workplace was the most consistently cited emerging "issue of the future" in a survey of corporate communications officers by Burson-Marsteller, a worldwide public relations firm.[18] Today it is an accepted reality and necessity in most organizations. Managing diversity involves helping managers and employees deal with issues of prejudice and stereotypes as nontraditional workers are hired, developed and promoted in organizations. Openness, a willingness to learn about others' culture and values and visible role models all make acceptance and change easier.

The increasing diversity of the workforce is a symptom of marketplace changes as well. Wise organizations will take advantage of the new breadth in their ranks to better understand these markets and to provide new products and services to meet their diverse and changing needs.

Changes in Job Requirements

Unemployment resulting from prior recessions tended to mask a fundamental change in the job market of most industrial nations. Opportunities in manufacturing are both shrinking and changing. Meanwhile, new jobs are surfacing in the high-technology and service sectors—jobs requiring skills that many employees simply do not possess. The semiskilled industrial worker, previously the backbone of smokestack industries such as auto, rubber and steel, is becoming an expensive burden as technological advances such as robots reduce the number of employees needed to produce goods and services.

Equally profound changes are coming to the service and clerical sectors. ATMs have replaced bank tellers, and Internet shopping is beginning to supplant retail clerks. Computers have taken over not only arithmetic previously performed by low-level clerks, but also design work that formerly was the province of graphic artists and engineers. Of greatest significance, technology has created new jobs and an economic boom—and made many millionaires of workers on the bottom rungs and mid-levels as well as in executive suites of high-tech industries.

Issues of the social responsibilities and costs of applying new technology now are being addressed. Retraining workers is likely to become as high a priority as retooling machinery. Legislation has been passed, which requires advance notice to both employees and the community about plans to close a plant or another major facility resulting in heavy job losses. Employers can reduce unemployment tax costs in some areas—and buy public goodwill—by aggressively helping to place their laid-off workers in other jobs. Addressing and communicating such profoundly personal issues may be among our most difficult challenges in the next decade.

Declining Promotion Opportunities

As a result of the baby boom, a large number of workers—most of whom are better educated than their predecessors and approach their work differently—are impatient to move up the organizational ladder. On the opposite end of the spectrum, the trends toward raising or eliminating the retirement age and postponing payment of social security benefits have resulted in older workers wanting to hold on to their jobs. The result is a serious conflict of interests: Women, minorities and younger workers want more and better jobs, but older employees are not leaving their posts and creating openings.

Exacerbating the difficulties are the recent rounds of restructuring, flattening, outsourcing, downsizing and rightsizing in many organizations. As *Fortune* put it, "In this climate the hot new skill for leaders has become the ability to manage chaos—culturally, structurally, emotionally—while participating in the radical transformation of the way your company does business."[19] Promotional possibilities are more limited, and the gap between what people want at work and what is available is widening. To avoid layoffs and create movement, organizations are designing special incentive programs that encourage early retirement. The trick is to avoid losing too many good people or violating age discrimination laws. Again, intensely sensitive and personal concerns are involved.

Quality of Work Life

Organizations must also learn to manage "the new worker"— employees who think of themselves as individuals first and employees second. They bring their own special talents and skills into the workplace, but they also bring a deep concern for how they are treated. Beyond fair play, employees today—regardless of their ages—seek simple trust. They want to be respected enough to be counted on to do right—on their own. They want to put their personal imprint on their work, actively participate in decisions shaping the content of their jobs, and have a significant say in the standards that measure their contributions.

"Quality of Work Life" programs—commonly known as QWL—refer to systematic efforts to involve employees in designing and carrying out improvements in their work conditions. They cover a wide range of areas from different measurement methods to job-sharing proposals. While employees seek more responsibility and involvement in business decisions affecting their lives, their employers are pursuing a different goal: improved productivity and service, plus continuing profit growth. The two objectives are not mutually exclusive. Organizations pioneering in QWL have discovered that involving workers in day-to-day decision making can lead to improvements in productivity and profits as well as service and employee morale. QWL—sensitively and honestly implemented—can become an organization's competitive edge.

Security of Computer Files

The widespread use of computers has made it simpler for businesses and associations to process information rapidly and accurately. Computers also have made it easier for people to make massive mistakes and to steal information. Ensuring the security and integrity of computer files is a fast-growing priority in many organizations. From inadvertent miscalculations of interest due bank customers to deliberate intrusions into a file to introduce "viruses" or to steal or destroy valuable business information, the losses—in terms of dollars and public confidence—can be great.

New insurance policies are being created to cover damage to information as well as property. A growing segment of this new market is malpractice insurance for companies that write software to tell a computer how to perform a particular task. Malpractice insurance is increasingly necessary as computers are used in such life-saving efforts as neurological diagnosis. Off-site storage of back-up computer tapes containing inventory and customer data, and reciprocal agreements between companies to process the tapes in case of a fire, major power failure or other disasters, also increasingly are being included in computer security plans.

Employee and Customer Privacy

With so much personal information stored in computers and other files, and masses of business conducted on the Internet, protecting the privacy of employee and customer information is a volatile issue. Electronic safeguards built into the computer system and its software are valuable, but the collection and retention of unnecessary, out of date and, in some cases, illegal information is what draws a great deal of the concern and attention of consumer groups, legislators and the media. Where we buy our clothes, what restaurants we patronize, how many miles we drive in our cars, whom we phone, how much insurance we carry, which hotels we stay in when we travel, how large our mortgage payments are—such routine yet intensely private information is available in electronic memories when we pay our bills by credit card or check.

Purging nonessential data and severely restricting access to computer files is being legislated where it is not voluntarily accepted as good business practice. The first signal of this trend was passage of the Fair Credit Reporting Act of 1970, a model not only because it was the first major U.S. legislation relating to privacy but also because it granted the individual the right to know what is on file and to disclaim or dispute the information. Subsequent legislation and intense media and consumer interest in the subject—particularly in Brussels where the European Union is establishing new laws for the unified European Community—attest to the importance of this very personal issue.

Protectionism and Other Free Trade Issues

Globalization and increased world competition has created new demands for curbs on imports of products and exports of technology as each country strives to save jobs for its citizens. In the United States, much of the protectionism sentiment is directed at Japan, as that country's products take an increasing share in the auto, electronics and other key markets.

Some governments subsidize their companies' competition in global markets with low-cost loans. In many basic industries, on the other hand, U.S. and Canadian workers' high wages have priced their companies out of world markets. Advances in information networks and transportation systems now allow businesses to set up offshore operations where employees do a variety of tasks from word processing to components manufacturing more cheaply than their North American counterparts.

In retaliation there is a growing movement that calls for a variety of restrictions on foreign competitors or use of overseas workers, requirements for specific percentages of U.S. or Canadian parts and labor in any goods sold in those countries, or aid to workers who lose their jobs because of imports. In the United States several state legislatures have passed procurement preference bills—called "local content" provisions—that would give an advantage to firms whose primary place of business is in that state. Others object to such restrictions, arguing that healthy competition and free trade agreements ensuring the free flow of goods and technology encourage a growing worldwide economy and exchange of scientific ideas.

An Integral Part of the Corporate Planning Process

Donald E. Procknow, retired AT&T technologies vice chairman, no doubt had in mind such a complex and varied group of issues when he said:

> Public relations people should not be used simply to write announcements of what we have decided—or, worse yet, to fancy up words someone else has written. We all benefit when public relations is brought in much earlier in the decisionmaking process. Public relations is a management tool just like any other in the company—a very, very important resource.[20]

Kenneth S. Jamron expanded on that thought when he was president of Deaconness Hospital in Milwaukee, Wisconsin: "I believe communications is such an important function that it cannot be filtered through anyone else. It has to have the highest level and sit in on management decisions."[21]

Charles Marshall, retired chief executive officer of AT&T Information Systems, called his public relations staff "not only the business' communicators, but the business' consciences as well." Paraphrasing the poet Robert Burns, he says we must help our organizations see ourselves as others see us to ensure top management is not insulated—even when hearing the public's or employees' views is painful. Further, he reminds us: "We cannot just react. We must be proactive. Your role is to determine how we want our various publics to view us, and then help us develop a game plan to make it happen. After all, you cannot make us look any better than we deserve to look."[22]

Marshall articulates a view held by an increasing number of CEOs who have given their public relations people a status in the corporate and nonprofit worlds comparable to production, marketing, human resources, legal and finance staffs, because their skills are recognized as vital to setting sophisticated strategies and meeting ambitious objectives.

The Teletype Case

An example of a direct contribution to the development of an organization's business practices by media relations professionals took place at the Teletype Corporation in Illinois. Further, the public relations and marketing people not only began working more closely together but also were integrated into the company's overall corporate business plan.

When John J. Pappas was named president of the corporation, Teletype had been in existence for almost 75 years and a part of AT&T for 50 years, The company employed about 5,000 people who designed, manufactured and marketed data communications products. Headquartered in Skokie, Illinois, Teletype had manufacturing facilities there as well as in Little Rock, Arkansas. In addition, it had a nationwide distribution and service organization. But it suffered from being a subsidiary of a subsidiary. Owned by Western Electric (now Lucent Technologies), which in turn was owned by AT&T, Teletype rarely was considered news by the national business and trade press. Like Cinderella, Teletype people often stayed home and tended house while sister companies garnered the publicity by going to the ball.

AT&T knew that Teletype would play a key role in its future because of its data communications experience. One sign of the company's new prominence was Pappas' appointment—it was the first time Teletype had been headed by a full executive officer from the parent company. That move spawned an active media relations program to generate wider media coverage of Teletype. National business and trade press reporters who cover the communications industry are veteran AT&T watchers, alert to reading between the lines for indications of a change in corporate strategy. No effort had been made to promote Teletype as a separate entity before. Astute reporters read the signals and asked why. Publications such as the *Wall Street Journal, The New York Times, Electronic News, Telephony, Datamation* and *Telecommunications Report* covered the change.

From a strict media relations viewpoint, then, the plan was a success. However, it was becoming clear that Teletype's media relations, sales promotions and employee communications people needed to better coordinate their efforts. As is the case in too many organizations, public relations and marketing were separated philosophically as well as organizationally. Each operated independently, rarely sharing plans or exposing their materials to each other's audience. They did not have management's blessing of their information plans, so they had no assurance their activities were supporting the corporate plan. Media relations responsibilities were split—sales promotions handled the trade press and public relations handled the local media.

Pappas created a six-person task force composed of media relations, marketing and public relations people to come up with recommendations for the corporation. Stressing that their charter was broad, he told task force members at their first meeting: "The areas you should consider are unlimited. I am not prejudging your work, except that I know the situation we are in today needs to be fixed."[23]

It was an assignment based on public relations considerations, to be sure: its objectives were to present a consistent image of Teletype in all media and to all target audiences; to ensure that everyone involved in producing media for Teletype understood the company's corporate objectives and had written, detailed, tactical plans to help achieve them; and to upgrade the professionalism of promotions and communications materials where necessary. The task was rooted in the economic imperatives facing all organizations in these times of scarce and expensive resources. Its overall goal was firmly focused on helping to achieve the corporate mission: To increase sales and to position Teletype as a high-technology market leader.

After two months of analysis, the task force recommended new communications strategies that offered a coordinated, unified approach to Teletype's wide variety of promotional materials—whether they traditionally were perceived as public relations, advertising or marketing media. Included was a new definition of Teletype's current and future business—in effect, a new mission statement—based on interviews with its top executives. The strengths that the company brought to that mission also were documented, later to be translated by its advertising agency into a broad advertising campaign with the theme "Value sets us apart." Media relations activities were expanded and targeted news release lists developed. Public relations and marketing responsibilities were delineated so the skills of both were allied to offer more specialized service to the media and better results to the company.

With its public relations and marketing functions reorganized to exploit each discipline's skills while at the same time pooling knowledge, Teletype was able to take full advantage of the visit to its headquarters of New York and Chicago financial analysts, investment advisors and portfolio managers. Pappas' keynote address became the basis of a news release that was picked up by the local and trade press. The media relations people in Little Rock got coverage in both local papers on their president's visit to the Arkansas plant to give the financial analysts' presentation to employees there. Reprinted in booklet form, Pappas' speech was distributed to employees, reporters, key customers and analysts around the country.

The Teletype case illustrates corporate America's growing belief that media relations and other communications skills can play an important role in increasing sales and contributing to business policy before it is made. That recognition has elevated these functions both literally and figuratively within most organizations to the point where they now are valued participants in top-level councils. As Pappas put it:

> You show me a market-driven organization and I'll show you a place where public relations considerations are an integral part of the

planning process. CEOs should take advantage of all the expertise they can gather before they make decisions. Public relations is a valuable management resource. Media relations specialists in particular can offer insight into the shifting demands of the marketplace as a result of their contacts with reporters, who often reflect our customers' opinions.[24]

The Denny's Case

In 1991, a group of African-American students was asked to prepay for meals at a Denny's Restaurant while a smaller group of white customers was not. The black group hired a civil rights attorney and filed a class-action suit in California against Denny's. That was just the beginning of the crisis that would lead to Denny's diversity turnaround. Two years later a group of African-American Secret Service agents complained that they were not served at a Denny's in Annapolis, Maryland. A second class-action lawsuit was filed, charging Denny's with racial discrimination.

Public relations played a major role in the resolution of this crisis and in the resultant dramatic turnaround in corporate culture at Denny's, demonstrating the value of involved and informed counsel when a company is facing a serious business challenge. In fact, the turnaround at Denny's was so sweeping that within four years, in 1998, Denny's parent company was ranked number two on *Fortune* magazine's list of "The Top 50 Best Companies for Asians, Blacks & Hispanics."

The problem Denny's faced was more than settling the class-action lawsuits; they actually were settled out of court in 1994 for a total of $46 million. The real issue was changing a corporate culture from one in which discrimination had occurred to one that embraced diversity in all of its manifestations and in which there would be "zero tolerance" for discrimination. Karen Randall, vice president of communications for Advantica Restaurant Group, Inc., Denny's parent company, was one of the key players in devising the strategy to create and communicate this new culture. James B. Adamson, Advantica's chairman and CEO, was told a turnaround in Denny's corporate culture would be good for business. "I really didn't care if it was good for business," Adamson said. "It's the right thing to do."

A corporate diversity officer was hired. Then a management team led by Adamson set six objectives: To provide every employee from cook to senior manager with racial sensitivity training; to change the workforce composition to include more minorities and women, especially in middle and senior management positions; to change the composition of the company's board of directors to include more minorities and women; to change patterns of franchise ownership so that more minorities and women owned Denny's restaurants; to seek out and use minority suppliers; and to improve the chain's reputation in the minority community.

It is significant that Advantica's strategy was one of changing the company, not just changing the company's reputation or what key publics thought of it. Adamson and his senior management team knew that some very basic practices within the company had to change. Communications was key to implementing change, but the change itself was about a lot more than communications.

Part of the strategy was to have top-down insistence that change would occur. Adamson was unrelenting in his insistence that Advantica and Denny's would not tolerate discrimination and would insist on a climate where diversity was valued. Another key was admitting Denny's had made mistakes—and then moving forcefully and openly to correct those problems. Denny's used research to develop its turnaround strategy and monitor progress. In 1995, the company held focus groups with white and black customers. The research indicated Denny's needed to get out its message of a changed company—based on a new leadership team and minority involvement in decision making through ownership of franchises and positions in management.

Advantica and Denny's met their objectives, and Adamson says the company has made important strides toward its goal of creating a corporate culture that respects diversity and will not tolerate discrimination. Evidence of success:

- In 1999 the Advantica board of 12 included three African Americans, a Hispanic and a white female, compared to one minority board member in 1993.

- African Americans are returning to Denny's. Focus groups conducted in 1996, 1997 and 1998 showed a nearly 14 percent increase in blacks' visits to Denny's in 1998 over 1996.

- In 1999 almost half—45 percent—of Denny's senior management team was minority or female: three women, one of them black, are among the 11-member senior management team, and minorities make up 28 percent of Denny's managers.

- In 1999 more than a third—36 percent—of Denny's franchises were owned by minorities, compared to none in 1993.

- In 1998 Denny's did more than $25 million in business with minority vendors compared to none in 1993.

In addition to being ranked number two on *Fortune*'s 1998 listing of the best companies for minorities, Advantica also was featured on *60 Minutes* in a very positive segment on the culture turnaround and profiled in *The Washington Post* in an article headlined, "Denny's Serves Up a Sensitive Image: Restaurant Chain Goes on PR Offensive to Show Changed Ways with Minorities." Denny's national TV campaign, with the tagline "Diversity: It's about All of Us," was applauded by both the public and civil rights leaders.

Throughout this difficult and complex turnaround, company executives remained calm, patient and good humored—so much so that Adamson approached Jay Leno about the changes at Denny's. Leno responded by picking up the phone himself and promising not to do any more jokes about Denny's and discrimination.[25]

The Boeing-McDonnell Douglas Case

As with many major mergers, headlines relating to the union of The Boeing Company and McDonnell Douglas Corporation focused mostly on international politics, antitrust reviews and stock prices. But the two companies' communications teams made a major priority of concentrating on what the merged company would look like in the future to its multiple audiences. And their role was deemed vital by top management. In fact, immediately after the deal was drafted, the two merging companies' top 10 communicators were called in for a "communications only" meeting with Boeing CEO Phil Condit, demonstrating the importance of PR in the merger process.

Management was clear from the beginning about its goals: Get the deal done, prepare for operating successfully as a combined company beginning on "Day One," and set the foundation for the new Boeing with both internal and external perception of a productive merger that was in the public interest. Achieving these goals was the task of Harold Carr, Boeing vice president of public relations who was nearing retirement; Larry Bishop, his successor; and Fred Hill, then vice president of PR at McDonnell Douglas.

Everyone knew that the immediate need was to get the deal approved by regulatory agencies and shareholders. The longer-range need—the vision—was just as clearly defined: To focus the efforts of employees into one new culture, the team that would position the new Boeing to be the global aerospace leader. CEO Condit and the communicators quickly concluded that priority audiences for the merger announcement and relating news would be employees, investors, customers and the news media. Much research was aimed at employee audiences, with the resultant theme of their communications being to treat the merger as a celebration, not a funeral. Early warning systems were activated to monitor the world's news media that were reporting opinions on the merger—especially in Europe, where the European Union was home territory to rival commercial jetmaker Airbus and where there were many critics of the merger. In the United States, balanced news media coverage was considered crucial to getting acceptance of the merger among employees, regulators, vendors, customers and the general public. A plan to achieve media understanding and balanced reporting was developed.

To move quickly and stifle leaks, communicators decided to host an unusual Sunday news conference at the National Press Club in Washington, D.C. The city provided global news access; it was home to the federal government, a major customer of both companies; and it was the place where approval was necessary. The announcement included a two-way audio conference in key plant and headquarters locations. As well, financial analysts were called at home and invited to tune in. An employee video was taped over the weekend and rushed to plant locations for Monday showings. Web sites were updated. Information packages were distributed. Analysts were updated via a conference call. And courtesy calls were made to selected customers, union leaders and government officials.

For the first seven months of 1997, communications continued on an intense basis, with virtually every audience of the two companies targeted for specific communications. Extensive work was done with the business and trade press in the United States and Europe to build upon the positive early reviews and counter negatives raised by key parties in Europe. At home, news media tours of principal company sites in the Seattle, St. Louis and Southern California areas were set up to help reporters understand the new Boeing scope.

After more than five million pages of submissions, the mergers received approvals from the U.S. and European regulatory bodies as well as the two companies' shareholders. Immediately following approval, massive internal communications efforts were undertaken, including videos, town hall meetings and other face-to-face employee meetings with the two CEOs. Investors were briefed. Internal and external Web sites were merged, demonstrating the technical and communications integration of the two companies. Print and TV advertising told the message: "One Company, One Vision, Building the Future of Flight Together." Post-merger research indicated applause for the intensity and candor of the communications. As can happen with massive mergers like this, many operations problems came to the fore after the union. As this is written, the company is going through the difficult post-merger period, as surging commercial airplane orders have caused serious production problems and major loss of profitability.[26]

The American Century Investments Case

"How are my investments doing?" is the single-biggest question and ongoing concern most investors have about their investments. Although there is a wealth of information available about investment performance, it does not tell an individual how his or her personal account has fared. Performance figures for any given security are readily accessible, but what an individual investor actually earns may differ materially based on when the investment was made, withdrawals from the account, additions, and dividend action.

Given Americans' reliance on mutual funds to save for retirement, Kansas City-based American Century Investments made providing personalized performance information the centerpiece of a 1997 initiative to overhaul investor statements. While revamping account statements may seem mundane, no other direct-marketed (no-load) mutual fund group had provided personalized performance disclosure before. The effort would demand scarce information technology resources, as well as a willingness to manage the risks in trying something new and highly visible, which was not legally required.

Corporate communications led this year-long project, marshaling the resources and commitment from business partners in I.T., finance, marketing and the executive committee to make personalized performance reporting a reality for all 1.8 million of the firm's investors in September 1998.

American Century's research confirmed that investors wanted personalized performance information. However, the obstacles to providing it were substantial. There was no industry-standard methodology for calculating performance. There also was the question of whether displaying results, some of which could be negative, would cause investors to panic and make ill-advised sell decisions. The operational and technology-related risks of such an undertaking created additional concerns. If the statements were late or, even worse, inaccurate, the company's credibility would suffer, raising the specter of more serious legal and financial repercussions. Other companies had dismissed the idea of providing personalized performance due to the potential cost and the extensive computer programming involved.

The timing of the new statements also posed a challenge. The market was in a late summer correction, and there was a good chance the first statements introducing personalized performance would show negative numbers due to the market downswing. The company's decision was to proceed anyway, based on the belief that its long-term goal was to present a truer picture of investment performance regardless of market conditions. Later research would indicate investors found this approach demonstrated American Century's confidence and honesty, and that investors' needs were the company's top priority.

The overall goal of the program was to win investor loyalty and trust by being the first direct-marketed fund family to provide personalized performance statements. Related objectives included industry, regulatory and public recognition for American Century's pioneering efforts. The company relied on customer input and feedback to design the prototype statements so that they were easy to read, clear and communicative while providing more information than ever before. It also minimized implementation risk by relying on proven vendors and by building in extensive testing. As well, American Century communicated extensively about the initiative to key publics—especially customers—before, during and after the implementation. A media plan and materials also were developed, resulting in positive coverage of the new statement in key publications.

The result of providing personalized performance to investors was overwhelmingly positive. Customers praised American Century for taking a risk in providing information that had been deemed too controversial and cost-prohibitive by other companies. Quantitative research conducted after the rollout found that overall customer satisfaction scores were high, and satisfaction scores comparing the statements to those of competitors had increased.

Kiplinger's Personal Finance magazine listed the statement on its "Best List" for 1998, saying, "The American Century group of mutual funds comes up a winner with a redesigned mutual fund statement you can actually understand. In addition to being investor-friendly, it features nifty graphics. . . . Even when you've lost money, it still looks good."[27]

Earning the Right to Counsel

The right to offer candid counsel and expect confidence in your advice does not flow automatically from your role as the media relations spokesperson, however. It must be earned. To be credible you have to demonstrate a solid understanding of the business and appreciation for its operations problems. You must do as good a job of preparing a case to persuade your management, board or other decision makers as you do when you are preparing a case to persuade the public.

You can take a lesson from the world of advertising. Look at the hard, creative work that advertising agencies put into researching and presenting an advertising program to a client. Then compare it with too many public relations presentations to top executives. Where are the opinion polls, the editorial analyses, the examples of competitors' actions, the evaluation plans and the clear and dramatic visuals? A presentation does not have to be fancy—and it should not be expensive. It should be complete enough to back up your case, whether you are trying to sell a new media relations program or a new salary and recognition plan for employees. It must demonstrate a clear understanding of your organization's goals, both short- and long-term.

It also can be helpful to presell your programs to others in the organization who will benefit from them. They then are likely to support you in their own interest. All too often public relations people are in the position of selling not only programs but also the need for them. Make sure your priorities are the same as your top management's. Then work with others in your organization whose needs you are attempting to meet, and turn your recommendation into a joint solution.

In Bob Haldeman's book *The Ends of Power,* there is a story about Henry Kissinger that symbolizes the multiple roles of the media relations professional. Haldeman was very protective of access to President Nixon, and this was a continuing area of conflict between himself and Kissinger. One day Kissinger came into Haldeman's office saying he had to see the president right away. Haldeman asked why, and Kissinger pointed to a stack of pictures he had in his arm. "It's a Cuban seaport, Haldeman," Kissinger said, "and these satellite photos show the Cubans are building soccer fields. I have to see the president now. Who's in there with him?" Apparently it was an important meeting on the economy, and Haldeman thought Kissinger had taken leave of his senses. "Are you going to burst into the Oval Office and interrupt a critical meeting to tell the president the Cubans are building soccer fields?" Haldeman asked, incredulously. "Of course I am," Kissinger answered, as patiently as he could. "These soccer fields could mean war. Cubans play baseball. Russians play soccer."[28]

We too must be able to distinguish between "baseball fields" and "soccer fields"—and then, once we have made the determination, to understand the difference and recommend appropriate action. Only then will we have completed the circle that is—or should be—our job description: to work professionally with the media to *tell* our organization's story, and to take advantage of our daily contacts with reporters by listening not only to what they are *asking* but also to what they are *saying*. Whether you are from the school that believes the media leads public opinion or reflects it, the opportunities are the same: Reporters are a key window to the world's view of our organizations, our products and our people. Reflecting their interests, anticipating their concerns, adapting our media relations efforts and suggesting new courses of action as a result of their input—that is what makes us valuable to our companies and clients. That is also what makes us true media relations professionals.

Building Respect for Our Role

We sometimes complain that we do not get enough respect within our organizations. But so many of us who aspire to greater recognition do not fulfill management expectations. On occasion we are carried away more by mechanics and methodology than by substance and measurable results. We cannot afford to confuse motion with progress—nor to do well that which should not have been done at all. We cannot claim authority merely from our place on the organization chart. Rather, we must prove we have skills that make us a valued part of the management team by using those skills to anticipate and then help solve the problems that keep our bosses and CEOs awake at night. Only then will we forge the close ties with our CEO and other decision makers in our organizations that are essential for achieving our counseling role.

We live in an environment of such complexity that almost each activity we confront requires new thought and sensitivity in applying the old principles. As Chester Burger, a PR veteran and long-time counselor to many Fortune 500 companies, cautioned, "Perhaps too many of our corporate messages are being framed in exactly the same way they were presented a quarter-century ago. We seem to pretend that the cynicism and changed values of a new generation don't exist."[29]

We need to help our organizations and clients see the world through a wide-angle lens, so that even those things that are far away or on the sidelines come into focus. We have a responsibility to assimilate, interpret and clarify information we gather from the media and our publics, and get it to the right person or group. We should be measured not by the amount of news coverage we generate or number of briefing papers we prepare but by our ability to mobilize the appropriate response within our organizations as well as externally. We need to be experts in influencing behavior.

We should ensure that our companies and clients have long-range plans reflecting both economic and social objectives, just as we provide guidance and discipline for making better decisions today. We should take care that our plans are operating like an architect's drawing: changes can be made and arrangements altered while the basic structure remains a strong, workable blueprint for action.

Beyond that, we should put the same effort into the long-term "storm warning" job as we do into the short-term activities. We must become, as management consultant Harry Levinson puts it, "organizational radar taking soundings and helping to steer rather than expecting to be piloted."[30] We must gain the confidence of the top management of our organization or client so that when we disagree with them they know it is *not* because we are argumentative or do not understand their goals but rather because we feel we would be abdicating our responsibility if we were to remain silent while they launch an unguided missile. We must gain their confidence so that we earn the right to offer counsel by persuasion, negotiation or exhortation. The trick is to rock the boat without making everyone sink. Yet we must retain our humility. Our value lies not so much in our knowledge as in our sources of information and our ability to come up with questions that ensure thoughtful evaluation and reasonable answers by other experts in the organization.

At the time of Anwar Sadat's death, Henry Kissinger wrote a moving obituary for *Time* magazine in which he described the characteristics that propelled the Egyptian president to the center of the world's stage. He was writing about great leaders in a lofty context, of course. Yet, the same qualities should be our ideal if we are to become effective organizational counselors. According to Kissinger:

> The difference between great and ordinary leaders is rarely formal intellect but insight. The great man understands the essence of a problem; the ordinary leader grasps only the symptoms. The great man focuses on the relationship of events to each other; the ordinary leader sees only a series of seemingly disconnected events. The great man has a vision of the future that enables him to place obstacles into perspective; the ordinary leader turns pebbles in the road into boulders. . . . But a statesman must never be viewed as starry-eyed. He must have vision and depth; he must also translate his intuition into reality against sometimes resistant material."[31]

Managing for the Future

The environment in which our organizations and clients operate is not one filled with easy managerial decisions to make in isolation or at a leisurely pace. The competitive global marketplace has little tolerance for complacency. To succeed, our organizations must offer products and services that meet customers' expressed needs—not assumptions of those needs.

As counselors, we should help our organizations manage for the future by establishing programs that detect emerging public issues and demands early, analyze their ramifications, track and respond to them as they develop, evaluate the results and modify activities based on this knowledge. We must demonstrate that we have a solid grasp of both our organization's objectives and the world in which we are operating, so that we can provide concrete assistance in articulating and dealing with the complex problems top management faces in relating to this ever-changing environment.

Edward M. Block, a PR veteran and retired senior executive at AT&T, put it this way:

> Counseling is what got us into top management in the first place. And counseling is what will keep us there, not withstanding the great changes that now envelop our companies or the ever-changing fashions of management consultants and business school theorists who presume to tell top management how to stay the course. . . . Problem solving is what management is all about, and corporate management will always have a need for—and respect for—constructive advice and timely action initiated by public relations people who know the business from the inside out as well as the outside in. To whatever extent public relations may have been disenfranchised by other management disciplines or by the unintended consequences of reorganizations and restructurings, I think it's because we have come to be viewed as communicators rather than problem solvers. Communications is *overhead*. Problem solving is *value added where it really counts*.[32]

We should help our organizations view themselves in a larger context, ensuring that they are not isolated from the mainstream of cultural, political, economic and social thought. We should not only react wisely to changing circumstances but also, when appropriate, help create them. We should embark on a continuing search for the tools and talents required to help both our companies and our clients deal with immediate issues and plan for future challenges.

Stuart Z. Goldstein, managing director-corporate communications at National Securities Clearing Corporation in New York, summed it up well:

> In the next century, companies will need professional communicators who have all the requisite writing skills, but see themselves as leaders. People who can help senior management understand how their decisions may be viewed externally and add value in guiding corporate strategy. People who think strategically about message management, corporate positioning and branding. Professionals who are equally capable of . . . conducting an on-camera media interview and guiding the use of technology to strengthen a company's ability to protect and enhance its reputation.[33]

We would never let our executives walk into a news media interview without preparing them for tough questions we expected from the reporter. By the same token, we cannot let our organizations move unprepared into next year—or into the next decade.

Advice from Top Executives, Academics

We asked experienced public relations executives, consultants and academics the question, "What skills and qualities are the most valuable for a media relations professional to develop in order to become an effective counselor to management?" Here are their replies:

> Management today is seeking out and depending upon public relations professionals who can see down the road and point out the likely outcomes of a course of action. This requires good risk management skills. It also is increasingly important to know both the business you are working in and the language of that business in order to understand the unspoken motivations and the backdrop for decisions that need to be made. As you learn to "read" the management group you are counseling, you need to understand the peer group of each executive, who she/he respects, etc. This will add rich perspective to the counsel you give. Today's public relations professionals need solid skills in working with the media and being able to build ongoing strong media relationships. This clearly is on the list of top concerns of corporate management—and can be the ticket to credibility as a counselor to management.
>
> **—Ann H. Barkelew**
> **Senior Vice President and Partner**
> **Fleishman Hillard, Inc.**
> **Minneapolis, Minnesota**

> Everything in my own long experience has taught me that a good counselor possesses at least three attributes that are not particularly well developed or rewarded in the other management disciplines: The first is an intimate understanding of the business, its culture, its goals, or, as we used to phrase it, "The Big Picture." The second is a confident understanding of what a company's various publics are thinking or may think about the company's policies and actions. And the third is the assertiveness to make certain these perspectives are heard, understood and heeded when management seeks to solve problems that exist or head off problems that may emerge.
>
> **—Edward M. Block**
> **Senior Vice President (retired)**
> **AT&T**
> **Key West, Florida**

> The effective counselor to senior management needs to bridge the quantitative demands of business to the more qualitative demands of key audiences—employees, customers, investors, communities. To build that bridge, communications counselors need a solid

understanding of the business, strong communications skills, the confidence and courage to speak the truth, and the ability to build alliances to get things done—while keeping a sense of humor.

—Pat Brozowski
Vice President-Communications
FMC Corporation
Chicago, Illinois

Counselors to management must step beyond the narrow role of being merely a "wordsmith" and a disseminator of messages to media. They must become truly sensitive to all the trends and developments inside and outside of their organization, which have the potential to affect its reputation. They also must be familiar with the full range of communication tools and technologies at the disposal of the organization—including the many techniques of advertising and marketing, and their potential interrelationship with traditional public relations approaches—so that they can help ensure that the public "face" of the organization is presented in a properly integrated manner. By developing this broad base of knowledge and skills, counselors can see "the big picture," integrate different aspects of communication to ensure that they work in harmony, appreciate the varying roles and problems of other professionals in the organization, ensure that communication efforts are tuned in to the concerns of both internal and external audiences, and above all demonstrate to senior management that they are genuinely useful contributors to management decision making. The good counselor is therefore a true "image police officer" (of the "good cop" variety) who helps to align corporate reality with desired corporate image, keep everyone out of trouble, and build positive on-going relationships with all the people and groups important to the organization's future.

—Graeme Domm
Senior Consultant
Fenton Communications
Melbourne, Australia

My easy access to top management always stemmed from the ability to write effective speeches tailored to fit the personalities of the speakers. You can't write their speeches without knowing what's going on, and what you write for them to say often triggers policy. It happened this way for me from my first assignment as a 2nd Lieutenant in the Air Force writing for a general on through my career with three Fortune 500 companies. I not only wrote for the CEO but other top officers too. This is probably how I survived twenty some years and five complete changes of top management at my last company, which held me an extra year beyond by retirement age.

—**John W. Felton, APR, Fellow**
President & CEO
Institute for Public Relations
Gainesville, Florida

The most essential qualification for a corporate communications counselor is a thorough and detailed knowledge of the company's business, its strategy, and its financial issues and track record. This knowledge, together with the full range of communications skills and an understanding of the media and how to work with reporters and editors, make up the communicator's tool kit. In addition, there must be a rapport between the communicator and the CEO. This, on the communicator's side, is aided by tact, respectfulness, and a willingness to take a firm stand, back it up with facts and logic, and accept the boss's final word.

—**Gale L. Griffin**
Vice President-Corporate Communications
Bestfoods
Englewood Cliffs, New Jersey

A principle espoused by Arthur Page, the first corporate public relations officer, is "Listen to the customer." The management pioneer Peter Drucker pointed to the number-one management objective: "Create a customer." Tom Peters, modern management's gadfly, recommended that every management strategy begin with a *listening* strategy. I've listened to these folks for so long they feel like friends and I agree with my friends. The counselor learns to listen. Listen, interpret, initiate. That's the essence of counseling. Consider publics—employees, the news media, stakeholders of all stripes—to be "customers" who must be created and re-created constantly. You can only sell to customers your product, service or message if they understand, want and are ready to deal with you. You can only sell when you understand them. To understand them you must listen to them. That's why public relations begins with research. It is the listening strategy. The counselor to management will do well to consider management as a customer, or potential customer to be created, which you can achieve if you listen well, interpret well (within the context of stakeholders to whom you have listened) and initiate. Listen a long time before you talk.

—**E. Bruce Harrison**
Senior Advisor, O'Connor and Hannan
Washington, D.C.
Executive Director, Arthur W. Page Society
New York City

PR professionals first and foremost need to be business people who understand corporate finance, operations and strategic planning. It is not enough to be an accomplished practitioner of any one public relations skill, such as media relations, employee communications and the like—those skills should be a given for any senior professional. But, reading a balance sheet, understanding cash flow and why it's important, knowledge of SEC regulations that apply to your business/industry and the like will convey to your colleagues and to senior management—your CEO, company president, operating division heads—that you are their peer and speak their language. Add to this, an understanding of issues that affect or might affect your business and your industry, experience in operating divisions, broad and deep knowledge about what's going on in the world as well as in the business world, the ability to listen and to articulate complex ideas in understandable language, and the ability to inspire trust and support from your colleagues and your subordinates, and you will have at least a reasonable chance of achieving that enviable position of *effective* counselor to management.

—Carol B. Hillman
Principal
Hillman & Kersey Strategic Communications
Framingham, Massachusetts

The skill that is most important to develop—and most misunderstood—is consulting techniques. The best public relations programming in the universe won't be accepted or utilized if practitioners can't persuade managers of its value. These techniques are not natural, but must be studied and learned. For instance, too often practitioners feel they must give specific *advice* on what to do in a situation (the *counselor's* solution)—when what is most often effective is providing the *options*, and letting the *manager* select the solution. That way, when the boss charts the course, but with guidance from the professional, chances are infinitely better something will get done.

—Patrick Jackson
Senior Counsel, Jackson, Jackson & Wagner
Editor, *pr reporter*
Exeter, New Hampshire

I look for people who excel in traits essential for counseling or taking a leadership role in public relations: Personal integrity; lucid and compelling writing; the strength to tell the truth to powerful people; the ability to see the big picture and make the connections that help others see that picture as well; interpersonal skills that encourage confidence and candor in others; enjoyment of change; enthusiasm for technology; deep knowledge of and interest in the operations of the business; and no problem saying, "I made a mistake."

—**Marilyn Laurie**
Laurie Consulting
New York City

The practice of corporate communications is subjective and directly reflects a corporation's chief executive officer. The top communicator's success is based upon (1) developing the capacity (tactical skills and business knowledge) to accomplish what is required, (2) enjoying a personal chemistry between the communicator and chief executive, and (3) establishing a mutual trust between the CEO and communicator based upon competency, reliability and sincerity of commitment. Competency is the assessment that you are able to perform the actions necessary to fulfill a commitment. Reliability is the assessment that you are able to fulfill the commitment on time, over time and as promised. Sincerity is the assessment that you are honest and not holding back on the commitment.

—**Curtis G. Linke**
Vice President-Corporate Communications
Deere & Company
Moline, Illinois

I believe good listening skills, courage and confidence are critical qualities of a PR person who is counseling senior executives. I've found that it is most important to be able to recognize the underlying concerns or issues (not just what's said out loud), not only from the CEO, but from employees, customers and shareowners. Then, you need to have the courage to bring these perspectives or issues, good or bad, to the forefront. And, you've got to be confident enough to take executives out of their comfort zones by really serving as the voice of your constituencies. Don't think of communications as reporting on an organization. Think of it as driving the organization. After all, communication and leading a company are really the same thing.

—**Maril Gagen MacDonald**
Vice President-Corporate Communications
Navistar International Transportation Corporation
Chicago, Illinois

Here is what I believe it takes to use the skills we are assumed to possess as a key element in the management matrix required to maximize an organization's performance: First, work continuously to apply and improve your communicative and creative skills on a scale that ensures that managing public perceptions of your organization is consistent with the expectations of senior management. Second, develop a keen understanding of senior management accountabilities and priorities. Know the business as well as is humanly possible. Third, cultivate relationship(s) with executive/leadership mentors, and absorb yourself in the wisdom and judgment available from the mentor(s). And fourth, square your communications planning perfectly with the organization's strategies, goals and priorities as defined by the senior management team of which you should be an integral member.

—**Richard R. Mau**
Senior Vice President (retired)
Rockwell International Corporation
LaJolla, California

The most important three skills are listening, honesty and the ability to bring solutions, not just problems. These skills work together like this: As the company's senior communicator, we talk with the media, investors and employees about their perceptions of our company. It's important to listen carefully to what they are saying, and not shut them out because they "don't get it," you're short on time, or they may have a negative slant. Sometimes you'll even hear a positive! Assuming the comment is legitimate, a senior communicator should tell management—in an honest, straightforward and constructive manner—about the issues. But that's not enough. If it's a problem, bring a potential solution to the table. If it's good news, suggest a way to share it as positive reinforcement.

—**Ruthellyn Musil**
Vice President-Corporate Relations
Tribune Company
Chicago, Illinois

Counseling is more than just being a professional communicator, although that's an important prerequisite. It requires always being on top of your game, both internally and externally, anticipating the good as well as the bad, and being able to offer constructive advice in a timely manner. You must also have the ability to earn the trust and confidence of those in senior management who may look to you for sage counsel in achieving the goals of the company. Without that trust and confidence, your message, no matter how good, will likely fall on deaf ears.

—**Edwin F. Nieder**
Partner
Nieder & Nieder Associates
Montclair, New Jersey

Skills needed to counsel management? Nontraditional, very varied and too often unappreciated attributes: To balance—even break through—the comfortable, myopic mindset of too many senior executives, the public relations counselor must read widely (not just business books), troll for ideas everywhere and analyze pragmatically. A solid liberal arts grounding, ability to think outside conventional wisdom, convincingly argue a position, and even gently educate others in the principles and possibilities of public relations are essential. Also important are understanding operational management and fostering personal chemistry with the CEO.

—**Dr. Marion K. Pinsdorf**
Senior Fellow in Communications
Fordham Graduate School of Business
New York City

Developed oral and writing skills are primary for PR counseling to management. As advocates for clients and their outside interests, you have to be convincing in your presentations. A broad perspective of the world through education, travel or experience helps. Loyalty to top management and to all employees on the staff—and knowing what to do when they are in conflict—also is important. Personal integrity is the glue that keeps it all together and humor helps you survive when things get tough.

—**Magda A. Ratajski**
President
MarassoCo.
Virginia Beach, Virginia

First, it is critical to be able to look broadly across the functions of a business—legal, finance, marketing, business development, etc. If you understand their roles and objectives, you'll be able to put yourself in their shoes and better understand their needs and concerns. PR leaders are uniquely positioned to see the big picture and bring diverse interests together to seek solutions. Second is the need to back up your position with facts and data. Without research to support the work and its results, PR will never be taken seriously by senior management.

—**Judi Servoss**
Vice President-Public Relations (retired)
MediaOne Group
Denver, Colorado

To be an effective public relations counselor to management, you must first have management's confidence in your ability to handle the basics of the business. To most CEOs, that means media relations. Do you know members of the press who cover your company or industry or government department? Have you gained their respect by being available and knowledgeable? Do they trust you? Are you ready for a crisis? Do you get results? If you can handle reporters, you can handle management.

—Robert B. Sims
Senior Vice President
National Geographic Society
Washington, D.C.

When CEOs are asked who they listen to on important issues, there is a great deal of consistency. They tell me they want people who deal well with ambiguity. They want an individual who, while having a balanced approach to a problem, sees both sides—and has a point of view, with the confidence to back it up. At the top of our profession, we have moved from a skill-based profession to a strategic seat at the table, and now we are being forced to view our jobs from a policy platform. Business people first—and then communications becomes one of the tools to solve the issue. The ability to know what is possible, and probable, comes from experience and practice. Basic skills will always be necessary to get in the door.

—Kurt P. Stocker
Associate Professor
Northwestern University
Chicago, Illinois

Strong writers must have a good understanding of how research can be used to develop and evaluate consistent, integrated and accountable strategic communications campaigns. They also must possess the ability to develop and nurture professional relationships with internal and external customers; the knowledge to align senior management's goals with external and internal communications needs; and have the talent and abilities to integrate public relations measures with the organization's business objectives. I'll take one additional step and suggest all of this will require solid undergraduate-level education—and perhaps graduate-level study backed up with appropriate professional development training—that focuses upon (a) a solid understanding of practical and theoretical aspects of communications and public relations; (b) a thorough background in liberal arts and sciences; (c) an awareness and understanding about technology, diversity, politics and culture; and, (d) an appreciation of the global business environment, ideally including the ability to read and speak foreign languages.

—**Donald K. Wright**
Professor of Communication
University of South Alabama
Mobile, Alabama
Director
Arthur W. Page Society PR Executive Forum

To bring real value to senior management, public relations professionals must be able to represent the "outside in" as well as the "inside out"; that is, PR managers must not only communicate the company's messages to external audiences, you must also communicate how those audiences view the organization and its decisions back to the management. That will not make you popular with your peers and superiors but is an absolutely vital management role. Otherwise, your organization will operate in a vacuum, oblivious to the public's impact on its ability to function.

—**C. Richard Yarbrough**
Vice President-Public Relations (retired)
BellSouth Corporation
Managing Director (retired)
Atlanta Committee for the Olympic Games
Atlanta, Georgia

Checklist: How Involved and Valuable Are You to Your Organization?

Following is a checklist that the public relations directors of The Reader's Digest Association were given at their Global Public Relations Conference in New York City in 1992 to help them evaluate their value as communicators and counselors to management. Test yourself to see how you measure up:

✓ Recognized by colleagues as having excellent communications skills.

✓ Knowledge of the company—mission, strategies, products, people, competitive strengths—to be a competent counselor to management.

✓ Member of significant committees and task forces within the organization.

✓ Close relationships with decision makers in all departments so your advice is sought by them.

✓ Always know of major news long before it breaks.

✓ Involved in counseling and planning as well as communicating.

✓ Offer advice—sometimes on own initiative—to CEO and other members of senior management.

✓ Advise senior management of upcoming PR opportunities and anticipate potential problems.

✓ Work with CEO and affected departments to create "just in case" communications plans when necessary.

NOTES

Chapter One

1. Grant N. Horne, "Brawling and Squabbling Towards the 21st Century," Hall of Fame lecture, Arthur W. Page Society 15th annual conference, 4–6 October 1998, Naples, FL.
2. Fraser Seitel, "1998's Six Public Relations Lessons," *Ragan Report*, 4 January 1999, p. 2.
3. Lesley Stahl, *Reporting Live* (New York: Simon & Schuster, 1999).
4. Robert MacNeil, *Breaking News* (New York: Doubleday, 1998).
5. Don Hewitt, 21st annual Frank E. Gannett Lecture, The Freedom Forum Media Studies Center, New York City, 10 December 1998.
6. "The Media," *Newsweek*, 8 February 1999, pp. 31–32.
7. "Slouching Toward Sanity," *American Journalism Review*, March 1999, p. 6.
8. "On Communications in the Next Century, with John Gilfeather," *Ragan Report*, 11 January 1999, p. 3.
9. "tomorrow.net," *The Chief Executive Guide: Beyond the Internet*, 1999, p. 5.
10. *Ragan Report*, p. 3.
11. Anne M. McCarthy, "Browsers Beware! The Passing Lane Is Open," *Journal of Integrated Communications*, Northwestern University, 1998–99, p. 24.
12. *www.usatoday.com*, April 1998.
13. *www.economist.com*, September 1997.
14. Stuart Z. Goldstein, "Information Preparedness: An Integrated Model for Communication in the Information Age," *Strategic Communications Management*, December/January 1999, p. 20.
15. Anderson Consulting, "The End of Innovation?" *Outlook*, 1999, No. 1, p. 9.

16. McCarthy, p. 24.
17. "Ten Reasons Why PR Is Entering a Golden Age," *PR Week*, 29 March 1999, p. 12.
18. Rem Rieder, "Playing to Their Strengths," *American Journalism Review*, April 1999, p. 6.
19. Ibid., p. 13.
20. "Things Researchers Pretty Much Know for Sure," *American Journalism Review*, March 1999, p. 54.
21. Ronald E. Rhody, "Business and the Media: A Status Report," remarks delivered to the Public Relations Society of America San Francisco chapter, 23 May 1993.
22. "Why Laissez Faire Is the Washington Line on Telecom Mergers," *Wall Street Journal*, 10 May 1999, p. 1.
23. "The Media," pp. 31–32.
24. Dan Rather, "An Anchorman's Views of the News on Television," *Wall Street Journal*, 5 August 1982.
25. Robert MacNeil, *The Right Place at the Right Time* (Boston: Little, Brown and Co., 1982), p. 129.
26. Quoted in *Peter's Quotations: Ideas for Our Time*, ed. Dr. Laurence J. Peter (New York: William Morrow & Co., 1977), p. 125.
27. Walter K. Lindenmann, "Measuring Relationships Is Key to Successful Public Relations," *Public Relations Quarterly*, Winter 1998–99, p. 19.
28. Kathleen Ladd Ward, "Evaluating Public Relationships," unpublished paper prepared for the Institute of Public Relations, 1998.
29. Randall L. Tobias, "Communications in a Time of Change," remarks delivered at the Arthur Page Society annual spring seminar, New York City, 4 April 1995.

Chapter Two

1. Lynne Masel-Walters, "Working With The Press . . .," *Public Relations Quarterly*, Fall, 1984.
2. AT&T Archives, Short Hills, NJ.

Chapter Three

1. Robert J. Samuelson, Washington Post Writer's Group, *Arizona Republic*, 18 June 1999.
2. James B. Stewart, book review, "America in the Age of Mixed Media," *The New York Times*, 4 July 1999.
3. Gang Box," newsletter of Daniel Construction Company, Greenville, South Carolina, April 1982, p. 3.
4. James B. Stewart, "Warp Speed," book review, *The New York Times*, 4 July 1999, p. 8.
5. "Quotes of the Day," *Ragan's Public Relations Journal*, March/April 1999, p. 64.

6. *PR Reporter*, vol. 25, no. 24 (14 June 1982), 1–2.
7. Eileen Prescott, "Behind the Camera on Morning TV," *Public Relations Journal*, November 1983, p. 17.

Chapter Four

1. Tina Koenig, "E-Media Relations—Same Routine or New Shtick?", *The PR Network*, 30 April 1999.
2. "How to Write an Op-ed," *PR Week*, 5 July 1999, p. 18.
3. "Picking Up on a New Signal in Electronic Publicity," *Ragan's PR Intelligence Report*, April 1999.
4. "Taking Your Press Conference On-line," *PR Week*, 16 August 1999, p. 36.
5. Annette Minkalis, "Answering Your SMT Questions," *PR Tactics*, July 1999.

Chapter Five

1. Larry Weber, "The Dawn of Experiential Public Relations," *Ragan's Public Relations Journal*, January/February 1999, p. 41.
2. John A. Meyers, "A Letter from the Publisher," *Time*, 14 November 1983.
3. Lesley Stahl, *Reporting Live* (New York: Simon & Schuster, 1999), p. 256.
4. "The Hot Zines," *PR Week*, 22 March 1999, p. 12.
5. "10 Steps to Becoming a Web Genius," *Ragan Report*, 10 May 1999, p. 7.
6. Ibid.
7. John A. Meyers, "A Letter from the Publisher," *Time*, 17 May 1982.
8. *PR Week*, p. 12.
9. Ibid., p. 13.
10. Dennis Holder, "*The Los Angeles Times* Reaches for the Top," *Washington Journalism Review*, July/August 1982, p. 17.
11. Marlin Fitzwater, *Call the Briefing! Reagan and Bush, Sam and Helen: A Decade with Presidents and the Press* (New York: Times Books, 1995).
12. "Our Expectations of You: Your Expanded Role in Our Global Company," remarks by George V. Grune at The Reader's Digest Association's global public relations conference, New York City, 19 October 1992.
13. William Safire, "On Language: Exit Haigspeak," *New York Times Magazine*, 11 July 1982.
14. Ann Wylie, "Simplify, Simplify, Simplify," *The Editor's Worksheet*, May 1999, p. 2.
15. Quoted by Ken Roman and Joel Raphaelson, *How to Write Better*, Ogilvy & Mather Inc., 1978, p. 10.

16. *UPI Reporter*, United Press International, New York.
17. "Title Fight," *Fortune*, 21 June 1999, p. 88.
18. "Why Americans Hate the Media," *Atlantic Monthly*, February 1996.
19. Rem Rieder, "Getting Back to Basics," *American Journalism Review*, January/February 1999, p. 6.
20. Stahl, p. 405.
21. "Time to Send Embargoed News Releases to Jurassic Park?" *PR News*, 21 June 1993.

Chapter Six

1. Joseph Heller, *Good as Gold* (New York: Pocket Books, 1979), p. 77.
2. David Wallechinsky, Irving and Amy Wallace, *The Book of Lists* (New York: Bantam Books, 1977), p. 469.
3. John O'Toole, *The Trouble with Advertising. . .* (New York: Chelsea House, 1981), p. 112.
4. *PR Reporter*, 28 September 1981, p. 4.
5. "The Editor's Desk," *Fortune*, 14 November 1983, p. 4.
6. Quoted by Eliot Frankel, "Learning to Conquer 'Mike' Fright," *Washington Journalism Review*, July/August 1982, p. 32.
7. Ibid., p. 33.
8. Frankel, p. 32.
9. Quoted in "Why TV Interview Training?", The Executive Television Workshop, New York.
10. *The New York Times* staff, *Churchill in Memoriam: His Life, His Death, His Wit and Wisdom* (New York: Bantam Books, 1965), p. 160.
11. Ann Wylie, "Simplify, Simplify, Simplify," *The Editor's Worksheet*, May 1999, p. 1.
12. Lesley Stahl, *Reporting Live* (New York: Simon & Schuster, 1999), p. 315.
13. Cover story, *Time*, 30 August 1982, p. 74.
14. "How to Handle the Press," *Newsweek*, 19 April 1982, p. 90.
15. Quoted by Susan Astarita, "Handle the Press With Finesse," *Savvy*, June 1981, p. 58.
16. "Work Week," *Wall Street Journal*, 4 May 1999, p. 1.
17. *Newsweek*, 19 April 1982, p. 90.
18. William Safire, *On Language* (New York: Time Books, 1981), p. 138.
19. Chester Burger, "Truth and Credibility in an Era of Disbelief," *Ragan's Public Relations Journal*, January/February 1999, p. 13.
20. Materials provided by the Arthur W. Page Society, New York, NY.
21. Robert MacNeil, *The Right Place at The Right Time* (Boston: Little, Brown and Company, 1982), p. 10.
22. Bill Adler and Bill Adler Jr., "He Keeps His Wit About Him," *Parade* magazine, excerpted from "The Reagan Wit."

23. *Newsweek*, 19 April 1982, p. 90.
24. Dan Rather, "An Anchorman's View of the News on Television," 5 August 1982, *Wall Street Journal*.
25. *U.S. News & World Report*, 5 August 1982, p. 46.

Chapter Seven

1. "For a Reporter and a Source, Echoes of a Broken Promise," *The New York Times*, 11 April 1999.
2. "All the News That's Fit to Terrify," *Family Circle*, 9 March 1999, p. 148.
3. "PRSA board votes to end contact with Jack O'Dwyer," *PR Week*, May, 1999.
4. Bulletin items, *Chronicle of Higher Education*, 12 March 1999.
5. "Ethics in Public Relations," *Public Relations Journal*, December 1982.
6. Ivan Hill, "Compromise and Conviction—The Ethical Dilemma," speech delivered to the Associated General Contractors, Houston, Texas, March 15, 1982.
7. *"The Credibility Factor, Putting Ethics to Work in Public Relations"* (Chicago: Richard D. Irwin, Inc., 1993).
8. Jeanne Mann, "Improving Relations with the Media: Two Views," *Business and Media*, vol. 111, no. 2 (Summer 1981).
9. Louis C. Williams, Jr., letter accompanying "Lou Williams Seminars" brochure, Fall 1992.
10. Lanny J. Davis, *Truth to Tell: Tell It Early, Tell It All, Tell It Yourself* (New York: The Free Press, 1999).
11. "Honesty Is Best Policy in a Crisis," *Jack O'Dwyer's Newsletter*, Internet Edition, 28 June 1999, p. 2.
12. Mann, op. cit.
13. "Quotes of the Day," *Ragan's Public Relations Journal*, March/April 1999.
14. *communication briefings*, November, 1993, p. 2.
15. John Rosica, "To Comment or Not to Comment?," *Ragan's PR Intelligence Report*, June 1999.
16. Bill Harlow, "Conference Workshop Examines CIA's 'Shroud of Secrecy,'" *Communication World*, February/March, 1999, p. 6.
17. *The Business-Media Relationship*, An AMA Research Study (AMACOM), 1981, pp. 39, 43.
18. Foreign Press Center brochure, Washington, DC, 83–220(27).
19. Jim Byrnes, AT&T's *Media Relations Newsletter*, 6 March 1990.
20. *Time*, 17 December 1984, p. 69.

Chapter Eight

1. Thomas L. Harris, "Marketer of the Year," *MPR Update*, March 1999, p. 3.
2. "Picking Up on a New Signal in Electronic Publicity," *Ragan's PR Intelligence Report*, 25 January 1999, p. 3.
3. "Polaroid Takes to the Road with Youth-Targeted Effort," *PR Week*, 19 April 1999, p. 2.
4. "Quantas VNR Hits Twice the Viewers of $6m Ad," *PR Week*, 29 March 1999, p. 1.
5. "NBC Boosts Brokaw Book and Gets Boost Back," *Wall Street Journal*, 25 January 1999, p. B1.
6. "Excuse Me, Please, Do You Mind If I Sell You Something?", *Fortune*, 21 June 1999, p. 190.
7. "A New Hospital for Berkeley," *Independent & Gazette*, 21 April 1980.
8. "Herrick Hospital an Innovator in Health Care," *Oakland Post*, 1 May 1980.
9. Materials and information supplied by Bestfoods' Corporate Communications Department, Englewood Cliffs, New Jersey.
10. Lisa Siracuse, "Looks Aren't Everthing: Creating Competitive Advantage with Brand Personality," *Journal of Integrated Communications*, Northwestern University, 1998–1999, p. 10.
11. Materials and information supplied to the Arthur W. Page Society 1999 national awards program by Sondra A. Fowler, manager-corporate public affairs, Conoco Inc.
12. Materials and information supplied to the Arthur W. Page Society 1999 national awards program by Elizabeth Polenske, vice president/account supervisor, Ketchum Public Relations.
13. Materials and information supplied to the Arthur W. Page Society 1999 national awards program by Robert DeFillippo, vice president-corporate public relations, The Prudential Insurance Company of America.
14. Materials and information supplied to the Arthur W. Page Society 1999 national awards program by Ken Makovsky, principal, Makovsky & Company.
15. Materials and information supplied to the Arthur W. Page Society 1999 national awards program by Shelley Spector, president and creative director, Spector & Associates, Inc.
16. Materials and information supplied to the Arthur W. Page Society 1999 national awards program by Lee Dancy, Matlock and Associates, Inc.
17. "United Way Bypasses Cultural Differences" and "Technology Extends United Way's Reach," *IABC Communications World*, August 1982, pp. 1, 3, 14.

18. "Attention to Detail Crucial in Event Promotions," *IABC Communications World*, July 1983, p. 1.
19. "Media Tactics Proposed to Reagan by Think Tank May Translate for Use by Practitioners & Their CEOs," *PR Reporter*, 27 April 1981, p. 1.
20. "Attention to Detail Crucial in Event Promotions," p. 9.
21. "Publisher's Memo," *Business Week*, 3 October 1983, p. 10.
22. "The Integrated Bug," *PR Week*, 26 April 1999, p. 16.
23. "Packaged PR is Key to Branding," *PR Week*, 22 March 1999, p. 6.
24. "The Integrated Bug," p. 16.
25. "The Voice of Marketing PR," *PR Week*, 29 March 1999, p. 18.

Chapter Nine

1. "New Breed CEO Markets Locally—Worldwide," *USA Today*, 8 February 1996, p. B1.
2. "A Globe of Localities," *CEO Report*, a supplement to *Chief Executive* magazine, October 1997, p. 15.
3. "New Breed CEO Markets Locally—Worldwide," p. B1.
4. "All the World's a McStage," *Business Week*, 8 May 1995, p. 8.
5. "What the Leaders of Tomorrow See," *Fortune*, 3 July 1989, p. 48.
6. "The Stateless Corporation," *Business Week*, 14 May 1990, p. 98.
7. "When History No Longer Repeats Itself," *Forbes ASAP*, 25 August 1997, p. 28
8. "Marketing Expert Lists 5 Themes for Business Communications in the 21st Century," *Public Relations Quarterly*, Spring 1999, p. 22.
9. "What the Leaders of Tomorrow See," p. 48.
10. "Frozen Out in Japan? Join the Club," *New York Times*, 13 June 1993, p. E2.
11. "The Mice That Roared," *CEO Brief*, a supplement to *Chief Executive* magazine, October 1998, p. 5–7.
12. "Journalists' Opinions Shine Through, Study Says," *Ragan's Media Relations Report*, April 1999, p. 3.
13. Henry Erlich, *Writing Effective Speeches* (New York: Paragon House, 1992), p. 141.
14. "Trainers Help Expatriate Employees Build Bridges to Different Cultures," *Wall Street Journal*, 14 June 1993, p. B1.
15. *The Wirthlin Report*, December 1997, Volume 8, No. 10.

Chapter Ten

1. Robert MacNeil, *The Right Place at The Right Time* (Boston: Little, Brown and Company, 1982), p. 89.
2. Letter to A. G. Hodges, 4 April 1864, "Life and Works of Abe Lincoln," Century Edition, Volume 8 (New York: Current Literature Publishing Co., 1907), p. 124.

3. "News Crews, Expecting the Worst, Prepare To Cover a Major Earthquake in California," *Wall Street Journal*, 24 June 1983, p. 25.

4. "News Media Guide to the Oklahoma City Fire Department," Jon A. Hansen, assistant fire chief, April 1994.

5. "Toxic-waste Scare 'Killed' Small Town, Its People Complain," *Wall Street Journal*, 1 March 1983, p. 1.

6. "This Is No Way to Save the Earth," *Reader's Digest*, June 1993, p. 170.

7. *Wall Street Journal*, op. cit.

8. "Reagan Goal of Easing Environmental Laws is Largely Unattained," *Wall Street Journal*, 18 February 1983, p. 1.

9. "Western Conservation Drive Cuts Light Bill By $91,000," Gainesville, Georgia, *Times*, 12 October 1980.

10. "Recycling Plastic Trash into Treasure," *Design News*, 19 October 1981, p. 14.

11. *Telephony*, 7 September 1981.

12. "Raking It In," *Lexington* (Kentucky) *Leader*, 31 August 1981.

13. "Raking It In for Reuse," *Phoenix Gazette*, 5 August 1981.

14. "Don Procknow On: Energy Conservation As Corporate Policy," *Electronic Engineering Times*, Speakout Series, June 1981, p. 3.

15. "Who Scores Best on the Environment?" *Fortune*, 26 July 1993, p. 116.

16. Ongoing coverage in *The Journal*, West Columbia, SC, *The Record*, Columbia, SC, and *The Dispatch News*, Lexington, SC from 17 March to 28 April 1982.

17. Materials and information supplied to the Arthur W. Page Society 1998 national awards program by Meinolf Sprink, Bayer Corporation.

18. *Seattle Post-Intelligencer*, 15 March 1982, p. 1.

19. *American Banker*, 23 March 1982.

20. *Seattle Post-Intelligencer*, 31 March 1982, p. A9.

21. *Seattle Post-Intelligencer*, 31 March 1982, p. A12.

22. Ibid.

23. "1.5 Million May Feel Sexually Harassed, Study Says," *Globe and Mail*, 6 April 1983, p. 1.

24. Quoted by Lucille deView in a review of "Writing Without Bias," *Media Reporter*, Brennam Publications, England.

25. Quoted in the Baltimore *News American*, 25 June 1980, p. 11-A.

26. James Wolcott, "Son of Kong," *New York*, 11 October 1982, p. 80.

27. Materials and information supplied to the Arthur W. Page Society 1999 national awards program and the 1999 Public Relations Society of America Silver Anvil awards by Federal Express Corp. and Ketchum New York.

28. "The Alaskan Oil Spill: Lessons in Crisis Management," *Management Review*, April 1990, p. 15.

29. "Exxon's Public Relations Problem," *The New York Times*, 21 April 1989, p. D1.

30. Patricia Sellers, "Crunch Time for Coke," *Fortune*, 19 June 1999, p. 72.

31. "Anatomy of a Recall: How Coke's Controls Fizzled Out in Europe," *Wall Street Journal*, 29 June 1999, p. 1.
32. "Coke Scrambles to Contain a Scare in Europe," *Wall Street Journal*, 17 June 1999, p. B1.
33. "Coke Chairman Begins Campaign to Apologize to Belgian People," *Wall Street Journal*, 22 June 1999, p. A4.
34. "Coke Estimates European Volume Plunged 6% to 7% in 2nd Quarter," *Wall Street Journal*, 1 July 1999, p. A4.
35. "Coke Reports 21% Decline in Earnings," *Wall Street Journal*, 16 July 1999, p. A3.
36. "When the bubble burst," *The Economist*, 3 August 1992, p. 67.
37. "Sears's Brennan Accepts Blame For Auto Flap," *Wall Street Journal*, 23 June 1993, p. B1.
38. Ibid.
39. "Sears Ducks Then Tries to Cover," *The New York Times*, 17 June 1992, p. D1.
40. "Pepsi Weathers Tampering Hoaxes," *Advertising Age*, 21 June 1993, p. 1.
41. "The Pepsi Crisis: What Went Right," *Advertising Age*, 19 July 1993, p. 14.
42. "The Right Moves, Baby," *Business Week*, 5 July 1993, p. 30.
43. "Crisis Plans Tested in KC Hyatt Hotel Disaster," IABC *Communications Journal*, August 1981, p. 1.
44. "Robberies Help Inspire Bank's Crisis PR Plan," IABC *Communications Journal*, June 1982, p. 8.
45. James E. Lukaszewski, "The Six Dimensions of Crisis Communication Management," *Ragan's Public Relations Journal*, January/February 1999, p. 22.
46. Dan Cordtz, "Why Business Won't Talk," *Business and the Media*, The Media Institute, Fall 1980.
47. Conversations between the author and C. Richard Yarbrough, as well as John Budd's article, "Bombing Puts Top Olympics Communicator on Alert," *Tactics*, August 1996.
48. Ongoing coverage in the *Salt Lake City Tribune* and *Wall Street Journal*.
49. Alicia C. Shepard, "An Olympian Scandal," *American Journalism Review*, April 1999, p. 22.
50. Quoted in "Business Says Product Recall Makes Sense," *The New York Times*, 17 October 1981, p. 9.
51. Quoted in "Handle the Press with Finesse," *Savvy*, June 1981, p. 57.
52. Quoted in "Johnson & Johnson Officials Take Steps To End More Killings Linked to Tylenol," *Wall Street Journal*, 4 October 1982, p. 16.
53. Quoted in "Tylenol's 'Miracle' Comeback," *Time*, 17 October 1983, p. 67.
54. Quoted in "Solid Consumer Relations Can Defuse Crisis," *Public Relations Journal*, December 1982, p. 8.

55. Remarks by Terri Holbrooke at the 14th annual spring seminar of the Arthur Page Society, New York City, 7–8 April 1999.

56. "How to Work for a Kid," *Fortune*, 1 February 1999, p. 66.

57. "CEO Exposes, Sues Anonymous Online Critics," *Wall Street Journal*, 7 July 1999, p. B1.

58. S. S. Ross and D. Middleberg, "Survey on the Media and Information Networks," Columbia University Graduate School of Journalism, 1997.

59. George Stephanopoulos, "The New Rules of the Road," *Newsweek*, 8 February 1999, p. 34.

60. "Watergate's Shadow," *Newsweek*, 21 June 1999, p. 38.

61. Ronald N. Levy, "Turn-around PR: Techniques of Geniuses," *Public Relations Quarterly*, Spring 1999, p. 17.

Chapter Eleven

1. The Institute for Public Relations, Commission on PR Measurement and Evaluation, *Guidelines for Setting Measurable Public Relations Objectives*: University of Florida, 1999.

2. Dan Burgess, "What Price, Fame?," *PR Intelligence*, 11 January 1999, p. 1.

3. Dr. Lloyd Corder, "Answering The Age-Old Marketing Question: What Have You Done for Me Lately?," *Tactics*, May 1999, p. 12.

4. Angela Jeffrey, "Evaluating Media Coverage for Small Clients Now Has an Objective, Cost-Effective Solution," *PR Week*, 26 April 1999.

5. "Count Clips while You Make More," *PR Intelligence*, 11 January 1999, p. 4.

6. Mark Weiner, MediaLink, The PR Network, 26 March 1999.

Chapter Twelve

1. Materials from the Arthur W. Page Society, New York City.

2. Alexander Kendrick, *Prime Time* (Boston-Toronto: Little, Brown and Co., 1969), p. 456.

3. Randall L. Tobias, speech delivered to the Arthur Page annual spring seminar, New York City, 4 April 1995.

4. Peggy Noonan, *Simply Speaking* (Ragan Books: 1998), p. 78.

5. Conversations with the author.

6. Carl Sagan, "A Gift in Vividness," *Time*, 20 October 1980, p. 68.

7. George V. Grune, remarks at The Reader's Digest Association's global public relations conference, New York City, 19 October 1992.

8. *Who's in charge? CEOs and Boards Shuffle Power*, Richard M. Clurman, Whittle Direct Books, 1993, p. 2.

9. Ibid, p. 3.

10. "Battles in the Boardroom," *On the Issues*, PBS-TV, 18 June 1993.

11. "Executive Pay: Compensation at the Top Is out of Control. Here's How to Reform It," *Business Week*, 30 March 1992, p. 52.
12. "Executive Pay: The Party Ain't Over Yet," *Business Week*, 26 April 1993, p. 56.
13. "Stealth Compensation," *Financial World*, 18 February 1992, p. 74.
14. "Family Friendliness," *U.S. News & World Report*, 22 February 1993, p. 60.
15. Ibid.
16. "The List Factor," *The Chief Executive Guide: The War for Talent*, July-August 1999, p. 32.
17. "Winning with Diversity," *Nation's Business*, September 1992, p. 19.
18. "Communications Challenges of the '90s," Burson-Marsteller.
19. "Managing in the Midst of Chaos," *Fortune*, 5 April 1993, p. 38.
20. Donald E. Procknow, speech delivered to AT&T Western Electric public relations managers, Princeton, NJ, 15 October 1982.
21. "Communication Plays Key Role, Say Hospital CEOs," IABC *Communications Journal*, April 1981, p. 7.
22. Charles Marshall, speech delivered at AT&T public relations vice presidents' conference, West Palm Beach, Florida, 15 March 1983.
23. John J. Pappas, talk to Teletype Corporation Integrated Promotions Task Force, Skokie, Illinois, 3 August 1981.
24. Conversations with the author.
25. Materials and information supplied to the Arthur W. Page Society 1999 national awards program by Judy VanSlyke Turk, Advantica Restaurant Group.
26. Materials and information supplied to the Arthur W. Page Society 1998 national awards program by Larry A. Bishop, vice president-communications and investor relations, The Boeing Company.
27. Materials and information supplied to the Arthur W. Page Society 1999 national awards program by Patricia Harden, vice president-corporate communications, American Century Investments.
28. H. R. Haldeman and Joseph DiMona, *The Ends of Power* (New York: Times Books, 1978), p. 85.
29. Chester Burger, "Truth and Credibility in an Era of Disbelief," *Ragan's Public Relations Journal*, January/February 1999, p. 13.
30. Harry Levinson, lecture delivered to AT&T—Pace University Executive Management Program, New York City.
31. Henry A. Kissinger, "A Man with a Passion for Peace," *Time*, 19 October 1981, p. 12.
32. Edward M. Block, remarks to the San Francisco Academy, May 5, 1995.
33. Stuart Z. Goldstein, "Information Preparedness: An Integrated Model for Communication in the Information Age," *Strategic Communication Management*, December/January 1999, p. 21.

BIBLIOGRAPHY

AMACOM. *The Business-Media Relationship,* An AMA Research Study, 1981.

AT&T. PR *Indicators,* A Quarterly Summary of Data on Bell System Public Relations Departments, 1981.

"Best Practices in Corporate Communications." Media Relations Conference call August 25, 1998. PAG Group, Inc., Washington, D.C.

Brown, Jerry. "12 Steps to a Successful Media Relations Plan," *Ragan's PR Journal* (May/June 1999), pp. 18–28.

"Business News Releases Faulted in Editor Survey." *Editor & Publisher,* (6 June 1981), p. 86.

Cantor, Bill. *Experts in Action—Inside Public Relations.* New York: Longman, Inc. 1992.

Chapman, Ray. "Measurement: It Is Alive and Well in Chicago." *Public Relations Journal* (May 1982), pp. 28–29.

Chesapeake and Potomac Telephone Companies. *Making Media Relations Work, A Guide for C & P News Contact People.* Washington, D.C.

Codes of Ethics, International Association of Business Communicators and Public Relations Society of America.

communication briefings, "How to Get Results with Publicity." Blackwood, NJ: Communication Publications and Resources, 1992.

Getting Yourself Known in the Community. New York: Anderson Press, 1981.

Guidelines for Measuring Effective Public Relations, The Institute for Public Relations, University of Florida, Summer 1997.

Guidelines for Setting Measurable Public Relations Objectives, The Institute for Public Relations, University of Florida, 1999.

Honaker, Charles. "News Releases Revisited." *Public Relations Journal* (April 1981), pp. 25–27.

Hunter, William. "Progress Showing in Business/Media Battle." *IABC News* (June 1981), p. 9.

Measuring Relationships, The Institute for Public Relations, University of Florida, October 1999.

Moskal, Brian. "Why Companies Avoid the Limelight." *Industry Week* (21 July 1980), pp. 53–57.

Nager, Norman R., and Allen, T. Harrell. *Public Relations Management by Objectives*. New York: Longman, Inc. 1984.

The National Center for Business and Economic Communication. *The American University Newsletter*, 11 (1 May 1982), p. 9.

Ricklefs, Roger. "Despite Some Gripes, Bosses Say Business Press Is Generally Good." *Wall Street Journal, (*21 September 1982).

Rossie, Chuck. "Writing News Releases: Some Free Advice." *The Journalist* (Fall 1983), p. 16.

Stevenson, H. L. *UPI Reporter,* newsletter (23 April 1981).

Warm, Al. Media Relations Workshop conducted at annual conference of International Association of Business Communications. Chicago, 1982.

Weber, Samuel. "A Basic Training Document: What the Press Feels We Should Know About Working with the Press." *Tips and Tactics,* a supplement of *PR Reporter*, 19 (22 June 1981), p. 13.

Western Electric. *Media Relations, A Guide for Western Electric Spokespersons*, May 1980.

Yale, David. "External Relations Require Careful Planning." IABC *News* (November 1981), p. 11.

Yale, David R. *The Publicity Handbook.* New York: Bantam Books, 1982.

INDEX

ABC, 172, 256, 259,
ABC World News, 148
Accidents/catastrophes, 244–62
Adamson, James B., 301–3
Advantica Restaurant Group, 301
Advertising, 144–45
Advertising Age, 205, 251
ALS Awareness Campaign, 170–71
America in the Age of Mixed Media, 29–30
American Cancer Society, 83, 173
American Century Investments, 305–7
American Express, 290
American Journalism Review, 3, 5, 81, 260
American Society of Newspaper Editors, 31
Arthur Page Society, 184, 266, 314, 320
Associated Press, 74, 262
Associated Press Stylebook and Manual, 49
Atlanta Journal Constitution, 172
AT&T, 77–78, 81, 87, 119, 120, 153, 155, 175-76, 222-25, 239, 286–87, 288, 290, 297–301, 312
AT&T Teletype Corporation, 298–301
Audio news releases, 52–53

Audits, 281

Background briefings, 63
Backgrounders, briefings and seminars, 63
Background pieces, 19–21, 83–84
Baker, Lee W., 135
Baltimore News American, 239
Baltimore Sun, 5, 81
BancOhio National Bank, 252–53
Bank of America, 261
BankAmerica Corp., 6
Barkelew, Ann H., 312
Barnes and Noble, 95
Barre, Benedicte, 211–12
Batiste, Bobby, 103, 221
Bayer Corporation, 225–26
BBC World News, 196
Beatty, Clyde, 136
Beeder, Dave, 102
Behaviors, changing, 9
BellSouth Corporation, 320
Berlitz Translation Service, 199–200
Berra, Yogi, 224
Bestfoods, 164–65, 188–89, 314
Birkmeyer, Dick, 239
Bishop, Larry, 303
Block, Edward M., 310–11, 312
Blood drives, 35
Bloomberg, L.P., 4
Bloomberg, Michael, 4

Bloomberg Radio Network, 172
Bloom, Jonah, 5
Boeing-McDonnell Douglas, 303–5
Bosshard, Hans, 213
Branding, 179, 188–89
Brinkley, David, 113
Broadcast range, 40
Brokaw, Tom, 31, 148, 205
Brozowski, Pat, 312–13
Brukardt, David, 176
Burger, Chester, 120, 134, 309
Burgess, Dan, 273
Burke, James, 261
Burlingame, Harold W., 288
Burns, Robert, 298
Burrelle's, 263
Burson-Marsteller, 286, 293
Burson, Harold, 286
Business and the Media, 137
Business Week, 175, 177–78, 189,
    291–92
Business Wire Global, 199

Cable television, 41
Cameron, Carey, 102
Capdeville, Henri, 211
Carroll, John, 5
Carr, Harold, 303
Case Studies
  ALS Awareness, 170–71
  American Cancer Society, 173
  American Century Investments,
      305–7
  AT&T Bell Laboratories, 209
  AT&T coal phone, 175–76
  AT&T Nassau Recycle
      Corporation, 223–25
  AT&T Teletype Corporation
      298–301
  Bank of America, 261
  Bayer Corporation, 225–26
  Bestfoods, 164–65
  Boeing-McDonnell Douglas,
      303–5
  Coca-Cola, 247–48

Conoco Inc., 166–68
Denny's Restaurants, 301–3
Exxon Valdez, 245–46
Federal Express Corporation,
    241–44
Firestone Tire & Rubber
    Company, 261
Herrick Memorial Hospital,
    162–64
Honeywell, 25–28
Hyatt Regency, 252
JI Case, 176
Johnson & Johnson, 261–62
Nike, 165–66
Olympic Games, Atlanta,
    258–60
Olympic Games, Salt Lake City,
    258, 260
Pepsi-Cola Company, 251–52
Perrier, 248-50
Philips Consumer
    Communications, 171–72
Prudential Insurance Company
    of America, 169–70
Reader's Digest Association,
    The, 201–8
Schwab Rehabilitation Center,
    174
Sears Auto Service Center,
    250–51
Seattle-First National Bank,
    226–30
United Way, 173–74
Visa USA, 168–69
CBS, 172, 217, 259
CBS Marketwatch, 71
CD-ROM, 42
Chancellor, John, 113, 291
Chat rooms, 57, 129
Checklists
  Advice from PR pros in
      international markets,
      209–14
  Advice from top executives,
      academics, 312–20

Alternatives to "No Comment,"
138–40

Announcements in international
markets, 201–8

Attitudes for successful media
relations, 22–23

Broadcast and print media
terms, 67

Characteristics of news, 31–32

Crisis, self-test, 269

Crisis plans, 253–57

Determining newsworthiness,
33

Does it pass the Coors tests?, 98

Environmental plans, 220

Equal employment opportunity
cases, 232–35

Equal employment opportunity
cases, telling the
positives, 235–37

Events in international
markets, 159–61

Global media relations,
191–201

Guidelines for media events,
153–59

Hints for news conferences,
126–29

Hints for television
appearances, 123–25

Hints from journalists, crises,
266-68

Hints from journalists, dealing
with reporters, 101–3

Hints from journalists, media
events, 184–85

Hints on interview techniques,
112–22

Hints on op-ed pieces, 56

How involved and valuable are
you?, 321

How to avoid interviewing
tricks, 131

How/when to say no, 95–99

Interview no-nos, 129–30

Layoffs, 238–41

Media events master list,
151–52

Miscellaneous helpful hints,
99–100

Press kit ingredients, 177

Suggestions for news releases,
49

Test your knowledge,
involvement, 85–86

Timeline for new product
announcements, 180–84

Using the media relations tool
kit, 65–66

Writing for the ear, 54

Chicago Tribune, 82, 172

Chief Executive, 187, 292

Chiquita Brands International,
133

Churchill, Winston, 114, 122

Cincinnati Enquirer, The, 133

Clinton, Bill, 3

Clippings,
    Analysis, 276–79
    Services, 274
    Software, 279

Clurman, Richard M., 290

CNBC, 148, 184, 268

CNet News.com, 81

CNN, 5, 70, 259, 268

CNN Headline News, 103, 221

CNN International, 148

CNNfn, 165, 185, 267

Coal Age, 175

Coal Industry News, 175

Coca-Cola, 188, 189, 245, 247–48

Colgate-Palmolive, 190

College of the Canyons, 134

Columnists, 37

communication briefings, 37, 54

Communications policy, 12–13

Condit, Phil, 303

Conference Board, 292

Conoco Inc., 166–68

Construction news, 35

Contact names/numbers, 48
Cooke, Janet, 135
Coors Brewing Company, 98
Copeland, James E., Jr., 195
Corder, Lloyd, Dr., 273
Cordtz, Dan, 256
Corrections, 94
Counseling,
  Building respect for the role,
    308–11
  Earning the right, 307–8
  Prerequisites, 284–85
CPC International Inc., 164–65
Crisis planning, 253–58
  Accidents, 245–46, 252–53
  Emergency contact lists, 78
  Environmental issues, 217–30
  Equal employment
    opportunity, 230–38
  Fraud, 250–51, 260
  Hints from journalists, 266–68
  Internet, curse and blessing,
    263–64
  Layoffs, 79–80, 238–41
  Lessons learned, 265–66
  News conferences, 62
  Product recalls/tampering,
    247–50, 251-52, 261–62
  Strikes, 241–44
  Terrorism, 258–60
  Wire services, power of, 262–63
Cronkite, Walter, 2, 130
Crown Center Redevelopment
  Corporation, 252–53
Crystal, Graef S., 292
C-SPAN, 123
Cyberspace, 71, 189

Dallas Times-Herald, 81
Datamation, 299
Davidow, William, 189
Davids, Fay, 212–213
Davis, Lanny J., 137
Deadlines, 70–73
Deere & Company, 316

Delahaye Group, 196
Deloitte & Touche, 195
Denver Post, 103
Design News, 222
Directories, 42
Directory format, 43
Doe-Anderson PR, 273
Domm, Graeme, 313
Donahue, 261
Donosky, Lea, 124
Dow Jones Newswire, 74, 75, 262
Doyal, Steve, 252
Dunn, Gloria, 162–64
DuPont, 166–68

Eagle Tribune, 102
Economist, The, 196, 248–49
Edelman Public Relations
  Worldwide, 81, 279
Electronic clips, 275
Electronic Engineering Times,
  222
Electronic News, 299
Eli Lilly, 9, 287, 290
Emergency contact lists, 78
Employee communications,
  100–101, 150
Employee publications, 83–84
Environmental issues, 217–30
Equal employment issues, 230–38
Errors, how to handle, 92–95
Ethics, definitions, 134–35
Ethics Resource Center, 134–35
European Community, 187–188,
  192
Executive biographies, 100
Exxon Valdez, 245–46

Fact sheets, 83
Federal Express Corporation,
  241–44
Feinberg, Bob, 261
Felton, John W., 313–14
Fenton Communications, 313
Fernandez, Ligia, 212

Financial Times, 66
Financial World, 292
Finding news, 34
Firestone Tire & Rubber Company, 261
Fitzwater, Marlin, 82
Fleishman Hillard, Inc., 312
FMC Corporation, 313
Foote, Cone & Belding, 106
Forbes, 145
Fordham Graduate School of Business, 316
Fortune, 95, 111, 149, 165, 189, 222–23, 247, 263, 292, 295, 301, 303
Foster, Jodie, 129
Foster, Lawrence C., 261
FOX, 165, 172
Freedom of the press, 134

Gallagher, Michael, 133
Gault, Stanley C., 291
Gehrig, Lou, 170–71
Gelbart, Debra, 22–23, 67
General Motors, 136, 289, 290
Generating media interest, 37
Gharib, Susie, 184, 267
Gifford, Walter, 286–87
Gilfeather, John, 4, 189
Giveaways, 201, 205
Goals/objectives, 13–14
Goizueta, Roberto, 188
Golden Rule, 146
Goldstein, Stuart Z., 4, 311
Golightly, Holly, 77
Goodyear Tire and Rubber Company, 291
Grant, John L., 290–91
Griffin, Gale L., 164–65, 314
Griswold, Barbara E., 161
Grune, George V., 86–87, 290
Gwinnett Daily News, 102

Haig, Alexander, 88
Haldeman, Bob, 307–8

Hansen, Jon A., 217
Hard news, 32
Harlow, Bill, 139
Harris, Lou, 219
Harris, Thomas L., 179, 180
Harrison, E. Bruce, 314
Hasse, Judy, 252–53
HealthSouth Corporation, 263–64
Heller, Jamie, 185
Heller, Joseph, 105
Henahan, Donal, 115
Henderson, Nina, 188–89
Herrick Memorial Hospital, 162–64
Hewitt, Don, 2–3
Hillman & Kersey Strategic Communications, 315
Hillman, Carol B., 315
Hill, Fred, 303
Hill, Ivan, 135
Hobbies, 35
Holbrooke, Terri, 263
Holtz, Shel, 76
Home files, 78–80
Hooker Chemical Company, 218
Horne, Grant N., 2
How to Get Results With Publicity, 37
Humpty Dumpty, 119
Hyatt Regency, 252

Iacocca, Lee A., 116
IBM, 290
Independent, The, 196
Institute for Public Relations, 314
Integrated marketing communications, 178–84, 299-300
International Association of Business Communicators, 76, 189, 193
International Herald Tribune, 196
International Public Relations Association, 193
Internet, 3–5, 29, 71–72, 263–64

Interviews, 54, 88–92
  Briefing reporters, 89
  During the interview, 111
  Followup, 91–92, 111–12
  Handling requests, 88–89
  Hints for news conferences,
    126–29
  Hints for on-line chats, 129
  Hints for radio, 126
  Hints for television, 123–25
  How to avoid interviewing
    tricks, 131
  How/when to say "no," 95–99
  In-person, 90–91
  Internet, 90
  No-nos, 129–30
  Phone, 90
  Preparation with
    spokesperson, 110–11
  Techniques, 112–22
  Video conference, 90
Investor relations, 149–50, 255
Issues management, 8–9, 216,
    290–97
  Changes in job requirements,
    293–94
  Corporate governance, 290–91
  Declining promotion
    opportunities, 294–95
  Diversity, 293
  Executive pay, 291–92
  Free trade, 297
  Privacy, employee and
    customer, 296–97
  Protectionism, 297
  Quality of Work Life, 295
  Security of computer files,
    295–96
  Work and family balance, 292–93
Ivester, M. Douglas, 248

Jackson, Jackson & Wagner, 315
Jackson, Jesse, 124
Jackson, Patrick, 315
Jamron, Kenneth S., 298

JI Case, 176
Job description, xvi–xvii, 7, 8–10,
    11, 87, 286, 308
Johnson & Johnson, 261–62

Kelly, Gerri, 81
Kennedy-Nixon debate, 123
Kennedy, John F., 287
Kerchner, Kathy, 67
Keresztes, Peter, 212
Kerr, Drew, 81
Ketchum Public Relations, 9,
    168–69, 241–44
Ketter, William, 237
Kiplinger's Personal Finance, 307
Kissinger, Henry, 88, 307–8, 310
Knight, Jerry, 262
Koch, Markus, 268
Kodak, 290
Kovach, Bill, 30
Kutner, Lawrence, Dr., 172

Landers, Ann, 81
Larry King Live, 251
Lasswell, Harold, 12
Laurie, Marilyn, 315–16
Layoffs, xiii, 238–41
Lazard Freres & Company, 119
Leaks, 177–78
LeCarre, John, 195
Lederman, Judith, 137
Leno, Jay, 303
Letters to the Editor, 58, 92, 95
Levinson, Harry, 286, 309
Levy, Ronald L., 265
Lewinsky, Monica, 3, 29
Lexington Leader, 222
Lindemann, Walter K., 9
Linke, Curtis G., 316
Los Angeles Times, 82, 88
London Times, 81
Love Canal, 218
Lucent Technologies, 171, 298
Lukaszewski, James E., 33, 253
Lying, 136–38

MacDonald, Maril Gagen, 316
MacNeil, Robert, 2, 7, 121, 216
MacNeil/Lehrer News Hour, 121,
    251
Magazines, 39
Mailing lists/directories, 42–45
Makovsky & Company, 170–71
Manahan, David V., 175–76
MarassoCo., 318
Mark, Reuben, 190
Marshall, Charles, 298
Matlock & Associates, 173
Mau, Richard R., 316–17
McAlpine, Stephen, 245
McCallum, Martha, 184, 268
McCarthy, Anne M., 4, 4–5
McCatherin, E. Zoe, 252–53
McDonald's, 189, 195
Measurement,
    How to measure, 272–76
    What to do with results, 276–79
    What to measure, 271–72
    Measuring actions/attitudes/
        behaviors, 279–82
Media audits, 87, 281–82
Media events,
    Alternatives, 174–76
    Events in international
        markets, 159–61
    Master checklist, 151–52
    New facility, 150–52
    Planning and implementation
        guidelines, 153–59
    Press kit, 177
Media mix, 6
Media relations program, 11–12,
    15–17, 84–85
Media terms, 67
MediaOne Group, 318
Meeting the media, 21–24
"Mercator effect," 194
Merrick, Arthur P., 228–30
Meyers, John A., 70, 80
Michaelangelo, 148–49
Michigan State University, 31

Mining/Processing Equipment,
    175
Minneapolis Tribune, 81
Miss Piggy, 114
Mitchell, Elizabeth, 174
Mitsubishi Motor Manufacturing
    of America, 137
Mobil Oil Company, 145
Monitoring services, 274
Morgenson, Gretchen, 267–68
MSNBC, 148
MSNBC.com, 148
Mueller, Liz Dingwall, 210
Murrow, Edward R., 287
Musil, Ruthellyn, 317

Nader, Ralph, 30, 289
Nashville Tennessean, 81
National Geographic Society, 319
National Securities Clearing Corp.,
    4
Navistar International
    Transportation Corporation,
    316
NBC, 136, 172, 259
NBC Nightly News, 148, 205
Nevin, John J., 261
New York Times, The, 1, 6, 82,
    115, 175, 194, 251, 268, 298
News conferences, 58–62, 156–57
    Hints, 126–29
    On-line, 60
    Radio, 51–53
    Television, 51–53
News features, 64
News leaks, 177–78
News releases, 47–54, 99
    Components, 48
    Electronic, 51
    Features, 63–64
    International, 199
    Timing, 49, 73–75, 199
News, definition, 29–34
Newsletters, 38
Newspaper readership, 5–6

Newspaper Readership Project, 31
Newspapers, 37
Newsweek, 3, 7, 81, 124
Nieder & Nieder Associates, 317
Nieder, Edwin F., 317
Nightly Business Report, 184, 267
Nike, 165-66, 202–3
Nixon, Richard, 135, 307–8
"No Comment," alternatives, 95, 118, 138–40, 233–34
Noonan, Peggy, 288
North American Free Trade Agreement, 188
North American Precis Syndicate, Inc., 265
Northwestern University Medill School of Journalism, 179, 319

Objectives, 13–14
O'Connor and Hannan, 314
O'Dwyer, Jack, 133–34
Off the record, 143–44
Office coverage, 24–25
Office setup, 17–21, 100
Ogilvy, David, 149
Oklahoma City Fire Department, 217
Olympic Games, Atlanta, 258–60, 320
Olympic Games, Salt Lake City, 258, 260
Omaha World-Herald, 102
Op-Ed pieces, 55–56
Organizational milestones/awards, 36
Ostberg, Ullastina, 213
O'Toole, John, 106

Pacific Northwest Bell, 237–38
Padmore, Tim, 102
Page, Arthur, 120, 286–87, 314
Pappas, John J., 298-301
Patriot Ledger, 237
Payne, Billy, 259

PBS, 291
Pepsi-Cola Company, 245, 251–52
Perrier, 245, 248–50
Pfister, Walter J. Jr., 131
Philips Consumer Communications, 171–72
Philips Electronics, 171
Phoenix Gazette, 222
Photographs, 64, 81, 109, 110–11, 141–42, 154, 155, 222
   Model releases, 141
Pierce, James R., 178
Pinnacle Worldwide Inc., 118
Pinsdorf, Marion, K., Dr., 317–18
Polaroid, 4, 147
Porter/Novelli, 138
Positioning, 202–3
PR News, 99
PR Newswire, 74, 215
pr reporter, 315
PR Week, 5, 178–79
Press kits, 155, 177
Prodigy, 129
Procknow, Donald E., 297
Production records, 35
Prudential Insurance Company of America, 169–70
Prudential Intercultural Services, 195
Public Radio International, 196
Public Relations Journal, 31
Public Relations Society of America, 9, 133–34
Public service announcements, 53–54, 76–77
Pulitzer Prize, 135
Pyramid style, 50

Qs and As, 64–65
Quality of Work Life, 295
Quantas Airlines, 147–48

Radio, 39–40
   News release, 51
Rafe, Stephen C., 131

Ralston Purina, 147
Randall, Karen, 301
Ratajski, Magda A., 318
Rather, Dan, 7, 31, 130
Rawl, Lawrence G., 245–46
Reader's Digest, 81, 149, 218
Reader's Digest Association, The,
     81, 86–87, 161, 190, 198,
     269, 290, 321
Reagan, Ronald, 121
Reiman, Mark, 170–71
Relationships, 9, 69–70, 266,
     281–82
Rhody, Ronald E., 6
Rieder, Rem, 5
Riggio, Leonard, 95
Rockwell International
     Corporation, 317
Rogers, Will, 8
Rohatyn, Felix G., 119
Rohne-Poulenc Rorer, 170–71
Rooney, Andy, 142–43
Roper, Jo, 210
Roper Starch, 169–70, 171–72
Rosenstiel, Tom, 30, 88
Rubenstein, Helena, xiv
Ruder Finn, 178–79
Rush, Louise, 292–93
Russell, Anita, 98
Russell, Mark, 87

Sadat, Anwar, 310
Safire, William, 87, 119
Sagan, Carl, 289
Salt Lake Tribune, 260
Samaranch, Juan Antonio, 259,
     260
Samuelson, Robert J., 29
San Francisco Examiner, 65
Satellite media tours, 62
Schaffler, Rhonda, 185, 267
Schmertz, Herb, 145
Schubert, Michael, 179
Schwab Rehabilitation Center, 174
Schweitzer, Albert, Dr., 134

Scott, Jim, 102, 125
Scrushy, Richard, 263–64
Sears, 290
Sears Auto Service Center, 250–51
Seasonal events, 35
Seattle Post-Intelligencer, 229
Seattle Times, 172
Seattle-First National Bank, 226–30
Securities and Exchange
     Commission, 99, 166, 258
Seitel, Fraser, 2
Seltzer, Frank, 54
Service projects, 35
Servoss, Judi, 318
Sevareid, Eric, 124–25
Sexual harassment issues, 230–38
*Shadow: Five Presidents and the
     Legacy of Watergate*, 265
Shapiro, Irving, 113
Shepard, Alicia C., 260
Siconolfi, Michael, 185
Sills, Beverly, 115
Simpson, O. J., 30
Sims, Robert B., 318–19
Siracuse, Lisa, 165–66
60 Minutes, 2, 142–43, 261, 303
SmartMoney.com, 81
Smith, Kerri S., 103
Soft news, 32
Spector & Associates, Inc., 171–72
Speeches, 99
Spokespersons
     Characteristics of, 107–8
     Choosing the right one, 106–8
     Interview techniques, 112–22
     News conferences, 126–29
     On-Line chats, 129
     Preparation for, 108–11
     Radio appearances, 126
     Television appearances, 123–25
     Training for international,
          200–201
Stahl, Lesley, 2, 70, 114
Standby statements, 64–65,
     150–56, 181–82, 220

Stephanopoulos, George, 137, 265
Stewart, James B., 29
Stocker, Kurt P., 319
Strategic planning, 8–9
Stylebooks,
　Associated Press, 87
　Ayer, 87
　New York Times, The, 87
　United Press International, 87
　*Wired Style: Principals of
　　English Usage in the
　　Digital Era*, 76
　Writing for the Wired World, 76
Suggestion award winners, 34
Sullivan, Joseph, 137
Swoboda, Frank, 137

Tabloid journalism, 2–3, 29
Tag line, 48
Talk shows, 41, 56–57
Technology, 7, 75–76, 161, 279
Telecommunications Report, 299
Telephony, 222, 299
Television, 40–42
　Interview techniques, 124–25
　Releases, 31
　What to wear, 123–24
The Ends of Power, 307–8
The Trouble with Advertising, 106
TheStreet.com, 185
Time, 70, 80, 103, 115, 119, 310
Tobias, Randall L., 9, 287
Tracking services/agencies,
　275–76
Trade shows, 197–98
TRAKWare, Inc., 279
Tribune Company, 317
Turner, Ted, 5
Twain, Mark, 88, 113
Twisk, Russell, 214

Ungeheuer, Frederick, 103, 119
United Press International, 88
United Way, 173–74
University of Notre Dame, 117

University of South Alabama, 320
USA Radio Network, 172
USA Today, 4, 6, 172, 251, 260
U.S. Central Intelligence Agency,
　139
U.S. Foreign Press Center, 143
U.S. Information Service, 208
U.S. Justice Department, 144
U.S. News & World Report, 292

Vail, Theodore, 12–13
van der Rohe, Mies, xv
Vancouver Sun, 102
Venton-Ross, Bonnie, 211
Ventura, George F., 133
Video, international standards,
　196–97
Video news releases, 52–53
Visa USA, 168–69
Visiting dignitaries, 36
Volkswagen, 147, 178-79

Wall Street Journal, 1, 6, 71, 75,
　79-80, 130, 145, 166–67,
　175, 176, 185, 247–48, 264,
　299
Wallace, Mike, 113
Ward, Kathleen Ladd, 9
Warner, Dan, 102
Washington Journalism Review,
　113
Washington Post Writers Group,
　29
Washington Post, The, 82, 135,
　137, 262, 265, 303
Watergate, 135, 137
Weatherup, Craig, 251
Web sites, 75–76, 94
Weber, Larry, 69
Wederspahn, Gary, 195
Weinstein, Harold, 263
Westinghouse, 290
Williams, Lou, 136
Wire services, 262–63
Wired, 81

Wired Style: Principals of English Usage in the Digital Era, 76

Wirthlin Worldwide Monitor, 202

WISH-TV, 102

Woodward and Bernstein, 130

Woodward, Bob, 265

Workforce 2000, 293

Working Mother, 292

World Press Encyclopedia, 193

Wright, Donald K., 319–320

Writing for the Wired World, 76

Wylie, Ann, 114

Yahoo!, 81

Yankelovich Partners, Inc., 3, 4, 189

Yarbrough, C. Richard, 258-60, 320